PERSONAL MYTHOLOGY

Also by David Feinstein:
Rituals for Living and Dying
(with Peg Elliott Mayo, in press)

Also by Stanley Krippner:
Human Possibilities: Mind Research in the USSR and Eastern Europe

Song of the Siren: A Parapsychological Odyssey

Dreamworking: How to Use Your Dreams for Creative Problem-Solving (with Joseph Dillard)

Healing States (with Alberto Villoldo)

The Realms of Healing (with Alberto Villoldo)

Dream Telepathy: Experiments in Nocturnal ESP
(with Montague Ullman and Alan Vaughan)

PERSONAL MYTHOLOGY

The Psychology of Your Evolving Self

Using Ritual, Dreams, and Imagination to Discover Your Inner Story

David Feinstein, Ph.D. and Stanley Krippner, Ph.D.

Foreword by June Singer, Ph.D.

JEREMY P. TARCHER, INC.
Los Angeles
Distributed by St. Martin's Press
New York

Art in Prologue: *Mirth* by William Blake. Reproduced by courtesy of the Trustees of the British Museum.

Art in Chapter 1: Madras Rameshwaram, *Corridor of the temple* (17th–18th century).

Art in Chapter 2: Drawing by Andrew Lang from *The Andrew Lang Fairy Tale Book* (New York: Signet Classics/New American Library, 1986).

Art in Chapter 3: *The Fall of Man* by Albrecht Dürer. Reproduced by courtesy of the Trustees of the British Museum.

Art in Chapter 4: *Jacob's Dream* by William Blake. Reproduced by courtesy of the Trustees of the British Museum.

Art in Chapter 5: *The Creation of Adam* (detail) by Michelangelo.

Art in Chapter 6: *Drawing Hands* by M. C. Escher. Copyright © 1988 M. C. Escher Heirs/Cordon Art—Baarn—Holland. Reproduced with permission.

Art in Chapter 7: *The First Probe* by Rob Vanderhorst. Copyright by Rob Vanderhorst. Reproduced with permission.

Art in Epilogue: *Earthrise.* Photo courtesy of NASA.

Library of Congress Cataloging in Publication Data

Feinstein, David.
Personal mythology: the psychology of your evolving self / David Feinstein and Stanley Krippner.
p. cm.
Includes index.
ISBN 0-87477-483-7.
ISBN 0-87477-484-5 (pbk.)
1. Attitude (Psychology) 2. Mythology—Psychological aspects. 3. Self-perception. 4. Attitude change. 5. Self-actualization (Psychology) I. Krippner, Stanley, 1932– . II. Title.
BF327.F45 1988
155.2—dc19 88-10056 CIP

Jeremy P. Tarcher, Inc.
5858 Wilshire Blvd.
Los Angeles, CA 90036

Design by Rosa Schuth

Manufactured in the United States of America
10 9 8 7 6 5 4 3 2

For Sol and Edith Feinstein

Contents

Acknowledgments

Discussions with Rosie Adams, Sharon Doubiago, Joel Elkes, Richard Evans, Steven Goldstein, Joel Heller, Jerry Jud, Steve Kierulff, Don Klein, Ron Kurtz, Danielle Light, Bill Lyon, Gene Mallory, Rollo May, Reid Meloy, Stella Monday, Paul Oas, Tiziana de Rovere, Virginia Satir, Chuck Simpkinson, Meredith Spencer Foster, Katherine Yates, Carl Young, and the Wightman Men's Gathering all contributed to our thinking in ways that are gratefully acknowledged. Dan P. McAdams offered many wise and productive suggestions on an earlier draft of this volume. Peg Elliott, who has been a constant source of perceptive and buoyant counsel, has contributed more of substance to this work than we can measure. Marj Davis gracefully offered spiritual respite along with her twinkling spirit. We also would like to express our gratitude to Rita Rohen and the late Richard Price, whose generous hospitality permitted us to write parts of this book in the beautiful surroundings of Esalen Institute.

Jeremy Tarcher has been a compelling and imaginative force in this effort to bring the ideas and methods presented in our seminars and professional writings to a wider audience. Our editors, Connie Zweig and Ted Mason, have been generous in talent and good humor.

The love, understanding, and inspirational presence of our partners in marriage, Donna Eden and Lelie Krippner, are appreciated beyond words.

Foreword

Personal myths are not what you think they are. They are not false beliefs. They are not the stories you tell yourself to explain your circumstances and behavior. Your personal mythology is, rather, the vibrant infrastructure that informs your life, whether or not you are aware of it. Consciously and unconsciously, you live by your mythology. In this remarkable book, the authors challenge you, through the use of ritual, dreams, and story, to become aware of the mythology you are living, to confront it, and in the end to gain some mastery over it. The book is an exercise in the "evolution of consciousness"—your consciousness and the consciousness of the culture in which you are embedded.

To live mythically means to become aware of your personal and collective origins. In the process of learning to do this you will discover, or affirm, that you are not an isolated independent being, but the end product of the millennia of acculturation and maturation of the human race. Personal mythology is but the flower on the bush: the family myth is the branch, society's conventions form the stem, and the root is the human condition.

Personal myths structure our awareness and point us in the direction that becomes our path. If we are unacquainted with the contents of our personal mythology we are carried by it unconsciously, with the result that we confuse what exists objectively in the world with the image of the world supplied to us by our own distorted lenses. Based on an unconscious personal mythology, or a mythology rigidly imposed by our social group, we tend to see only one correct path. We do not see it as *our* way, but as *the* way, and we do not see that it could lead to disaster as easily as to contentment.

The book has its roots in a research project at The Johns Hopkins University School of Medicine in which Feinstein compared several emerging systems of personal growth therapies with more traditional therapies. He found a common denominator: each therapy, in its own way, attempted to influence how people construct their understanding of themselves and their place in the world. He used the term *personal mythology* to describe this "evolving construction of inner reality" and to emphasize that all human constructions of reality are mythologies.

Krippner's role in this book has been one of offering inspiration and insight to the primary author. He brings to the collaboration thirty years of pioneering research on human consciousness, particularly his studies of dreams, healing, and altered states. Over the past decade the authors have conducted workshops and developed methods through which people can become aware of the mythologies that have guided them in the past. With that understanding, it is possible to move on to guiding myths that are more vital and viable. The process is systematically arranged and comprises the major portion of this work. Step by step, the book sets forth a guide to personal transformation through explanation, participatory experiences, and case material. It not only provides the necessary conceptual information, but helps the reader integrate the knowledge through rituals and practices and then apply the new awareness to everyday life.

An approach that delineates five stages of growth is offered. The stages are informed by sources encompassing many schools, all the way from ancient Greek philosophy to the methods and theories of Freudian and Jungian psychology to the practical approaches of contemporary behaviorism and cognitive psychology. None of these systems is applied uncritically, and the authors have managed to integrate a coherent synthesis of a tremendous body of psychological theory into their work.

The first three stages echo the Socratic thesis, antithesis, and synthesis. Stage One involves recognizing and defining one's own personal myth and discovering to what degree this guiding myth is no longer an ally. Stage Two requires the identification of an opposing personal myth, one that creates a conflict in the person's psyche. The conflicting myths are brought into focus and examined to see how each is linked to the past. The person will soon recognize that the myths of childhood are rarely appropriate to serve the adult.

Stage Three, synthesis, entails conceiving a unifying vision. Here the old myth and the counter-myth are brought into confrontation. They may be personified so that the conflict can be worked out as a drama of the inner life, and so that, as Feinstein and Krippner so nicely put it, it does not have to be "played out on the rack of life." In the process, obstacles to harmony are re-visioned as opportunities for growth.

Stage Four begins where many modes of therapy end. It is called "From Vision to Commitment." Here is where the insights are tested and reinforced so that the process envisioned can move from the hypothetical or imaginal realm into the phase of intention and then into action. Stage Five entails weaving the new mythology into life. Here a series of practical steps is suggested whereby the inner transformation can be demonstrated in the world. The butterfly emerges from the chrysalis and is (and is not) a new being. From here on, the process continues both as inner work and as living in the world in a new way, more free of the constrictions of unconscious assumptions.

Personal Mythology's great contribution, it seems to me, lies in the way it facilitates individuals in recognizing the root causes of their difficulties and then taking responsibility for their own healing process. In this age, information is more accessible to more people than ever before, and individuals are better informed about what is needed to gain and maintain a healthy state both physically and psychologically. Consequently the physician, the psychiatrist, and the psychotherapist are no longer held up as the only people who can lead us to better health. In many situations it is possible and also desirable for individuals to take responsibility for their own well-being. This is done through such practices as exercise, good nutrition, and maintaining a variety of interests. Feinstein and Krippner point the way and provide some very good guidance for attending to one's psychological health and development. Each person who reads this book is challenged to undertake the journey in whatever way is appropriate: alone, with a partner, with friends, or in a group committed to a growth process.

At some point along the way, personal myths converge with cultural myths to govern every human activity. There comes a time, as we work on our personal issues, when we realize the degree to which our personal concerns are of limited significance. The "independent individual" is a myth gone bankrupt. We have always depended upon others for our most basic needs: food, shelter, security, and affection. How much more do we need one another to supply all the complex requirements of life today! You are a participant in the creation of whatever will happen next on this planet. Looking toward the future, the authors point out that a rigid nationalism, "the fiercely independent ego writ large," is losing its feasibility as a social form. In the emerging Global Village, as Marshal McLuhan called it, allegiances transcend regional and cultural boundaries. Information, business, the arts, the media, the news, all know no national limitations.

We can no longer separate ourselves from the destiny of the planet, be it a global society in which people may live in mutual trust and high productivity, or nuclear annihilation. The next challenge, which Feinstein and Krippner raise in closing, is to apply to the human community the principles derived from observing the way individuals think mythically. Can the methods the authors have presented for dealing with intrapersonal conflict be used in dealing with the cultural myths that foster intergroup and international conflicts? As in any open system, the solution of one series of problems opens the door to working with a set of higher-level problems. That challenge may well lead us to the next step in the "evolution of consciousness."

—JUNE SINGER

Prologue

Expanding Your Mythology Beyond Limiting Cultural Images

Mythic images . . . are pictures that involve us both physiologically in our bodily reactions to them and spiritually in our higher thoughts about them. When a person is aware of living mythically, she or he is experiencing life intensively and reflectively. —NAOMI GOLDENBERG[1]

To be aware of living mythically is to understand your life as an unfolding drama whose meaning is larger than your day-to-day concerns. It is to nurture a ripening appreciation of your cultural and ancestral roots. To live mythically is to seek guidance from your dreams, imagination, and other reflections of your inner being, as well as from the most inspiring people, practices, and institutions of your society. To live mythically is also to cultivate an ever-deepening relationship with the universe and its great mysteries.

Since the mid-1970s, we have taught some two thousand people a system for learning to live more mythically. In this book we present that system as a series of "personal rituals" designed to bring greater awareness to the submerged mythology that shapes your thoughts, emotions, and behavior. The quiet guidance of your personal mythology gives meaning to every situation you meet and determines what you will do in it. Your personal mythology acts as a lens that colors your perceptions according to its own assumptions and values. It highlights certain possibilities and shadows others. Through it, you view the ever-changing panorama of your experiences in the world.

People often live their lives with very little awareness of the lens through which they are looking. According to Jungian analyst Frances Wickes, "modern man is unaware of the myth that lives itself within him, of the image, often invisible, that dynamically impels him toward choice."[2] It is possible, however, to step back and begin to inspect the lens, the mythology that is directing your choices. For Wickes, the art of living is, in essence, a development of the power of inward choice. She believed this to be "of all creative arts the most difficult and the most distinguished."[3] Developing the power of inward choice is the challenge this book sets before you. We offer this challenge with the conviction that examining your personal mythology will strengthen your ability to make choices that are more creative and empowering.

Much of the psychological suffering people experience is entangled in personal myths that are not attuned to their actual needs, potentials, or circumstances. Attempting to follow a personal myth that is not in harmony with who you are or with the world in which you live is painful, and a mythology that is unable to serve as a bridge to deeper meanings and greater inspiration than you can find in the outer world is often accompanied by a deep and nameless anxiety. As you develop greater awareness of your emerging mythology, you experience increased intimacy with your inner being. To "know thyself" in this informed and substantial manner inoculates you against at least one strain of the generalized anxiety of the day by engaging greater support from your deeper self.

Your personal mythology is the distinctive, although sometimes imperceptible, self-psychology[4] that guides your behavior and prepares the way as you evolve in the world. *Personal Mythology: The Psychology of Your Evolving Self* presents an integrated set of psychological principles and procedures you can master for promoting your personal development. The book can help you examine, revise, and revitalize the private theories that shape your life. Kurt Lewin, who was distinguished for his ingenious application of psychological knowledge to social problems, was fond of pointing out that "Nothing is as practical as a good theory." His observation is valid not only for scientific theories, but also for the private theories or personal myths we all hold. Such theories are more than just intellectual constructs; they are ingrained models of reality that determine how you see your world and understand your place within it. When such models are flawed or out of date, they lead to unrealistic expectations, poor choices, and emotional distress. When they are serving you well, you have better access to your inner wisdom and greater understanding of your environment.

Myths, in the sense that we are using the term, are *not* legends or falsehoods. They are, rather, the models by which human beings code and organize their perceptions, feelings, thoughts, and actions. Your

Expanding Your Mythology
Beyond Limiting Cultural Images

personal mythology is rooted in the very ground of your being, and it is also a reflection of the mythology held by the culture in which you live. We all create myths based on sources that are within us and sources that are external, and we live according to those myths. Psychologist Henry Murray thought of myths in this way: myths serve to inspire, generate conviction, orient action, and unify a person or a group by creating the "passionate participation of all functions of the personality (*individual* myth), or of all members of a society (*collective* myth)."[5]

Through your personal mythology, you interpret the experience of your senses, give order to new information, find inspiration and direction, and orient yourself to powers in the universe that are beyond your understanding. Without your mythology, your experiences would be disjointed and chaotic. Myths, in this broader sense, are not properly understood as being true or false, right or wrong. They are ways of organizing experience that may ultimately be judged as more or less effective for the well-being and performance of an individual or group.

Our approach is organized around three basic premises:

1. Myth-making, at both the individual and the collective levels, is the primary though often unperceived psychological mechanism by which human beings navigate their way through life.
2. People in contemporary cultures are more capable of constructing distinctively *personal* mythologies and reflecting upon those mythologies than in any previous period of history—and the need to become conscious of the mythologies we are living out is more urgent than ever before.
3. By understanding the principles that govern your underlying myths, you become less bound by the mythologies of your childhood and of your culture, and you may begin to influence patterns in your life that once seemed predetermined and went unquestioned.

MYTHOLOGY IN A CONTEMPORARY CONTEXT

There recently has been a resurgence of interest in mythology as a path to a richer inner life and a more sophisticated spiritual outlook. Bruno Bettelheim, Robert Bly, Jean Shinoda Bolen, Joseph Campbell, Joan Halifax, James Hillman, Jean Houston, Robert Johnson, Sam

Keen, Rollo May, Arnold Mindell, Paul Rebillot, William Irwin Thompson, and Barbara Walker are among the contemporary figures who have offered more vital psychological perspectives by calling upon mythology. We like to think of our work as also helping to revive this powerful, ancient concept and applying it in a contemporary and somewhat novel manner. Besides suggesting that mythologies function in the modern world as much as they did in earlier times and that they operate at personal as well as cultural levels, we are emphasizing that it is possible for you to develop a set of skills for revising your personal mythology in ways that will benefit you. When you alter a guiding myth, decisive changes in your perceptions, feelings, and behavior follow.

Your mythology is, to an extent, your culture's mythology in microcosm. Everything you do and every thought you have bears the distinctive mark of the mythology of the culture in which you were raised. Even activities that might seem natural or universal are dictated by the basic assumptions and underlying images that are reflected in your culture. What you eat and the way you eat it, what you wear and how you wear it, whether your thinking is oriented toward the present or the future, whether your experience of the moment accents thoughts or feelings, how you greet strangers and receive friends, and how you acquire, accumulate, and display material possessions are all fashioned, in important ways, by the mythology of your culture.

Today's myths appear in less distinguished guises than the elaborate stories and exotic rituals of tribal and ancient peoples. The spirits and deities whose authority was unrivaled in tribal, classical, and medieval cultures have faded into antiquity. Now we find an abundance of mortal heroes and heroines, both real and imaginary, in novels, comics, movies, and television stories. While these images are less than venerable—rather than reaching back through the generations, they appear suddenly and fade abruptly—they are disseminated through powerful media and leave strong impressions. The lyrics of popular songs often provide compelling mythic messages that may later appear word for word in a teenager's protestation of love, statement of defiance, or suicide note.

Myths permeate all areas of modern life. They are reflected in and transmitted through stage, screen, and song; education, religion, and politics; literature, art, and architecture; advertising, fashion, and design. They are intertwined with our child-rearing practices, sexual norms, and social systems. They are maintained by the slant of our history books and news stories and exposed by the salary differential between a good schoolteacher and a good salesman or a movie star. The myths operating in modern societies tend to support material progress and the control of nature, rather than the attunement and participation with natural cycles that characterize more classical mythologies. Because technologically oriented cultures have discounted the mythological dimension that underlies the material realm, we have as a society become less adept in our commerce with the deeper levels of existence.

The logic of Western mythology, according to Sam Keen, has been dictated by "the erotic obsession with the machine."[6] He identified some two dozen articles of faith that grow out of this mythology, such as: sensation, intuition, and feeling are primitive, immature forms of thought; females, like nature, are to be controlled and excluded from positions of power; human life is organized around the laws of the market; and knowledge and power are the twin pillars of human identity. These axioms are now being challenged as they are followed by a trail of increasingly hazardous ramifications.

A primary role of myth always has been to carry the past into the present. Through this binding of time, a culture's accumulated knowledge and wisdom are brought to each new generation. Today, however, the circumstances for which our mythologies must provide guidance are changing at an unprecedented rate. Long-enduring myths have been cracking under the strain of abrupt shifts in the very foundations of social organization, such as overpopulation, diminishing resources, and increasing jeopardy for future generations. Cultural myths have been drifting toward obsolescence more swiftly since the midcentury than in any previous period of history. The half-life of a valid guiding myth has never been briefer, and we see new myths being hammered out daily on the anvil of people's lives.

Writing about the experience of being a young American in the 1980s, Wanda Urbanska observes that the boundaries of imagination were

> defined by the grim prospect of worldwide nuclear annihilation, not the sense of a better tomorrow. . . . We grew up with the disgrace of Vietnam and Watergate, not the stability of the Eisenhower presidency. We grew up with the odd urgings of the Moonies and the fear of political terrorism and airline hijackings, not the certainty of church on Sunday and American supremacy. We grew up with punk rock and MTV, not the Lennon Sisters and "Father Knows Best.". . . We are a generation raised on Jack-in-the-Box hamburgers and Diet Pepsi, not home cooking and whole milk.[7]

The guiding values and cherished convictions of recent generations are often all but useless in dealing with contemporary issues. The myths that supported large families were not concerned with overpopulation. Expectations of continual upward mobility with larger homes and greater consumption assumed a boundless supply of natural resources. Cultural images that exalted the compliant female defined her as an appendage to the male. The belligerent foreign policies that were traditionally thought to convey a nation's strength have created a Damocles sword of nuclear destruction that reverberates in the nightmares of children and the disquieting suicide rate of adolescents. Guiding myths that were workable in recent memory have lost their viability at a dizzying pace. As history has advanced more rapidly, so has the need to become more facile in revising the myths that guide us.

The diversity of the mythic images we encounter through electronic and other media can also be overwhelming. For most of the history of civilization, the myths held by the individuals in a society were relatively uniform, allowing for little question or variation. To stand out was to risk censure and even death. Ancient mythologies were bound by tradition or, perhaps, altered by a shaman's sacred vision. However, no single unifying force in today's complex civilizations is powerful enough to preserve cohesion amid the multitude of competing myths and fragments of myths people are exposed to now.

It is likely that your attitudes and values differ from your neighbors' in ways that could not even have been conceived in tribal cultures. In addition, you have been obliged to learn how to reflect on the fit between your myths and the situations you encounter with more agility than your parents or the generations before them. Never have so many visions been available to choose from, nor has there been media so capable of parading those visions in front of you. Growing up is no longer a matter of following in the well-tried footsteps of ancestors who may for generations have been in the same trade, held similar religious convictions, and considered the tradition-bound roles of men and women to be part of the natural order.

The need to unshackle ourselves from outmoded myths is becoming ever more pressing. Rollo May has commented that "the old myths and symbols by which we oriented ourselves are gone, anxiety is rampant. . . . The individual is forced to turn inward."[8] In our disillusion with the spellbinding cultural images of the past, combined with the capacity of our imagination to soar beyond the real and the present, we can each envision a range of possibilities for ourselves whose scope was previously unthinkable. In short, mythology has become an increasingly personal affair, and one of the distinguishing features of modern life is the rate at which that development is accelerating.

We are all called upon to participate in selecting, realigning, and updating the myths that we follow. This book outlines a system for teaching yourself to become more adept in contemplating your direction. We believe that a well-articulated, carefully examined mythology is one of the most effective devices for countering the disorienting grip of a world in mythic turmoil. Such a mythology also points the way back to the deeper world of the psyche. Because you are less able to rely on the myths of the past or of the society in which you live, you are compelled to establish a greater degree of self-reliance. People who are effective at what they do instinctively use creatively conceived myths to deal with the problems they face. The renowned inventor R. Buckminster Fuller, late in his life, described the significance of his severely impaired eyesight as a small child. Everything he saw was extremely fuzzy until, at age four, he was given eyeglasses and was astounded by how the world suddenly came into focus. This modern Renaissance thinker speculated that receiving those glasses might have accounted for his lifelong conviction that even if ideas and relationships seemed fuzzy to him at first, they would eventually become clear. That was, for him, a positive, effective, and realistic guiding myth.

As you become more aware of your developing mythology, you become more capable of finding creative guidance from within and of drawing dependable conclusions from the lessons of your personal experiences, rather than being compelled to follow antiquated beliefs, family codes, or cultural images. Gaining a measure of autonomy from the limiting mythic images of your culture and from other early influences increases your psychological freedom and strengthens your ability to cope within a rapidly changing world. This book offers a set of tools to help you better understand and constructively work with your ever-evolving mythology.

PERSONAL MYTHOLOGY IN A PSYCHOLOGICAL CONTEXT

Psychologists have offered numerous terms and concepts for helping people think about their inner lives. We turn to mythology because myth *is* the language that most closely approximates the natural workings of the psyche. "Personal mythology," however, is sometimes misunderstood because "myth," in its vernacular usage, has come to mean a mistaken idea. Yet we know of no better term than *personal mythology* for capturing the way that human consciousness reflects deep mythological images while simultaneously being shaped by the mythology of the surrounding culture. Unlike terms such as *scripts, attitudes,* or *beliefs, myth* is able to encompass the archetypal dimension of the unconscious mind, which transcends early conditioning and cultural setting. A mythic outlook also reminds you that you are part of a larger picture than your immediate concerns. Bringing a mythological perspective to psychology yields a framework that is more potent in its facility with unconscious processes, in its sensitivity to cultural forces, and in the dignity it lends to the act of examining the human story.

The term *personal myth* was first introduced into the psychiatric literature in 1956 by Ernst Kris, who used it to describe certain elusive elements of human personality that psychoanalysts must account for if the effects of therapy are to be lasting.[9] Similar concepts, however, can be found in the work of Sigmund Freud, Alfred Adler, and Carl Jung. Freud was fascinated by mythology, selecting the Oedipal myth to portray the pivotal dilemma in human development. Adler believed that an individual's early recollections revealed a "private mythology." The striking parallels found by Jung in dreams, works of art, and cultural myths led to his penetrating studies of the psychological relevance of mythology, and he discussed his own "personal myth" in his autobiography.[10]

The psychotherapeutic approaches that trace directly back to the work of Freud, Adler, and Jung are collectively thought of as depth psychology because of their emphasis on unconscious processes. Depth psychology, according to James Hillman, is "today's form of traditional mythology, the great carrier of the oral tradition."[11] He stresses that "myths talk to psyche in its own language; they speak emotionally, dramatically, sensuously, fantastically."[12] Depth psychology offers a framework and a method for examining the human psyche—the "organ" of psychological life, operating both within the field of conscious awareness and far beyond it, balancing innumerable desires, impulses, and intuitions, and capable of expressing itself in images, feelings, thoughts, and actions. The promise of depth psychology is that as you become more conversant with your psyche, unconscious impulses become less menacing and unconscious wisdom becomes more accessible.

While psychoanalysis and other depth psychotherapies were initially the property of the privileged, a wider interest in and accessibility to approaches that promote an understanding of unconscious motivation have now become a mass phenomenon. Growing numbers of people are systematically thinking about their psychological development. For many individuals, supporting their inner growth has become a guiding value that influences key choices in areas ranging from career to family to the use of leisure time. In the United States, this emphasis on the evolution of the self traces back at least to the transcendentalism of Emerson and Thoreau. An avalanche of new techniques for pursuing personal growth has been witnessed since the mid-1960s, proffered by psychotherapists, healers, self-proclaimed gurus, growth groups, and self-help books and tapes. We view this mass phenomenon, in part, as being an outgrowth of the widespread anxiety and disorientation that accompanies the gnawing realization that existing mythologies are leading us toward destruction. However, we also believe that it is a call to the individual's deeper creativity. The trend has produced some innovations that are of genuine value, leading to greater insight, inspiration, and ability to productively participate in society, as well as to self-indulgent activities that further isolate people from inventively meeting the culture's mythic crisis.

Our work had its origins in a research project designed to compare some of the emerging systems of personal growth with more traditional therapies.[13] One of the common denominators among the approaches examined was that each, in its own fashion, attempted to influence the way people construct their understanding of themselves and their place in the world. In a paper published in *The American Journal of Orthopsychiatry* in 1979,[14] David Feinstein used the term *personal mythology* to describe this evolving construction of inner reality and presented a five-stage model designed to assist individuals in working with their inner mythologies. Later that year, Stanley Krippner organized a symposium for the American Psychological Association that examined some of the issues raised in that paper.[15] The theory has been developed further in seminars and in a series of professional reports.[16]

Beyond the understanding and procedures adapted from the practice of depth psychologists, we also have drawn from the fields of cognitive and humanistic psychology in developing our model. George Kelly's personal construct theory[17] was a forerunner of the contemporary cognitive trend in psychology that teaches people to overcome emotionally disabling thought and behavior patterns by altering their internal representations of the world and their place within it. By insisting that cognitive psychology must bridge the gap between the rational and the imaginative, Jerome Bruner has expanded the field's boundaries to include the study of narrative, meaning, and myth.[18] The approach we have developed also was directly influenced by Carl Rogers's respect for the ability of individuals to direct their own growth,[19] and by Abraham Maslow's insistence that the field of psychology, which was oriented toward psychopathology and stimulus-response relationships, concern itself as well with psychological health and "the farther reaches of human nature."[20]

USING THIS BOOK TO EXPLORE YOUR PERSONAL MYTHOLOGY

This program is presented with the hope that it will help you to more consciously and systematically participate in the evolution of your unique mythology. The program adapts numerous techniques from the practice of psychotherapy. Psychotherapists offer diverse approaches for helping people with problems that result from the failings of what we are referring to as personal myths. Therapists, in fact, perform many of the functions that in earlier times were reserved for shamans, priests, and other spiritual leaders. However, psychotherapy is often practiced within a framework that limits a full response to the complex psychological and spiritual needs of modern people. We believe that many forms of psychotherapy would be better conceived in the context of the individual's evolving mythology than in the medical model of illness and treatment. Carl Jung's approach to psychotherapy, which maintains a mythological perspective, was distinguished, among other things, for its appropriateness with people who could not properly be given a psychiatric diagnosis yet were suffering from the sense of meaninglessness and emptiness that has been called "the general neurosis of our times."[21]

This book is a guide for learning to live more mythically and for dealing more effectively with the mythic dilemmas that are central to adjustment and personality development. It is neither a substitute for psychiatric treatment nor an attempt to facilitate major personality reconstruction. While some of its goals may parallel those of psychotherapy—such as increased insight, the resolution of inner conflicts, and decision making that is more psychologically informed—we do not see the book as a surrogate therapist. In the face of emotional turmoil, persistent depression, overwhelming life crises, or recurrent patterns that prove to be destructive, psychotherapy can be of immense value. It is one of the most direct ways to gain access to the existing storehouse of behavioral science knowledge and technique designed to help people adjust and develop.

Many of the methods presented in this book are adapted from

clinical practice and may have a strong emotional impact. While they will not cause new emotional problems, any potent experience can bring underlying difficulties to the surface. A number of steps you can take if the program becomes too unsettling are presented in Appendix C. If you are currently in psychotherapy or have reason to believe that you need psychiatric care, we request that you use the program presented in this book in consultation with a therapist. Psychotherapy and this program are, in fact, quite complementary.

Like many of our professional colleagues in psychology, we have been concerned about the superficiality and glib promises of many of the "pop psych" books that have been flooding the market since the 1960s. In designing this book, we have attempted to conform to the principles for self-help books implicit in the guidelines published in the journal *Contemporary Psychology.*[22] For instance, after working with some two thousand people in educational, clinical, and community settings as the program was developed and refined, we engaged an additional thirty participants specifically to test and revise the program in the self-guiding format presented here. We have framed the book's assertions within our understanding of the limitations of a self-help format and the dilemmas involved in working with unconscious personality dynamics. We must also emphasize that while the program arose out of more than a decade of development in a range of settings, our premises and methods are yet to be evaluated by systematic scientific investigation.[23]

We believe it is possible, through the methods presented here, for you to initiate the following types of changes: (1) to begin to *identify* outmoded or otherwise unproductive personal myths that have been operating largely outside of your awareness; (2) to begin to *revise* them; and (3) to *experiment* with ways of bringing your life into greater harmony with these revised myths. In addition, by coming to understand your own mythology, you become more able to understand the mythology of your culture and to participate more effectively in its evolution. In teaching people how to examine and recast the deep-seated myths that govern their lives, we have repeatedly observed the practical benefits of simply becoming able to articulate the myths that are operating. The periodic crises of faith, courage, and identity that punctuate life may be treated as calls for renewal in your mythology, as unending a task as that of the paint crew on the Golden Gate Bridge, whose work is never finished.

This program introduces you to a particular terminology and methodology for bringing a mythic perspective to the lifelong process of reflecting on your inner experience. It is, of course, only a beginning, and even at that it calls for a substantial commitment of time and energy. However, reading the book without performing the personal rituals can also be of value, and an understanding of the basic concepts can still be gained. You will become more attuned to the mythic dimension of your inner life, and you will be exposed to a set of instructions that you can adapt to your own needs or return to at a later point. We encourage you to survey the entire book so you will have an overview before deciding how to proceed. Below are some preliminary points about the program:

Personal rituals. A ritual is a symbolic act that celebrates, worships, or commemorates an event or a process in the individual's or the community's life. Human beings are extraordinarily flexible, and all societies have created rituals that shape the individual's development, a consequential feat in human engineering. Character traits that served the needs of the clan could be fostered, and the individual's passions and spiritual aspirations could be directed to benefit the community.

Rituals may strengthen rapport with the rhythms of nature, delineate the tasks of individual or community development, or establish a connection with aspects of the cosmos that are held to be sacred or divine. A ritual can be centuries old or devised for a contemporary occasion.[24] It might be performed regularly, occasionally, or only once. A ritual can be carried out privately or with others. A private ritual might consist of writing a farewell letter and ceremoniously burying or burning it. Public rituals are typically performed in a prescribed manner and in a certain order, such as a graduation, wedding, or funeral. They may be conducted by a family, a small group, or an entire community. Rituals may or may not be accompanied by words, music, or mind-altering techniques such as the whirling dance of Sufi dervishes, Native American peyote ceremonies, or the delirious frenzy of a rock concert.

Modern people crave fresh rituals, attuned to the times and capable of responding to their higher sensibilities. A growing number of innovative approaches are helping individuals and communities rediscover ancient ceremonies and create new rituals.[25] Our focus has been on developing a set of essentially private rituals to systematically guide you in identifying a core conflict in your mythology and finding a resolution to that conflict. The rituals in this book will also help you make contact with the inner symbolism your psyche is continually generating. Robert Johnson explains that when we experience such images, "we also directly experience the inner parts of ourselves that are clothed in the images."[26] Each of the rituals presented in the following chapters builds on those before it, so it is important to carry them out in the order given. They may be conducted privately, with a partner, or within a small group.

Using a personal journal. Psychologist Ira Progoff pioneered the "intensive journal" as a tool for assisting people in working with their inner lives and discovering deeper levels of meaning in their experiences.[27] You will be using a personal journal throughout the program. The instructions will guide you in recording your experiences with each of the rituals, as well as your reflections upon them. Most people use a spiral notebook or an aesthetically pleasing diary, and some use personal computers. Describing your thoughts and feelings in a journal will help you fix your insights in your memory and foster the unfolding of unconscious processes into your awareness.

Your journal will provide a record of your discoveries and your growth during the program, and you will periodically be asked to review it as you proceed. As you engage yourself with your journal, extend your experience beyond the ritual you are describing. Let your journal entries emerge in their own way. Journal work can take you into a deep, contemplative state. Give voice to your imagination and spontaneously describe the associations you have to your memories, emotions, and ideas. Sense where your writing wants to lead you and follow it. This may feel awkward or forced at first, but you will eventually begin to uncover deeper feelings and contact earlier memories. Allow your journal work to become a process unto itself and it will enrich your experience in the program as well.

Guided imagery instructions. Many of the personal rituals take you on "guided imagery" journeys. Some preparation is necessary for these experiences. You might, for instance, read the instructions into a tape recorder and let the tape guide you through the experience. You might arrange to have another person read the instructions to you. Or you might thoroughly familiarize yourself with the instructions and allow your memory to lead you through the ritual. You can also purchase a cassette recording that has the instructions for these imagery journeys, along with meditative background music, prerecorded on it (see page 269).

If you tape the instructions yourself, we suggest you follow a few simple guidelines. Read the instructions slowly and deliberately. While it may be necessary to experiment a bit with tone and tempo, the most common error is to read too rapidly. When you read the instructions into the tape, or if you are reading them to a partner, pause for about ten seconds each time you come to the word "Pause," each time you come to the end of a paragraph, and after each word that is in uppercase letters (as in: ". . . breathing deeply, ONE, TWO, THREE, FOUR, FIVE").

Where the instructions ask for a 20-second pause or longer, these are estimates that are most useful for reading the instructions to a group. If you are working alone or with a partner, it is best to say "Pause" or use a chime or clicker at these points. Then, if you are using a tape, you can simply stop it for these pauses and resume whenever you are ready (a hand-held remote switch or a microphone with an on-off switch is ideal). If you are working with a partner, establish a hand signal to indicate when you are ready for further instruction. Also, at any point where you need more time to carry out an instruction, freely indicate this to your partner or stop the tape.

Pacing the program. There are several reasonable ways to structure your time as you work with the personal rituals presented in the program. One recommended way of pacing the program is to allow yourself one to two weeks to complete each of the five stages. It is usually best to go through each chapter in several sittings; each typically requires four to seven hours. These estimates will vary, however, depending upon your natural pace, whether you are working with a partner, the amount of attention you give to exploring your dreams, and how much detail you choose to put into your journal. Another way to pace the program is to go off for a few days and plunge into it intensively. You also may go through the program any number of times, each time exploring a different area of your personal mythology.

An attitude toward resistance. The same resistance that may seem such an obstacle to personal development also may serve as a powerful teacher. Recognize that resistance is natural in the face of change: it is one of the ways that we maintain our equilibrium. There may be good reasons that a part of you is resisting. We encourage you to appreciate the resistance and approach it with an attitude of curiosity and the sense that if you can penetrate to its core, you will gain greater self-understanding. Perhaps you find yourself frittering away time you have set aside for the program, or keep losing your journal, or find that you are unable to concentrate when you sit down to work. Such unintentional actions can provide you with information about a part of yourself that has been outside your awareness. Perhaps you are pushing yourself too hard, or trying to change qualities about yourself that hold symbolic meaning you have not recognized, or you need more time to relax rather than to undertake another concentrated task. Listening to what the resistance is attempting to tell you can reveal new understandings that ultimately enhance the program. By using resistance as a gauge that points to areas of your life that are in need of greater attention, it becomes a teacher rather than a tyrant.

Working with your dreams. Working with your dreams is a supplementary track throughout this program that can substantially enrich your experience. You are encouraged to record your dreams. We have found that the dreams people spontaneously recall as they go through the program often parallel themes relevant to the stage of the program in which they are working. Each stage of the program includes one or two "dream focus" instructions that will suggest you review your journal to find themes in recent dreams that relate to that stage of the program. The "dream focus" segments also provide instruction for requesting dreams to clarify specific questions, a process called "dream incubation." These are optional instructions, and the book is arranged so that the personal rituals can stand alone, with no special attention given to your dream life.

The appendices. The three appendices are to be consulted at any point in your work. Appendix A offers specific suggestions for enhancing the program by building habit patterns that anchor and support the work, creating an inspirational setting, engaging other people in your efforts, using retreat settings, and intensifying the personal rituals. Appendix B provides a primer for remembering and working with dreams. It gives an overview of some of the most useful approaches we have found for investigating the significance of dreams as related to personal myths. Appendix C provides suggestions for you in the event that your work in the program arouses painful feelings or other troubling emotions. Please skim these appendices before starting the program so that you will know what they contain and can consult them when they would be most useful.

Chapter 1 presents our basic assumptions concerning the nature of personal myths, how they evolve, and how they affect people. It also leads you through two personal rituals that initiate you into the program. Chapters 2 through 6 will guide you through our five-stage model, one stage per chapter. Chapter 7 provides a theoretical framework for understanding the ongoing evolution of your personal mythology and closes with a review of the program. The Epilogue places the model into a broader context by exploring its implications for understanding and working with mythic processes at the cultural level.

1

Into Your Mythic Depths

Myth is the secret opening through which the inexhaustible energies of the cosmos pour into human cultural manifestations.[1]

It has always been the prime function of mythology and rite to supply the symbols that move the human spirit forward.[2]

—JOSEPH CAMPBELL

Through your personal myths, you interpret the past, understand the present, and find guidance for the future. Your myths address the broad concerns of identity ("Who am I?"), direction ("Where am I going?"), and purpose ("Why am I going there?").

This chapter will present our assumptions about the nature of personal myths and how they evolve. It opens with an imaginary journey back to your ancestors and will then introduce you to some people whom you will come to know through the myths that have orchestrated their lives. Issues that arise as people attempt to change their mythologies are discussed, and several preliminaries to working with your own mythology are addressed. The chapter closes with a ritual that introduces you to your "Inner Shaman," a wise companion from the invisible world who will assist you as you make this journey into your mythic depths.

A JOURNEY BACK TO YOUR ANCESTORS

We begin with a personal ritual that will give you an experiential sense of how personal myths operate. You will be using your imagination to locate the roots of your own mythology in the mythology passed down through your family. Personal myths are laden with the hopes and disappointments of prior generations. Your mythology is your legacy from the past, as well as a source of guidance and inspiration for the future. The family is the crucible in which genetics and cultural mythology are amalgamated into the unique mythic framework that shapes personal development. It is the institution charged with creating a person-sized mythology for each of its young. Family myths evolve as they are passed from one generation to the next, and the development of the individual's mythology must be viewed against the backdrop of the family's mythology.[3]

Personal Ritual: "Remembering" the Myths of Your Ancestors

This opening ritual will make it possible for you to understand your later explorations in the context of your forebears and the mythology they passed down to you.[4] Read the instructions into a tape that can then lead you through the experience, or have someone else read the instructions to you, or familiarize yourself with the instructions well enough that you can perform the ritual from memory with only glances at the book.*

Stand where you can move several feet in any direction. Find a comfortable posture and close your eyes. Take a backward step and imagine that you are stepping into the body and the being of your father if you are a man, or of your mother if you are a woman. (If you were adopted, make a choice between your biological parent and your adoptive parent for this experience.) Then take a few moments to get a sense of what it must have felt like to be in this body and this personality.

Take another step backward and step into the body and being of your parent's parent, your same-sex grandparent. After sensing this grandparent for a few moments, take another step backward and enter the body and being of your same-sex great-grandparent.

Finally, take another step backward to become your same-sex great-great-grandparent. You might be a late-seventeenth-century craftsman's wife in downtown London, a foot soldier in the army of the Czar, or the slave of a tobacco farmer in Virginia in the 1830s.

Physically assume the posture that you imagine might have been

*See box on page 269 for information on ordering prerecorded tapes of the guided imagery instructions.

Into Your Mythic Depths

a typical posture for your great-great-grandparent. Dramatize this posture until it begins to symbolize what you know and imagine about this person's life. You will be reflecting upon the person's perceptions of self, environment, and purpose.

Even though it is unlikely that you will have access to the facts that would allow you to answer these questions with certainty, the answers your great-great-grandparent gave to them shaped your family's mythology and echo in your own psyche. Assume that these echoes are registered so deeply in your being that the answers your intuition offers now will, if not factually precise, be instructive as metaphors for further understanding your heritage. Consider the following questions as if you were your great-great-grandparent:

1. What are your major concerns?
2. What are your primary sources of satisfaction?
3. How do you understand your position within your society—its limitations, privileges, and responsibilities?
4. If you look to a nonhuman authority to explain human destiny, what is its nature? [60-second pause]

Once you have answered the four questions, take a step forward and assume a posture that you imagine to be typical of your great-grandparent when he or she was your current age. Dramatize this posture until it begins to symbolize what you know and imagine about this person's life.

Consider the same questions as if you were your great-grandparent:

1. What are your major concerns?
2. What are your primary sources of satisfaction?
3. How do you understand your position within your society?
4. If you look to a nonhuman authority to explain human destiny, what is its nature? [60-second pause]

When you have answered these questions, take another step forward and assume a posture that might be typical of your grandparent when he or she was your current age. Dramatize this posture until it begins to symbolize what you know and imagine about this person's life.

Again consider the four questions as if you were your grandparent:

1. What are your major concerns?
2. What are your primary sources of satisfaction?

3. How do you understand your position within your society?
4. If you look to a nonhuman authority to explain human destiny, what is its nature? [60-second pause]

When you have answered these questions, take another step forward and assume a posture that represents your parent when he or she was your current age. Dramatize this posture until it begins to symbolize what you know and imagine about his or her life.

Again consider the four questions as if you were your parent:

1. What are your major concerns?
2. What are your primary sources of satisfaction?
3. How do you understand your position within your society?
4. If you look to a nonhuman authority to explain human destiny, what is its nature? [60-second pause]

Now, step forward into yourself. Find a posture that represents the statement your own life is making. Hear this statement as an actual phrase or sentence. Say it aloud.

Let your posture become animated as you continue to repeat your statement. Explore and experiment with the movement and the statement. If you have a sense that you need a greater statement or expanded posture, stretch your movements or your words to represent this new statement. [60-second pause]

When you have explored the statement and the movements to your satisfaction, come to a resting point and reflect on your observations during this ritual. Finally, describe your experiences in your personal journal.

As you identified with your progenitors, you may have begun to sense how they perceived themselves, how they understood their circumstances, and what they valued and trusted—core questions at the heart of your own mythology as well. By reflecting on how they might have related to these issues, you are also opening yourself to new insights about the mythology you are living out.

Can you see patterns that have been carried to you from your parent's generation? Are you likely to pass these patterns along to your children? At some point, you may wish to repeat this exercise, stepping into the lives of your opposite-sex parent and ancestors, or, if you were adopted, stepping into the life of the biological or adoptive parent whose lineage you did not explore the first time. This speculation on the mythologies of those who preceded you will provide a reference point as we begin to discuss the nature of personal myths. Your understanding of the concept will further unfold as you explore your own personal mythology through the sequence of personal rituals in the following chapters.

WHAT IS A PERSONAL MYTH?

During the visit to your forebears, you began to explore the relationship among personal myths, family myths, and social change. You considered several questions that are at the core of the mythologies all people live. Here we will examine in greater detail the characteristics of personal mythologies and the way they develop.

How can you recognize a personal myth? Would you see it in images? Would it come through as thoughts that tell you what to do? Would your heart race if it were challenged? Does it unfold like a story? Are you the main character in that story? We want to take you into the mind of a single individual, a young boy, to demonstrate how personal myths develop and come to be expressed in all of these ways.

The boy is a bundle of impulses, experiences, aptitudes, uncertainties, ideas, needs, fears, and longings. He depends upon models from the outer world to help him order this highly charged interior and give him direction. The cultural heroes who touch him emotionally are powerful influences in helping him organize his life. If the boy was born in the United States in the World War II era, one of his mythic heroes would be the ruggedly individualistic cowboy, personified by figures such as John Wayne. This strong, tough, and confident image was at the core of the personal myths that showed innumerable little boys, who are now in positions of leadership, how to behave and what to expect of themselves. Many little girls also internalized the John Wayne image, but as a model of what to expect in a man and what to avoid in their own behavior.

Our little boy will mimic the heroes to whom he is most strongly drawn. How does he incorporate the John Wayne image into his own identity? Because of the human capacity to make comparisons, he will see analogies between the image portrayed by John Wayne and his own life. He will find or create opportunities, often unconsciously, for behaving according to the image. When he acts tough, brave, or independent, engaging a situation the way John Wayne would have, he feels affirmed for having lived up to his ideal. The qualities and behaviors he associates with John Wayne provide reference points as he maps his personal world.

Once he has incorporated that image, however, he is controlled by it. Consider him in a situation that he finds threatening, such as encountering the class bully. He may feel fear and uncertainty, but the image so strongly prohibits such feelings that he represses or denies them. He may even become ruthlessly aggressive in an unconscious attempt to defeat his fears. Punished for having injured the bigger boy with a rock, he defiantly responds, "Nobody's going to beat me up!" Unnamed myths may decisively shape our feelings, thoughts, and behavior.

The image at the core of a personal myth is generally far more complex than in the John Wayne example. Rarely in our diverse culture, with its daily onslaught of media figures, is a personal myth organized around a single image. The boy has probably been influenced by the qualities of other heroes he has admired—people in his life as well as media figures—and he will modify the John Wayne image to blend with the models they provide. The model will also be challenged and altered over time. Since the boy was first exposed to John Wayne, in fact, the John Wayne image has been changing within him, interacting with other models and ideas, and becoming tailored to his unique character and circumstances.

What is it that makes some images more attractive to the boy than others? What early experiences would predispose him toward John Wayne? Figures that are idolized by his peers and venerated by the "myth-maker machinery"[5] of his culture have powerful appeal. More personally, perhaps he resents an ineffectual father and has desperately been looking for someone he can admire who is as different from his father as possible. Or maybe he has already internalized the cultural message that men are to appear brave and strong, and he seizes the John Wayne image as a model for his attempts to manifest those ideals. As he makes the model his own, it guides his activities, and he measures himself against it.

However, what if he has learned to accept his fears and show his sensitive side? What if he is repulsed by pretense and bravado? The John Wayne image may have little emotional appeal for him. He will flounder until he is able to find or invent other models. Ideally, his culture will be bountiful in providing constructive alternatives. Today the range of available heroes to teach him about strength extends from Rambo to Gandhi. The culture's spotlight, however, persistently shines on the figures that are more dramatic and arrogant. A sensitive boy finds himself in the midst of difficult choices.

You can see how uniquely personal your myths can become. You do not simply adopt all the myths of your culture. And the myths you do adopt evolve with time. The boy's mythology will be further shaped by what happens to him when he acts in accordance with the John Wayne image. Some parts of it will be supported and others will not. Perhaps his toughness will get him into fights. If he wins the fights, he may adopt the image in even greater detail. If he loses, he may stop acting so tough, but also experience an inner crisis as he is forced to reconcile the discrepancies between the way he feels he is supposed to be and who he is. We all face many such crises during our lives.

Myth has been described as "the dramatic representation of our deepest instinctual life . . . capable of many configurations, upon which all particular opinions and attitudes depend."[6] At the core of a personal myth is a central theme. You organize new experiences around such themes. The theme serves as a template, a bare motif, a map, a skeleton without flesh. But rich imagery, complex beliefs, passionate feelings, and powerful motivations attach themselves to this framework and fill in its character.

A *personal myth* is a constellation of beliefs, feelings, and images that is organized around a core theme and addresses one of the domains within which mythology traditionally functions. According to Joseph Campbell, these include: (1) the urge to comprehend the natural world in a meaningful way; (2) the search for a marked pathway through the succeeding epochs of human life; (3) the need to establish secure and fulfilling relationships within a community; and (4) the longing to know one's part in the vast wonder and mystery of the cosmos.[7] Personal myths explain the world, guide personal development, provide social direction, and address spiritual longings in a manner that is analogous to the way cultural myths carry out those functions for entire societies. Personal myths do for an individual what cultural myths do for a community.

Your *personal mythology* may be thought of as the system of complementary and contradictory personal myths that organizes your sense of reality and guides your actions. The theme at the core of a personal myth is a composite, usually built from many sources. Because the theme is symbolic and abstract, it is versatile. It provides a structure that allows images reflecting the culture's diverse mythology to be blended with the varied impressions of daily experience and sculpted into the uniquely personal myths by which you live. The images provided by your culture, from John Wayne to Michael Jackson, are evaluated and organized according to your existing mythic structure. Media images may add new features or even change the direction in which your mythology will develop. So did the examples provided by your parents, teachers, and peers. Your personal myths are also responsive to the rewards and punishments you receive for your behavior or appearance. In addition, images that originate in the deepest parts of your being may be reflected in your mythology. Such images may be foreign to your previous experiences, yet they often provide inspiration that is sound, creative, and durable.

Often your personal myths will be in conflict. This underlying conflict may become evident when your beliefs do not match your behavior. Many people think of themselves as lazy, even though they consistently push themselves beyond the point of exhaustion. The statements they make to themselves may echo the words of a parent who long ago was frustrated with them for not being more responsive to the parent's desires. The enormous suggestive power of a father's or mother's emotionally charged remarks leave indelible images. Perhaps, because of a father's goading, a boy works diligently and as an adult accomplishes more than might be expected of him, although always with the whip of his father's admonitions, now internalized, echoing at his backside. His image of himself as lazy may be countered by another model that is outside his awareness. That model may portray him as being capable of pushing through his acknowledged "laziness" and working prodigiously. Even though he cannot articulate this model and continues to think of himself simply as lazy, the new model may be running the show and driving him to herculean efforts. The personal myths with which we consciously identify are not the only influences at work.

Personal myths are intimately connected with deep feelings. If you argue about politics, religion, or social change with a friend, you quickly begin to sense that personal myths run much deeper than mere rationality. You may, in fact, have to conclude that the emotional dimension of your friend's passionately held mythology carries more weight than the rules of logic. Although your myths will inevitably seem quite sensible to you, at least until you have reason to challenge them, they are complex products of your culture, experiences, and temperament. You may have such a strong emotional investment in them that it is difficult even to entertain explanations and possibilities that are based upon different premises. There seems, in fact, to be a nearly universal tendency to denounce "myth as falsehood from the vantage-point of a rival myth."[8] Understanding how your own myths function helps you relate more productively with family, friends, colleagues, and adversaries whose mythology may in important ways differ from your own.

To summarize, your personal myths address themselves to your past, present, and future, as well as to your identity and purpose in the world. They typically operate outside of your awareness but have a powerful effect on your feelings, thoughts, and behaviors. They are influenced by your accumulating experiences, the guidance provided by your society, and visions that arise from your unconscious mind. Your personal myths reflect your culture's myths, yet they can be relatively independent from them. At the core of a personal myth is a motif that shapes your perceptions, guides your development, establishes your role in society, and helps you find spiritual meaning and connection. Your mythology fuels your emotions and shapes your beliefs. As you come to understand the principles by which your personal mythology operates, you will become more able to consciously participate in its development.

THE SELF-FULFILLING NATURE OF PERSONAL MYTHS

The personal myths that are central in your life tend to be self-fulfilling in the sense that you are drawn to live out their underlying themes. If a premise of your personal mythology is that you are bright, you are likely to use your intellectual capacities more effectively than if you believe you are dull. If "disappointment in love" is a dominant motif in your mythology, you will tend to select partners and make choices that bring it your way.

Such myths inhibit your development. Others, which once provided sound guidance, become outmoded. When they do, your psyche begins to cultivate alternative mythic images. This process, a natural part of your psychological development, is usually gradual and largely unconscious. The following stories illustrate how people's myths shape their actions, and how new personal myths can emerge at various points in life.

Dana. Dana was a middle child, the second girl between an older sister and a younger brother. Her father was conspicuous in his interest and affection for his older daughter. The brother aroused the father's jealousy, while Dana simply did not seem to elicit much attention from her father. She longed for his affection, however, and constantly witnessed the spirited relationship between her father and sister.

Dana's sister was uncomfortable with her father's intimacies. When the sister recoiled at his approach, Dana intently observed her father's pain and figured out ways that she could help him to feel better. This became her role in the relationship. While she could not obtain her father's impassioned affection, she took pleasure in receiving a growing number of appreciative words and glances. This relieved some of her desire for deeper contact with her father, but she still wondered if something was wrong with her because she never received the rapt attention he had for her sister. Dana continued to find ways to comfort her father, and even if he seemed disinterested in her for herself, she was finally receiving some of the attention she craved. She became adept at comforting others as well. It made her feel good to make them feel good. Dana found great solace in Sunday School stories about the life of Jesus. Like Jesus, she thought, she would devote herself to loving others without expecting anything in return.

When the older sister became a teenager and attracted the attention of boys, the father turned his fond overtures into an irritated disapproval of his older daughter's activities. Dana had developed an unusual capacity for empathy, and she saw the anguish of everyone involved. She could sense how each of them felt, and she tried to respond in ways that would comfort them. She was particularly attentive to her father. No matter how cross or unreasonable he might be, she always could understand his feelings. Even when she was very young and he would spank her, she would think, "Poor Daddy, he just doesn't know any better."

Dana could listen to others with such compassion that they would be inspired to share with her their most intimate thoughts and feelings, and she would continually find herself in the middle of their problems. She might be the confidant of two girlfriends who were themselves in the midst of a disagreement. After talking with Dana, each would feel affirmed in her own feelings and position. Then each would feel betrayed when it became clear that Dana also was championing the other. The only truth that mattered to her was the one that took away pain and made people feel good about themselves.

In romance, Dana felt at home with men who admired her for how good she could make them feel. This mirrored her experience with her father, and she would further ensure the pattern by avoiding relationships with men who showed too much romantic interest. Their overtures collided with her mythology that nothing about her could evoke a good man's passion, and she was never drawn to them. Her affection was most easily elicited if a man was in need of support and affirmation. She expected nothing in return, and her relationships were markedly one-sided.

Dana stayed acutely attuned to other people's pain, responded competently, and gained a reputation as a selfless helper. When another person was hurting, she hurt as well, and she would continue to hurt until she had helped the other person feel better. What she did not do well was set limits. She collected a cadre of "best friends" wherever she lived. Once there were so many people clamoring for her attention that she actually moved to a new city to avoid their demands without having to hurt their feelings. Her mythology entangled her so deeply in their pain that she could see no other way to get out from under the impossible expectations people placed upon her.

Dana's personal life was overrun with the needs of the many people who depended upon her. She was genuinely valued in her community and widely sought as a resource, but she was always overinvolved and overtaxed. A man who was interested in marrying Dana nearly left her, protesting that there was too little space for him. He complained, "There are five hundred people in this town who think you are their best friend!" A series of events, including confrontations with him, a health problem, and continual exhaustion, caused Dana to begin identifying the dysfunctional elements in her myth. She reported the following dream as a turning point as she began to recognize and question the myth that had been governing her relationships:

> The dream was horrendous. Spokespeople for the world come to me with a plan. They say they have a way to heal all the people in the world . . . and that if I truly love unconditionally, I will go along with it. They tell me they have an amazing formula that can make my body feed everyone. They want me to give up my life and be made into white bread that could feed the multitudes. They know how to bottle "Dana Essence" and they plan to squirt one drop into each loaf with an eye dropper. Then all the people would be healed. This, they say, is a much better plan than the present arrangement where I am using up my essence by stretching myself too thin and trying to help too many people.
>
> I agree to let them kill me "mercifully," as they put it. The scheduled time for my killing is 10:30 A.M. But at 10:15 I know I don't want to give up my life essence to go into white bread to feed the multitudes. I go to this warehouse to see if I can call off the killing. I hear people talking, and I know that it is too late. They have their solution to the world's problems, and they will not listen to me now. I feel in such danger that I hide in the warehouse, not knowing what my next move will be.
>
> I don't know how the dream would have ended because I woke up at that point with my nose bleeding. I had developed an open sore on the side of my nose that sometimes appears when I am

stressed. It had become raw and blood was squirting out of it, reminding me of the stigmata. I couldn't stop the bleeding for a long time. Finally, when it did stop, my sheets were red with blood.

The dream left Dana with images of Jesus feeding the multitudes. She vividly recalled a scene from the musical *Jesus Christ Superstar* in which Jesus screams at the crowd, "Heal yourselves!" She played the record over and over that morning, and it was as if he were speaking for her as well. The dream was a strong stimulus for committing herself to change the way she related to others. As she painstakingly traced the roots of her interpersonal style back to her relationship with her father, her accommodating responses to others became less automatic. A new personal myth gathered strength, which asserted that she should respond to her own needs as well as to others, that people are best served when they are able to take care of themselves, and that she is worthy of passionate as well as appreciative interest.

Michelle. While growing up in an upper-middle-class family with an alcoholic father, Michelle was unhappy. By her mid-teens she had run away from home numerous times. After her parents discovered that she had been sleeping with her boyfriend and smoking marijuana, they managed to have her involuntarily committed to a psychiatric hospital.

Michelle could hardly believe what was happening to her. She became disruptive on the ward, screamed at the nurses, and was given medications that sedated and confused her. The experience was like a nightmare for her, and she began to wonder if she was indeed going crazy. On her last day there, she overheard one of the few staff members she had come to trust tell someone, "People who have been in mental hospitals always return to them."

Michelle was released from the hospital after three weeks. There was no evidence that her behavior had been a sign of mental illness. But the statement, "People who have been in mental hospitals always return to them," stayed with her. She recalled it whenever she heard of the relapse of anyone who had at one time undergone psychiatric treatment. She remembered the words whenever she read newspaper accounts of former mental patients who had committed acts of violence, and she was plagued by fears that she would have a bizarre psychotic break in which she lost control of her behavior. Any time she felt depressed, her distress was complicated by her fear that she was about to plunge into insanity. When she pulled out of her depression, she told herself that this was probably only a temporary reprieve. The statement by the staff member had become a personal myth for Michelle.

Michelle saw every emotionally difficult period of her life as further evidence of her impending mental breakdown. She was certain it would be only a matter of time. She began to consider her poor memory, her low tolerance for stress, and her penchant for daydreaming as further proof of her tendency toward insanity. Each indication of mental problems, no matter how slight, was thoroughly examined and analyzed for signs of her looming crash, thus magnifying her already existing stress. Michelle noticed that she had begun to take fewer emotional risks, narrowing her scope of activities by avoiding situations that might make her uncomfortable.

Her belief that she was mentally unstable was causing her, increasingly, to behave as if she were. After ten years of contending with these fears, she consulted a psychologist. She was given a battery of psychological tests which revealed that she had a high capacity for imagination and superior intelligence, but no signs of a serious mental disorder. As Michelle began to acknowledge that the preponderance of evidence from her life showed a basic emotional stability, she was able to take comfort in her strengths and to relax the concerns that had for a decade been keeping her anxious and limiting her development.

Fred. Like many men born in the first quarter of the twentieth century, Fred was a stern, hardworking husband and father. His personal mythology, the product of a youth spent in the rural South during the Depression, held that life is serious business. He believed that "you get what you earn and you earn what you get." He reasoned, "It is best not to be too positive lest you set up expectations that will result in disappointment." For Fred, there was little room for emotion because "feelings keep you from what is important and make you look weak." Unlike many of his peers, he had no use for religion. He was bitter about his early church experiences, and he found no assurance in promises of an afterlife.

At the age of fifty-five, Fred had a heart attack and was hospitalized. In the hospital, he had another massive coronary. His vital signs indicated eight times that he was clinically dead. But he was revived each time, and after the final episode he related a remarkable story:

> First I was up near the ceiling and I could see the medical team trying to resuscitate me. I heard a doctor say, "He's had it!" I yelled

> back, "Whatever it is, I don't want it!" but nobody heard me. Suddenly, I was walking over a bridge with a dry riverbed underneath. On the other side was an open field. Walking to greet me was Bart [a childhood friend who had died in his early twenties]. I was overjoyed to see Bart. He greeted me warmly and told me to observe everything. But he said that I had to go back. "Why?" I asked. "Because you haven't learned the most important thing, Fred. You haven't learned how to love."

As Fred became aware of being back in the hospital room, he opened his eyes and met the gaze of a concerned nurse. The words "I love you" came out of his mouth. He said, "I love you," to each nurse and doctor in the room. One doctor, according to family legend, uncomfortably replied, "That isn't necessary." His family was amazed. His daughter explains that Fred did not find it easy to say, "I love you," to anyone. He would sometimes walk out of the room when a song on the radio or a program on television "got too mushy."

For the remaining sixteen years of Fred's life, he seemed to be making up for lost time in cultivating an ability to listen, taking an intense interest in the lives of others, traveling extensively to other parts of the world to try to understand people from different cultures, making amends for the past with his intimates, and enjoying the company of his grandchildren. At his memorial service, the theme most dwelt upon was the loving spirit Fred had developed in the latter part of his life.

In each of these cases, you can sense the role that early experiences played in fashioning the person's mythology, and you can see how the mythology then shaped subsequent development. Dana's resourceful approach for winning her father's attention initially focused on his emotional pain, but it grew into a compulsion to respond to the distress of anyone around her. Michelle's self-limiting myth, formed on the basis of a comment overheard in an impressionable moment, maintained her long-standing belief that she was on the edge of insanity. It caused her to choose her goals and activities gingerly, as if she were indeed dangerously unstable. Fred had emphasized the value of hard work but, until his heart attack, had systematically neglected opportunities for loving contact.

The mythologies that Dana, Michelle, and Fred had been living out seemed logical to them, given their experiences to that point of their lives. But important aspects of who they were and what they might become were being inhibited. As they changed these mythologies—as

Dana questioned her "compulsion to help," as Michelle acknowledged her emotional sturdiness, and as Fred grew to learn about love—their lives changed accordingly.

CHANGING YOUR PERSONAL MYTHOLOGY

One quality of a vital personal mythology is its capacity for change. Your mythology is regularly challenged to incorporate information that contradicts its premises, to adapt to new circumstances, and to expand as you mature and accumulate new knowledge. There are many ways in which you can consciously participate in and cultivate its evolution. Some people, however, spend a lifetime attempting to live according to cultural images that never quite fit them. Joseph Campbell describes the dilemma: "Whenever a knight of the Grail tried to follow a path made by someone else, he went altogether astray. Where there is a way or path, it is someone else's footsteps. Each of us has to find his own way. . . . Nobody can give you a mythology."[9]

The goal of our program is to teach you to participate more effectively in the evolution of your mythology, both in your inner life and in its expression in the outer world. We are not, however, suggesting that it is possible to control or even fully understand your mythology. Jung succinctly summarized the stalemate that is inevitably met by such efforts: "The totality of the psyche can never be grasped by the intellect alone."[10]

A central aim of depth psychotherapy is to bring the conscious ego into increased accord with the deeper forces that undergird it. By developing greater awareness of your intuitions, feelings, and inner images, you gain a more complete view of the mythology that lives itself within you. That is the vantage point we ask you to seek as you enter into this program. We ask that you begin to recognize your inner life as the poetics of mythic themes vying for expression. James Hillman has suggested: "Let us reimagine psychodynamics as mythic tales rather than as physical processes; as the rise and fall of dramatic themes, as genealogies, as voyages and contests and respites, as interventions of Gods."[11]

By reaching imaginatively and persistently toward your innermost depths, you open a door to a more profound view of your daily concerns. You broaden the horizons of your self-knowledge, and you tap into a power that can transform you. Erich Neumann, the great Jungian analyst, offered an image for the inward journey: "The discovery of the reality of the psyche corresponds to the freeing of the captive and the unearthing of the treasure."[12] As you work with your personal mythology, you update and embellish your map for "unearthing the treasures" of your own psyche.

The journey requires effort. While the mythic world within you is rich in symbolism that can inspire and motivate, we modern individuals, enthralled with our new-found individuality and mastery over nature, have not been as attentive in tuning into the deeper mythic levels. As a result, we have become less versed in this realm and have alienated ourselves from it. On the other hand, in more ancient times, when consciousness was steeped in the mythological dimension, the ability to reflect and maintain objectivity had not yet been developed. Inhabiting one's rich inner world with volition and self-awareness was a possibility reserved only for sages, shamans, and seers. Now there is opportunity to make the journey into the interior even more extraordinary than had ever been possible as you use your rational capacities to reflect upon the miracle of your unfolding mythology.

Myths That Need to Be Changed

By understanding how your personal mythology developed, you can recognize outmoded myths and you can accept that their season has passed. Without the recognition that a particular myth is no longer serving you, you are likely to dissipate your energy with misdirected effort as you continue to live according to its guidance. You also bring about the problems bred by a dysfunctional myth. With the realization that the myth is deficient, and a compassionate understanding of how it became that way, you are more able to marshal your energies for changing it rather than to squander them on self-condemnation. To move forward, you are best served by appreciating rather than rejecting your past.

The desire to change an impoverished myth may be strong, but change does not occur in a vacuum. No one's mythology or behavior exists in isolation from its social and political context. Many people are trapped in circumstances so overpowering that they are blinded to any mythology but the one that dominates in their situation. They may remain in an unhappy marriage, unfulfilling job, or oppressive social role because societal conditions prevent them from conceiving of, no less moving toward, other options.

Even where external change is not possible, more sophisticated attitudes, values, and philosophies can help you persevere in a difficult situation, and often you do have freedom to bring about change. Freedom has been defined as the "state of mind you enjoy when you are aware of a choice and have the power to choose."[13] Your awareness of choice increases in a profound way when you recognize that undesirable patterns in your life are being supported by myths you had not previously questioned. Very early in your life, you began to create a mythology to cope with your unique circumstances. If you came to believe that the world is a loveless place, you may, for self-protection, have sensibly avoided intimacy. If, as an adult, you are able to recognize that you are living a mythology that is keeping you emotionally isolated, you then have a choice. If you challenge the myth and open yourself to greater closeness, you may be struck by how many more opportunities for choosing intimacy seem to come your way.

How do you know when a myth needs to change? On occasion, a single powerful experience will deal a mortal blow to a limiting myth, but more often a series of less momentous events leads to changes. Sometimes the feedback that a myth is not working is quite subtle. Harmful patterns that keep recurring in your life are particularly noteworthy. Underlying myths that play themselves out repeatedly may be found in difficulties with authority, explosive love relationships, or a tendency to grab failure from the jaws of success. Often the example of a parent's life sets a ceiling on a person's mythology regarding success or achievement, and breaking through that barrier is an important part of maturation. If you can recognize the mythic dimension of patterns you wish to change, you will be more effective in working with its deeper layers.

This relationship between early experiences and patterns in adult life has gained increasing recognition in recent decades. Adult children of alcoholics are articulating common themes, such as an unreasoned need to please a remote or abusive partner. Women are identifying the way an unfulfilled longing for their father's love may have left them addicted to men who are emotionally unavailable. Men are seeing how the models provided by the culture, and more specifically by their fathers, caused them to despise and repress vulnerable feelings. Adult victims of child abuse are finding ways to control their own abusive impulses. There is freedom in recognizing underlying themes. Rather than automatically living out these patterns, people can develop the ability to reflect on them and find new options. Psychologists have described numerous constellations of thought, feeling, and behavior that are arranged around a nuclear theme and cause problems in people's lives. These patterns are often called *complexes.*

Freud held that the Oedipus complex, organized around the theme of the son's competition with the father for the mother's erotic love, must be resolved if he is to go on to healthy relationships and a normal life. Alfred Adler emphasized the "inferiority complex" and the "power complexes" related to it. Henry Murray referred to the "Icarus Complex."[14] In the Greek myth, Icarus, son of Daedalus, had an inflated estimate of his capacities and flew so close to the sun that the wax on his artificial wings melted, carrying him to his death. The "Icarus Complex" leads people, particularly young adults, to reach too far and expect too much, until they fall and become psychologically disabled with fear or apathy. The "Jonah Complex," in contrast, was described by Abraham Maslow to portray the fear of attaining one's full potential.[15] Just as Jonah, in the biblical account, ran away from his call from God and ended up in the belly of a whale, many individuals avoid their inner callings and find that their vitality begins to atrophy. Carl Jung, who introduced the term *complex* to psychoanalysis, believed that each person has a number of core complexes that grow out of conflicts concerning archetypal themes.

The program you are about to begin will help you identify patterns of that magnitude in the language of your own psyche, understand them in the context of your past and your aspirations, and initiate changes in the service of your mythology's evolutionary capacity.

How Your Myths Evolve

Our most fundamental myths may be glimpsed through dreams and other products of the unconscious, and they are particularly evident during those life crises in which our ways of understanding the world and directing our actions are failing us. If a tragic illness occurs to someone we love, we may reel in despair, bewildered by questions we cannot answer: "What did he do to deserve such agony?" Embedded in the question is the belief that those who are visited by grave misfortune deserve it; those who are worthy will be spared. That myth once gave us comfort and security, but when it does not hold up, our sense of balance in the world may waver as well. Your personal mythology changes both through a gradual evolution and more dramatically through such crises.

A gradual refining of your mythology grows out of the inevitable conflict that will develop between existing mythic structures and new experiences. The two establish a feedback loop. Your inner models guide you toward particular actions, and the consequences of those actions either reinforce or challenge the original model. A married man who secretly believes he is a Casanova divorces, begins to pursue his fantasies, and is consistently rebuffed by the women he tries to lure. He is likely to suffer unwelcome shifts in the model he holds about himself. Perception is a match-mismatch process. If there is a close correspondence between your myths and your perceptions, both remain intact and equilibrium is maintained. But if your internal models and your experiences do not match, the imbalance leads to attention, thought, and action aimed at removing the mismatch and replacing it with a better fit.[16]

When your experiences and your myths do not correspond, there are two basic possibilities for handling the contradiction: alter your perception of the experience *or* change your myth. Jean Piaget used the term *assimilation* to describe how perceptions may be filtered or distorted to fit internal models, and the term *accommodation* to describe how internal models may be altered to fit new experiences. The man described above may interpret his rejections as a confirmation rather than a refutation of his myth, modifying his perceptions to fit his Casanova self-image (assimilation). He might, for instance, tell himself that his magnetism is so powerful and so overwhelming that a particular woman simply could not cope with it and was forced to make a hasty retreat, selecting instead a less manly suitor who didn't intimidate her. Or, after numerous rejections, he might adjust his self-image (accommodation). Thus you may unconsciously distort your perceptions so that they may be *assimilated* into the mythology you hold, or you may (also often unconsciously) revise your mythology to *accommodate* new or freshly perceived experiences. It is through a continual accommodation to experiences that contradict the premises of your mythology, or are altogether beyond its boundaries, that your mythology gradually evolves.

Your mythology also evolves through crisis. Erik Erikson used the term *identity crisis* to describe the transitional period between one stage of psychosocial development and another. Such crises occur naturally and periodically, and they accompany a breakdown in your mythology. One reason that such an event is called a "crisis" (represented in Chinese by a combination of the characters for "danger" and "opportunity") is that it is painful and threatening to give up a familiar myth, even when it is limiting your opportunities. Established myths are sometimes so central to your identity that to renounce them, though they are dysfunctional, means suffering what Elisabeth Kübler-Ross has referred to as one of the "little deaths" we face throughout our lives.

Jean Houston points out that in the ancient mystery schools, one is required to die to one story in order to be reborn to a larger one. The soul's development is said to begin "with the wounding of the psyche by the Larger Story."[17] Because our life had been organized around the old story, the wounding of the psyche by the Larger Story is a crisis of immense proportion. The Larger Story is infused with higher purposes and may shatter cherished values that were presumed in the old story. It demands worthier involvements than were imaginable within the old story, and it embraces parts of the psyche that the old story fearfully consigned to the shadows.

The Larger Story is immense beyond comprehension, so the crisis that assaults an old myth does not necessarily leave a new mythic image in its place. Jerome Bruner observed that "when the myths no longer fit the internal plights of those who require them, the transition to newly created myths may take the form of a chaotic voyage into the interior, the certitudes of externalization replaced by the anguish of the internal voyage."[18]

But, according to Houston, the wounding "becomes *sacred* when we are willing to release our old stories and to become the vehicles through which the new story may emerge into time." She points out that, in the Greek tragedies, the gods forced themselves into human consciousness when the soul had been wounded. "Wounding opens the doors of our sensibility to a larger reality, which is blocked to our habituated and conditioned point of view."[19] If we cannot open ourselves to this larger reality, we continually repeat the old story. The struggle between the prevailing myth that keeps you tied to the old story, and an emerging myth that is often kindled by glimpses into the larger reality, is the second way your mythology evolves.

It is at the points of conflict between prevailing myths and emerging myths that the most dramatic changes in your mythology are possible. And it is at these points that your mythology is the most ripe for your attention. The old and the emerging typically engage in a struggle deep within you, a contest between the dying and the unborn, for the dominance of your perceptions, values, and motivations.

While the first flights of the fledgling new myth will probably be tried outside your awareness, as its struggle with the old myth intensifies, it begins to break into consciousness, often through dreams, fantasies, unfamiliar impulses, novel ideas, or the emergence of a budding "subpersonality."[20] There will be much in the old myth worthy of preservation, and the emerging myth will hold promises that are not attainable. Ideally, a synthesis between the old myth and the emerging myth will incorporate the most vital elements of each and point you in new directions that are both realistic *and* inspired. By bringing the process to your awareness, you have a greater chance of working out the conflict as a drama in your inner life rather than having to play it out on the rack of life.

Participating in the Evolution of Your Mythology

Developing a framework for thinking about your personal mythology allows you to participate more effectively as it develops. You are less likely to cling to an outdated myth if you are able to envision the potential value of changing it. You are less likely to naively or desperately grab at untested alternative images when you are able to appreciate the constructive functions the old myth once served. Still, there are many dilemmas in attempting to revise one's mythology. When people enter psychotherapy, their presenting problem is often formulated according to the premises of the old myth. Rather than speculating that the old myth may be failing them, they assume that they are not adhering to it closely enough. When the conquering Spaniards laid waste to Mexico in the early sixteenth century, the Aztecs felt that they had failed to honor their gods, and they increased the number of victims they sacrificed.

In today's world, a long-standing myth might instruct a woman to maintain a friendly, cheerful disposition at all times—submerging her legitimate frustrations and resentments, her minor irritations about life, her responses to injustice, and generally creating a doll-like caricature of who she really is. If people do not treat her with respect, she may conclude that she is not following the old myth closely enough. Her self-criticisms and her motivation for "self-improvement" may be directed toward perfecting herself in that image. She may become even more agreeable, more passive, more falsely cheerful, regardless of the personal costs. Like the Aztecs before her, she may remain oblivious to the foibles of the old myth and scurry back to whatever psychological security it can offer.

We think of conflict or shortcomings in people's myths as the leading edge of their psychological development. As you reach new stages in your own maturation, and as your circumstances change, myths that once offered effective guidance may become unworkable and even destructive. Difficulties in making a decision, unfamiliar fears or anxieties, self-contradictions, puzzling dreams, nagging confusion, ambivalence, and even physical symptoms may signal mythic conflict. It is in those areas of your life where you are having difficulty or experiencing dissatisfaction that work with your personal mythology is likely to have the most impact.

As you will see, an early focus of the program involves identifying such trouble spots in your underlying mythology. You will then be shown, step by step, how to work with one of these areas. In renewing this aspect of your mythology, you also will be gaining a basic understanding of how your mythology operates and how to continue to constructively involve yourself in its evolution.

Each of the next five chapters provides guidance through one of the five stages in the program. In each chapter, you will be asked to carry out between five and seven structured procedures that we call "personal rituals." These rituals range from creating a symbolic shield and going on guided fantasy journeys to writing personal "Fairy Tales" and staging the enactment of a desired personal myth. The rituals will lead you through a systematic and practical exploration of your personal mythology. We turn now to a personal ritual that will introduce you to your "Inner Shaman."

MEETING YOUR INNER SHAMAN

Just as cultural myths may bring out the best or the worst of an entire people, personal myths affect each of us at this most basic level. One way of evoking your deeper wisdom and higher possibilities is to cultivate what we call the "Inner Shaman."[21] Shamans—the spiritual leaders, healers, and "technicians of the sacred" of tribal cultures—have been receiving increasing attention in recent years. They provide a model, rooted in nontechnological societies, for guiding the Western mind back to its estranged primal roots.[22]

The shaman's powers and ecstatic visions provided guidance and explanation to tribal peoples for natural events that were otherwise unfathomable. The shaman was an artist in relation to the culture's guiding mythology, adept at guarding, transmitting, and transforming it.[23] As myth-making has become more highly personalized, modern individuals are called upon to become skilled in developing such facility with their own personal mythologies. To cultivate the Inner Shaman is to develop within yourself the skills for becoming a thoughtful agent of your own evolving reality. Your Inner Shaman can be a guide to the hidden and unutterably rich landscape of your unconscious.

The Inner Shaman has three essential responsibilities. The first is to maintain a conduit between the waking consciousness of "Ordinary Reality" and the hidden reality of the "Other Worlds." Tribal shamans believe that people are influenced by the animal spirits of the "Lower World" (one's animal nature) and the godly spirits of the "Upper World" (one's spiritual nature). Just as shamans regularly entered the

Other Worlds, reemerging with new visions and direction for their people, your Inner Shaman can serve as a guide as you take periodic inward journeys to the Other Worlds. The ability to take such inward journeys can be developed, and a central feature of this program involves practice in accessing and using those altered states of consciousness that can be reached through deep relaxation, guided visualization, and imagery work.

The second responsibility of the Inner Shaman is to creatively and effectively bring new circumstances into accord with your guiding mythology. Traditional shamans used their powers to influence physical and social events toward outcomes that were harmonious with the culture's existing myths. The Inner Shaman taps into deep mythic guidance for approaching life's demands and opportunities. This requires an ability to selectively apply and adapt the existing mythology. The Inner Shaman is able to impartially observe your personal mythology and astutely bring its wisdom to changing circumstances.

Third, your Inner Shaman guides the evolution of your existing mythology. The tribal shaman had to find a balance between established customs and cultural innovation, serving as a guardian of tradition, while also introducing new mythic visions to the society. Flaws in the existing mythology may have become conspicuous, or the mythology may not have been able to adapt to new circumstances. New mythic images were periodically required. Sometimes, the shaman's visit to the Other Worlds resulted in a new and inspiring vision—a glimpse of the Larger Story—that refined or replaced an existing myth. But visions and insights encountered in altered states do not necessarily constitute sound mythic guidance. The Inner Shaman is challenged to bring you informed and seasoned judgment as you shepherd your mythology's development.

The program presented here calls upon you to develop and exercise your ability to carry out all three of these responsibilities. The Inner Shaman operates from the position that some psychologists call the "observing ego" and that meditators often refer to as the "inner witness." While you will not always need to invoke your Inner Shaman to work effectively with your personal mythology, drawing upon this inner witness will generally be empowering. There will be numerous times that you may call upon your Inner Shaman for assistance in maintaining a passageway between your waking consciousness and the Other Worlds, for creatively drawing upon deep mythic wisdom as you meet new situations, and for further refining your developing mythology.

Personal Ritual: Meeting Your Inner Shaman

The following personal ritual will introduce you to your Inner Shaman. The instructions are arranged so that you may have someone read them to you, make a tape, or become familiar enough with the words that you can lead yourself through the ritual from memory. As with all the instructions in this book, feel free to modify the following in any way that makes it more useful and appropriate for you.

When you meet your Inner Shaman—whether in the guise of a Wise Old Man, the Earth Mother, a known Master, a Celtic Priestess, Jesus, Confucius, or whoever else emerges into your awareness—it will be a significant moment in your life. It is probable that your Inner Shaman's appearance will suggest a spiritual connection, perhaps through a ceremonial setting, ritualistic objects, or by being surrounded in light. The scene will be markedly different from the mundane. Your sense of security and comfort will transcend the ordinary. Begin by finding a comfortable position, sitting or reclining.

Allow your breathing to become slow and deep. [Pause] Relax comfortably. Begin to release any tension in your body. [30-second pause]

Bring to mind people who have been inspiring models to you, such as good teachers, wise friends, or talented leaders. [Pause] Focus on one or two of them. [Pause] Consider the qualities that made these individuals important models for you. [30-second pause]

Now move more deeply into your appreciation of these figures and, searching your own vulnerabilities, discover your need for instruction and protection. Affirm to yourself your resolution to take this journey into realms that are usually hidden from you. Your efforts here are earning you the right to access deep wisdom.

In a few moments, you will imagine yourself becoming very small. You will find yourself standing on your own stomach. You will not be troubled by the ordinary laws of physics regarding size, speed, gravity, the presence of light where it is normally dark, or your ability to exist in two forms simultaneously. With your next three breaths, you will begin to become smaller until you find yourself standing on your own stomach. Feel yourself becoming smaller now. ONE. TWO. THREE. Explore your stomach. Find your navel. It is a magical entrance to your Inner World. Imagine yourself climbing inside your body through your navel.

You are in a timeless and dreamlike reality. It is dark as you feel your way and move bravely forward and downward on a path strangely familiar to you. Notice your sensations and feelings in this non-ordinary reality. Breathe deeply as you become more comfortable here.

You move forward for a long while. You are starkly alone, lacking landmarks, acutely aware of your vulnerability, need, and hope. Without knowing how, you find you have come to a monument, and on it are the beliefs and injunctions by which you have lived. Read one or more of them, and recognize that these have been your commandments. Take time to consider them. [45-second pause]

Gather your courage, for you must enter ever more deeply into the dark places of your being. The challenges make you worthy of the guidance you desire. The Inner Shaman is not revealed to the unprepared or casual seeker. Moving beyond the monument, you eventually find yourself on a stone prominence overlooking the Valley of Your Youth. Your sight and hearing are strong and you feel compassion as you survey the emotional world of your childhood. Without faltering, consider the terrors, deprivations, confusions, and blessings of your early years. Do not flinch or condemn, for your task is to affirm your stamina in having survived. [45-second pause]

Continue to move, one slow step at a time, until you come to a clearing surrounded by lush green plants. At its edge, the branches of two large trees touch and form an archway. You know that on the other side of that archway is the sacred setting of your Inner Shaman. It may be a mountaintop, a desert, a temple, or a forest. Walk to the trees and notice how they form pillars for the archway that leads to the dwelling place of your Inner Shaman. Now step through the archway and behold. [30-second pause]

Respectfully walk up to and greet your Inner Shaman. Use your senses to discover what you can of the appearance and temperament of this mysterious individual. [Pause] Thank your Inner Shaman for having met you. Use words, gestures, or silent intuitive communication. [Pause] Recognize your Shaman's bottomless affection for you and belief in your worthiness. A profound silence falls upon you as you gaze at your Shaman and your Shaman gazes at you.

Ask any question of importance about your life. You may well receive an unexpected answer. [60-second pause] Now ask about your ritual of return. You need to be able to visit your Shaman at will. Your return ritual will be described to you in the way in which you learn best, perhaps by speaking, movement, or imagery. Remember that the laws of ordinary physics do not apply here. You may be told to find your way back by visualizing the paths you have just taken, by using the sound of a gong, a ritualized movement, or with the repetition of a few chosen words. Now, with your Shaman's assurance that you can return, receive instruction for how to embark on your next visit. [60-second pause]

It is time to come back to Ordinary Reality. Be respectful in your leavetaking. [Pause] You will return in your own manner. Perhaps you will retrace your steps with the speed of a running deer, passing the Valley of Your Childhood, the monument, and coming up through your navel. Perhaps you will return by another route. Return now. [20-second pause] Now that you are back, you will with your next three breaths return to your normal size and your ordinary reality. ONE. TWO. THREE. Coming into waking consciousness, gently open your eyes. Record the experience in your journal, emphasizing especially the method you will use for your next visit.

Here is the journal account of Meg, a woman with whom you will become quite familiar in the following chapters:

> I greet him with "I knew you'd be here, and I am most grateful. You are revealing the path to me, reluctant as I've been to follow it." He's smiling at me. I don't know how to feel about being loved so much. I've never felt such absolute acceptance for who I am. His eyes are remarkable. They are infinitely wise and young and curious and laughing and forgiving. There is nothing for me to prove. Nothing is asked of me. He has said nothing, but I know these things in all my senses, wordlessly. My words are pale facsimiles of the experience. I ask, "Have I permission to return to you?" He makes a gesture, a shrug with upturned palms that I read as "Of course, silly." I sense a playfulness that enjoys my naiveté. I mimic his movement and hear myself say, "Though the path be dark, the goal is light." I don't know where these words came from, but they seem like a great teaching. I somehow know that repeating the phrase and the gesture will be the ritual for my return. For a timeless time I am in the cradle of my own center, in healing communion with my Inner Druid Shaman.

On to Stage One

The following chapters present a carefully arranged sequence of rituals that will teach you how to understand more of your life at the mythic level. Your Inner Shaman will assist you at various points along the way. We invite you to take this journey, by way of rituals, stories, ideas, and dreams, to the inner realms where your myths are made. In the process, you will have an opportunity to consider new perspectives on the myths that guide your thoughts and actions, and to apply these insights toward a more mythically informed life.

2

The First Stage: Recognizing When a Guiding Myth Is No Longer an Ally

Error is just as important a condition of life's progress as truth.

—C. G. JUNG[1]

We open this first stage of the program with a series of personal rituals that will take you into the past and help you understand your unique history in terms of your evolving mythology. From this perspective, you will begin to identify areas of your mythology that are not serving you well. While these personal myths may at one time have been the best inner guidance conceivable for facing the dilemmas that confronted you as a child, they are no longer allies. By the close of this chapter you will have selected one of these areas for your attention, and in the remainder of the program you will be mobilizing your determination and creativity as you transform that part of your mythology. The task of engaging yourself fully in this process will be challenging, perhaps at times discouraging; yet it holds the potential of yielding novel insights, greater meaning, and fresh direction as you consider central questions in your life from a larger perspective.

PERSONAL HISTORY FROM A MYTHIC PERSPECTIVE

Freud showed how the past creates the present; Erik Erikson, one of Freud's most innovative successors, showed how the present reorganizes the past.[2] Our self-identities, according to Erikson, are formed as we come to interpret experiences from the past in light of their meaning for our current lives. Consciously and unconsciously, each of us is continually creating an inner story to explain the past, understand the present, and anticipate what the future may hold.

That story forms the basis of your identity, your sense of who you are. When, in chapter 1, you took an imaginary excursion back to the lives of your ancestors, you were reconstructing history according to available facts and considerable conjecture. We all continually reconstruct our personal histories as we incorporate new experiences into them. Yet we may not realize the powerful influence exerted by the way we construct the past on our current convictions, doubts, and view of the future. Articulating your past from a new, spirited, and mythically informed vantage point allows you to begin to rewrite your life story in a manner that beckons to your higher possibilities while realistically accounting for your limitations.

Many motifs from classical mythology, such as Odysseus' heroic journey, Persephone's descent to the Underworld, the quest for the Holy Grail, the tale of Psyche and Eros, or the dialogues of Krishna and Arjuna in the *Bhagavad Gita,* speak to dilemmas that are still germane to the modern psyche. Any of them could provide a structure that would be meaningful to most readers for reviewing their own lives.[3] Our program draws upon the motifs of "Paradise" and "Paradise Lost" from the Eden myth to structure an initial examination of your life story.[4] Later, you will be telling your story with your own metaphors, but we have found it useful to begin by organizing the work around the stirring images of this fundamental cultural myth.

Although our pragmatic, materialistic culture has tended to redefine "Paradise" in terms of worldly riches, most of us are aware of deeper longings. Attaining a particular vision of Paradise (Heaven, Nirvana, Valhalla, Elysium, Devachan) is the ultimate goal of many religious systems. Not only do scriptures describe some version of Paradise, they also attempt to explain why life on earth does not correspond with that vision, along with what believers must do to enter through the celestial gates. Adam and Eve's story is, of course, firmly embedded in the deeper recesses of the Western mind. The progression from Paradise to Paradise Lost and then toward a vision of Paradise Regained, at the core of Judeo-Christian tradition, is also a mythological representation of a fundamental theme for the individual's psychological development. And it provides a fertile context for the line of exploration you are about to pursue.

The Eden myth recalls the time in humanity's development before individual consciousness progressed out of an idyllic identification with nature and the life of the body. With the fall from innocence came an awakening of *self*-consciousness, paid for, however, with an anxious sense of separation from community and from the natural order—Paradise Lost. Theorists who have noted parallels between the

Recognizing When a Guiding Myth
Is No Longer an Ally

early stages of humanity's development and the child's personal development have interpreted the Genesis story as psychologically representing the individual's "fall" from innocence during the journey through childhood.[5]

As the human embryo typically develops in an environment that provides for all its warmth and safety needs, so too do infancy and childhood often provide long stretches of time blessed by innocence and wonder. Even in those troubled homes and damaged families where childhood is hardly a carefree idyll, boys and girls often enter into fantasy worlds that provide a measure of security and hope, charged with images about the lives of children that are found in stories, television, and movies. Progressively, however, a disquieting awareness of separation from the nurturing environment and from the fantasies ensues as the child matures.

The infant's realization of separateness from the mother begins a sequence of differentiations that extend through the early years of life. Sometimes these separations are experienced as the achievement of independence, and they bring satisfaction and joy; at other times, the severance is a source of anxiety and grief. In either case, the increasing awareness of estrangement between self and environment is part of growing up and has been mythologically likened by Rollo May to "the time when each child re-enacts the 'fall' of Adam."[6]

But myths of Paradise Lost are accompanied by visions of Paradise Regained, the promise of recovering a secure and tranquil position in the order of things. People adhere to images of Paradise Regained passionately and, for the believer, they reveal the Larger Story. Some psychologists have equated the powerful motivation to pursue Paradise Regained, the religious impulse, with a primitive longing to recapture a sense of womblike peace and union. Others have argued vehemently that to understand this passion in anything but a broad spiritual context is blindly reductionistic.[7] Whatever the true significance of this longing may be, the great myths and religious systems of diverse cultures have portrayed it as the soul's yearning to awaken to its connection with powers that are beyond the visible world.[8]

Channeling this deep longing into an ever-maturing vision of Paradise Regained *in this lifetime,* an inspired understanding of where you are headed and why you are headed there, opens you to the Larger Story and keeps your journey on a more heartfelt path. Elaborating and supporting such a vision is a pivotal challenge for your personal mythology.

In the first four rituals of this chapter, you will explore the role of your own childhood version of Paradise (or its absence), your Fall from that buoyant moment in time, and the Quest you have pursued (or abandoned) toward a dimly perceived or well-articulated vision of Paradise Regained.

Personal Ritual: Your Lost "Paradise"

Slumbering in your unconscious mind may be dim recollections of a time prior to your awareness of separateness—a period when life was a rhapsodic dream. And you may recall childhood experiences that were permeated with a dreamlike sense of joy, security, or wonder. The purpose of this first personal ritual is to take you back, in your memory or imagination, to these pristine eras of innocence.

Where the instructions do not bring actual pictures to your mind, create the experience, as if you are telling yourself a story. For specifics your memory is unable to retrieve, embellish whatever you do recollect with your imagination. If you are unable to recall any serene or pleasurable early experiences, use your capacity to pretend. Treat this as an experiment in how things might have been. Fantasy is a practical tool in work of this nature.

Decide which of the methods for leading yourself through a guided imagery exercise you will use (asking someone to read the instructions to you, reading them into a tape, or becoming familiar enough with the instructions so you can guide yourself through them from memory). Also, recall that whenever you come to the end of a paragraph, to the word "Pause," or to words written in uppercase, a delay of about ten seconds is needed. For pauses of twenty seconds or more, consider using a chime, click, or a phrase indicating that the tape should be stopped at that point or that your partner should stop reading until you are ready to continue.

After choosing the method you will use and making the appropriate preparations, find a safe, secluded space where you are unlikely to be interrupted, close your eyes, take several deep breaths, and begin to relax:

As you settle into this safe, secure spot, focus on your breathing. Begin to release any areas of tension in your body. [Pause] Listen for and feel each in-breath and each out-breath. [Pause] Notice your belly and chest rising and falling. [Pause] Your breathing becomes slow and deep as you relax more and more completely with each of your next five breaths—ONE, TWO, THREE, FOUR, FIVE.

Thoroughly relaxed, re-create in your memory your last exchange with your Inner Shaman. Recall the instructions you were given for making another visit. Follow those instructions now. [30-second pause] When you have found your Shaman, exchange respectful, affectionate greetings. In your Shaman's company, sense the rightness of being together and attend to the sounds, colors, and forms in this sacred place.

Your Shaman lets you know that a pleasant experience awaits you. You are bid to prepare yourself for a journey to an earlier time when you were untested, innocent, and receptive. Your Shaman makes an evocative gesture and you are transported in time back to a pleasant moment of childhood. You view the world from the height of a child and with the curious eyes and inquiring ears of a child just come to the use of language and questioning.

You are revisiting the time of your very first joy-filled memory. See who is with you. Feel their touch. Sniff unashamedly the good odors around you. Sense how right it is for you to be alive. Move, skip, dance, or roll with the unfettered abandon of youth. Explore your world, unconscious of threat. Be fully present with this early experience. [60-second pause]

Now, focus on the most pleasant, peaceful feelings in that scene. Direct your breathing into them, allowing them to intensify and fill your body. Every cell comes to life as these positive feelings invigorate you from head to toe. [Pause] The feelings become deliciously vivid as they continue to build. [30-second pause]

Your Shaman has a lesson for you about this period of your life. Basking in the positive feelings, receive. You will remember in mind and body. [30-second pause] Take one last look at your Shaman and communicate anything you wish. [20-second pause] It is time to take leave of your Shaman. Express your farewell.

Prepare to return to your waking consciousness. Counting from five back to one, you will be able to recall all you need of this experience. When you hear the number 1, you will feel alert, relaxed, and refreshed, as if waking from a wonderful nap. FIVE, move your fingers and toes. FOUR, stretch your shoulders, neck, and face muscles. THREE, take a deep breath. TWO, bring your attention back into the room. ONE, open your eyes, feeling refreshed, alert, and fully competent to meet the requirements of your day.

In your journal, describe the scene you focused upon and the bodily sensations you experienced. Consider the degree to which the sense of an early Paradise was available simply by reaching inward according to the instructions. Reflect on how such early experiences, or the lack of them, may have influenced your ideas about yourself and about what you could expect from life. The lesson offered by your Shaman may have touched upon this question.

Many of our clients and workshop participants have, over the years, sent us copies of their journals. We've selected an account that is particularly lively and articulate to serve as an example as you lead yourself through the program.[9]

Meg was a fifty-five-year-old freelance writer when she went through the sequence of personal rituals presented in this book. Excerpts from her journal will provide you with a preview of each ritual you are about to perform. Read through the instructions for each ritual and the example following it before you perform the ritual. Because Meg is a professional writer, her images are especially vivid and her journal is unusual in its literary merit. While her writing lends rich example, be forewarned that it is not presented as a standard for comparison. The only relevant requirement for your journal is the degree to which it speaks from your deeper self.

During the Paradise fantasy, Meg returned to a happy childhood memory. She used the first person, present tense, to record it in her journal:

> I am seven and I am running around on Point Loma. There are no houses anywhere around me, just scrub brush on the cliffs above the ocean. I am limber and strong, with no sense of my own mortality, and I am recklessly clambering down the cliff to the exposed rocks below. My joints move freely, my hands are strong in finding crevices to grab onto, and my bare feet seek and find toeholds easily. The ocean is calm and the air is salty-sweet. The temperature is in the mid-70s and I am comfortably dressed in pants and T-shirt. Gulls are flying above and a line of pelicans surf the air currents over the incoming waves.
>
> I walk out on the rocks, my tough feet unhurt by the barnacles and mussels underfoot. I see the lovely tidepools, filled with riches in anemones, sea-hares, and shells. I pause and discover a perfect abalone shell. The outside of it is rugged and rocklike with seven little vent holes in the edge which, when the creature was alive, curled over to make a strong seal on the rocks. Inside the shell is a rainbow of sinuous, reflective forms in iridescent colors and

> complex patterns. I have never seen anything so beautiful in my life. The abalone shell is the most precious possession I have ever had, and I have no scruples about taking it from the tidepool and keeping it for myself. I am alone, happy, free and unmindful of time, demands, the past, or the future.

In tracing the influence this event had on her subsequent life, Meg reflected:

> The underlying theme I have carried forward from this early experience is the sense that there is always positive discovery ahead, that unimagined potential lies in the dullest-appearing object or circumstance. Also, my sense of myself as a participant in nature has never been lost.

By going on this brief journey back in time, Meg was left with a concrete Paradise image drawn from her own childhood. She recalls her escapade on Point Loma as an ecstatic union of body, mind, feeling, and spirit. The little girl is alone, contained, excited, yet there is no sense of relationship with anyone else. Each moment provided more than enough stimulation to keep her happy and engaged. With the abalone shell, she had, in her estimation, acquired a perfect possession. This memory reflects an internalized model that Meg carries within her, a standard against which she may now unconsciously measure the quality of her experiences. As you will see, the abalone shell also became a symbol on her Personal Shield.

Personal Ritual: Creating Your Personal Shield

We now invite you to construct a "Personal Shield." Many Native American cultures used Personal Shields for protection, healing, and reverence. An image received in a powerful dream or during a vision quest or other purification ceremony might be interpreted by the tribal shaman and painted on a circular hide, hung with feathers, fur tassels, or shells. The symbols on the Shield told who the person was and what he loved, feared, or dreamed.

For this ritual, your Personal Shield should be round, at least 10 inches in diameter, and you should be able to draw or paint on it. One way of making a Shield is to put white unbleached muslin in an embroidery hoop and use embroidery paints. Simpler methods include cutting a white piece of construction paper into a circle or using the back of a large paper plate. You will need several colored crayons, felt-tipped pens, or a paint palette.

Divide your Shield into five equal sections (drawing five spokes out from the center) and, on the outer rim, label the sections: "Paradise," "Paradise Lost," "Paradise Regained Vision," "My Quest," and "A Renewed Vision."

The following instructions will evoke the imagery that you will be drawing on your Shield. First reread your Paradise fantasy. Then make preparations for another guided fantasy experience by arranging to have someone read the instructions to you, tape-recording them, or familiarizing yourself with them well enough so that you can lead yourself through the exercise unassisted. Find a comfortable position, keeping your journal, your Shield, and the drawing implements nearby.

Take several deep breaths. [20-second pause] Look at the section of your Shield labeled "Paradise." [Pause] Close your eyes and recall your Paradise fantasy.

Thinking of your Paradise fantasy, notice the most pleasant sensations in your body. [Pause] Focus on your positive feelings. Breathe into them, allowing them to become more vivid. The positive sensations fill you.

Focus on the part of your body in which the pleasant sensations are the most intense. See the color of the sensations. Trace with your fingertips or in your mind the shape of these feelings in your body. Note their color. Explore the interesting texture. [30-second pause] In a moment you will see or sense a symbol emerging out of the shapes and colors.

Watch as a symbol appears that represents a time of personal Paradise for you. [Pause] You may actually see the symbol take form, or you may simply sense what it is. [Pause] It will further evolve over the next few moments. Relax as it becomes increasingly clear.

Once you have come upon a fitting symbol, open your eyes and draw it on the Paradise portion of your Shield. If after listening to these instructions, you still have no sense of having had even moments of happiness in your childhood, find a symbol that represents what you are feeling or remembering. Even leaving the Paradise portion of your Shield blank can be a powerful statement.

After you begin to draw your symbol, you may find that it is changing even as you are creating it, or that you have more than one image to draw. Or an additional image may occur to you while you are drawing. Draw whatever comes to you. Do not be concerned about what may be "aesthetic" or "correct." As long as the drawing is meaningful to you, you are doing it right. [If you are reading these instructions into a tape, add: "Now turn off the tape until you have finished drawing your symbol."]

After you have completed drawing your Paradise symbol or symbols, look at the Paradise Lost portion of your Shield. [Pause] Close your eyes and move forward in time to a point where the happiness represented by the Paradise portion of your Shield was interrupted. [Pause] This may involve a change in your circumstances, a betrayal by a loved one, a personal tragedy, or a memorable failure. [Pause] Feel your body's response to this event.

Focus on the part of your body in which you feel this loss. Trace with your fingertips or in your mind the shape of these feelings in your body. Note their color. Explore their texture. [30-second pause] In a moment you will see or sense a symbol emerging out of the shapes and colors.

Watch as a symbol appears that for you represents Paradise Lost. [Pause] You may actually see the symbol take form or you may simply sense what it is. [Pause] It will further evolve over the next few moments. Relax as it becomes increasingly clear.

Once you have come upon a symbol that represents this period of your life, open your eyes and draw it on the Paradise Lost section of your Shield. If you did not see a vivid image, create the symbol as you complete this second portion of your shield. [If you are reading these instructions into a tape, add: "Now turn off the tape until you have completed drawing your symbol."]

Now that you have drawn a Paradise Lost symbol on your Shield, allow yourself to consciously breathe out any unpleasant bodily sensations. [30-second pause]

After adjusting to a disappointment of the kind depicted on the Paradise Lost section of the Shield, we gradually formulate ideas and fantasies for restoring the sense of peace and contentment associated with Paradise. Look at the section of your Shield labeled "Paradise Regained Vision." Close your eyes and reflect upon the ideals or images you formed about the way you wanted your life to become. [Pause] As you begin to identify the ideals or images you formed at that time, sink into your feelings about them.

Focus on the part of your body in which these feelings are most intense. Trace with your fingertips or in your mind the shape of these feelings. Note their color. Explore their texture. [30-second pause] In a moment you will see or sense a symbol emerging out of the shapes and colors.

Watch as a symbol appears that for you represented your aspirations, your personal version of Paradise Regained. [Pause] You may actually see the symbol take form or you may simply sense what it is. [Pause] It will further evolve over the next few moments. Relax as it becomes increasingly clear.

Once you have come upon a symbol or a set of symbols that represents the hopes and aspirations you came upon early in your life, open your eyes and complete the Paradise Regained portion of your Shield. [If you are reading these instructions into a tape, add: "Now turn off the tape until you have completed drawing your symbol."]

Look at the progression of symbols on the "Paradise," "Paradise Lost," and "Paradise Regained" sections of your Shield. Now look at the portion of your Shield labeled "My Quest." [Pause] Once more close your eyes. Move forward in time from the Paradise Lost period of your life and consider the path you have taken toward Paradise Regained. Think about what you have done to attempt to make your life better—activities you have carried out, personal qualities you have developed, accomplishments you have attained. [Pause] Reflect on the dilemmas you were facing, what you attempted to do about them, and the outcome of those actions. [30-second pause]

Focus on the part of your body in which your feelings about your Quest are the most intense. Trace with your fingertips or in your mind the shape of these feelings. Note their color. Explore their texture. [30-second pause] In a moment you will see or sense a symbol emerging out of the shapes and colors.

Watch as a symbol appears that represents your actions in the world. [Pause] You may actually see the symbol take form or you may simply sense what it is. [Pause] It will further evolve over the next few moments. Relax as it becomes increasingly clear.

Once you have come upon a symbol or a set of symbols that represents your Quest, open your eyes and draw this on the section of your Shield labeled "My Quest." This drawing of your personal Quest is the last drawing for now.

If you would like to add details to your Shield, or to place borders on it, or to embellish it with some other decoration such as feathers or beads, do so now. Then sit back and inspect your creation.

The symbol on the Paradise portion of Meg's shield was of the abalone shell she had seen in her Paradise fantasy. Her Paradise Lost symbol was a hypodermic syringe. Her Paradise Regained image was the yin-yang symbol, a divided circle used in ancient China to represent the interplay of opposing tendencies. The symbol she drew for her personal Quest was a small coat-of-arms with the words *Freedom, Strength, Good,* and *Competent* written in its quadrants.

In the following personal ritual, you will be introduced to a technique for creatively examining the personal meaning of such symbols, and you will see the significance Meg found in each of the symbols on her Shield.

Personal Ritual: Exploring the Meaning of Your Shield

Choose at least one symbol from your Shield for deeper examination. Focus particularly on symbols that evoke discomfort, sadness, anger, or other unpleasant feelings. Examine the symbol and then begin to speak *as if you have become* that symbol. Give it a voice. You *are* the symbol; describe yourself in the present tense and in the first person.[10]

If the symbol is of a rowboat, you might begin by stating: "I am a small rowboat, I am blue, and I am on a stormy sea." Then continue to talk about yourself as a rowboat. Let your words come spontaneously and unrehearsed. If you are working alone, you may want to keep a record by talking into a tape recorder or writing your thoughts directly into your journal. If you are working with a partner, your partner's job is simply to listen, to gently remind you if you wander away from the first person present tense as you identify with the symbol, and to encourage you to go beyond the first few layers of associations. Discussion should wait until after you have explored the symbol in its own voice as fully as possible.

When you are finished, sketch the symbol in your journal and summarize the way you identified with it. Comment on the meaning the symbol seems to hold for you. Meg summarized her associations with all four of the symbols on her Shield:

> ***Abalone Shell (Paradise):*** I am an unblemished abalone shell in a tidepool on an unspoiled coast. A glorious natural phenomenon, a thing of beauty, I am utterly unstudied in my grace. It is clear that the hand of God created me.
>
> ***Hypodermic Syringe (Paradise Lost):*** I am the hypodermic syringe. I am a cold, efficient device for injecting drugs into the human body. I am a tool: mindless, efficient, disposable, benign or

deadly, depending on the use made of me. When Meg was a child, she knew me both by observation and use. She saw me putting morphine and adrenaline, alternately, into her mother's body. She was taught to use me to save her mother's life. I am indifferent about who uses me. I have no morality, no sentiment.

Yin-Yang Symbol (Paradise Regained): I am a symbol of unity. All contrasts are reconciled within me. I reflect the Tao, the One, the principle of unification. I encompass, without prejudice, all creation and all time. I am One with All: Godlike and Humble, Creator and Dissolver, Whole and Diffuse.

Coat-of-Arms with the words *freedom, strength, good,* and *competent,* written in its quadrants ***(the Quest):*** I am a strong protective covering, made of leather and oak, designed to protect Meg in her journey through life. Very few weapons can penetrate me, and Meg rarely lays me aside. I carry the emblems she values, even though she rarely lives up to them fully. What cannot be seen is my patched and shabby reverse side.

I speak of "freedom"—freedom of thought and action, freedom from convention and orthodox limitations. Behind me, however [on the back of the coat-of-arms], is "fear"—fear of censure and alienation. I keep my back side well hidden.

One of my sections is designated "strong"—strong in purpose, body, values, courage. The flip-side of "strong" is "rigid"—unwillingness, inability to yield without collapse.

Part of my front is "good"—I want to do good work and have a good heart, good will, good life, and good death. Good is defined as being a positive force. On the back, however, is its opposite: "self-serving."

My last quarter is for "competence"—development of my skills and facilities in a narrow range of activities (my artwork, mothering, writing—all easy stuff for me). On the back is "laziness and defensiveness"—being unwilling to challenge myself with difficult or boring tasks and unwilling to admit my incompetence at money management, at many human relations situations, or at physical challenge.

Frank, a thirty-five-year-old investment counselor, used this technique to explore the symbolism of a fist he had drawn on his Shield:

The symbol in the Paradise Lost portion of my Shield is a picture of a fist striking an innocent belly—specifically my belly, when I was four and a half. Okay, I am a fist. I am clenched. I am moving very rapidly. I have anger in me. I have incredible anger in me. That anger just wants to express itself. Wants to hit out. That anger is strong. And there is this kid playing with my toys. I have an excuse to put my anger right into his stomach. And that's what I'm doing. Wham! That felt good. I feel my power—instead of my usual helplessness. I feel contact instead of isolation. I feel dominance instead of feeling dominated.

Going from the warmth and safety of a loving, nurturing, and I guess overly protective home into kindergarten was totally overwhelming. I never seemed to know what was going on or what was expected of me or how to relate to the other kids. One day, one of the tougher boys was playing with a wooden train set. He went away and I started to play with it. Now I wasn't certain he was through with it, but he had left it, so with a shade of trepidation I went over and played with it. But he returned, saw me playing with the trains, and without a word, belted me in the stomach. I don't think I ever knew anything could hurt that much. All my breath was jerked out of me and I found out what it means when they say someone "sees stars."

It never occurred to me that it was wrong for him to have hit me—I always assumed he was justified because I should have known he was coming back and shouldn't have been messing with the toys he was using. For me, that fist represented an arbitrary authority that has always kept me in my place. I couldn't comprehend what was going on when I got hit, so I just took on a sort of unquestioned sense of being oppressed around strength or authority. I never really thought about what was on the other side of the fist.

"Becoming" the fist humanized it for me. I believe that my associations to the fist may have been very similar to what was going on for that kid. While I don't remember thinking of his fist for decades, I believe it represents a sense that I must be overly careful, a kind of self-oppression that I carry with me to this day. Somehow I believed I was bad because I was playing with those toys. So I accepted moral restrictions: I shouldn't ever break any rules; I must even abide by unwritten, imperceptible, and invisible rules. So now I put a lot of energy into second-guessing what might offend someone, what might cause someone to be angry with me, and I wind up stifling my spontaneity, and then I'm very uneasy around other people.

I tried real hard never to make the teacher or the principal or my classmates mad at me, and I still try not to make others, even strangers, uneasy around me or to give them any reason to judge me as doing something wrong. What a burden! What's striking is how I gave the kid that hit me so much authority to judge me.

You can see how Frank's elaboration upon this single symbol from his Shield began to reveal a persistent, self-limiting aspect of his personal mythology. Since childhood, he had given other people's opinions unwarranted authority in determining his own self-evaluations. In particular, the ways he imagined people might react to him caused him to sternly police his spontaneity.

This method, which begins with "becoming" a symbol and dramatizing it, is called *creative projection.* We encourage you to practice its use by exploring any symbolism—dream or waking—that emerges throughout the program. Creative projection is also a valuable tool for examining your reactions to artistic, spiritual, or other cultural images. For example, if you have access to a Tarot deck, pick a card, find the image on that card that you respond to most strongly, and use the creative projection technique to explore its symbolism. With this technique, you can develop your capacity to link symbols that move you and the personal meanings they hold.

Dream Focus: "My Quest"

The events that make up the Paradise and the Paradise Lost portions of your Shield occurred in the past. The Quest segment of your Shield symbolizes an ongoing story. The following optional dream instruction may provide further insight into your personal Quest.

If you have been recording your dreams, scan your journal to identify any dream images or sequences that might provide a glimpse into the nature of your personal Quest. Reflect on these dreams. If you would like an additional dream that might reveal more about your Quest, use the following instructions to "incubate" a dream tonight before going to sleep:

As you relax, reflect upon the Quest portion of your Shield. What bodily sensations resonate with the feelings you have about your Quest? Focus on these sensations. [Pause] Repeat to yourself, or out loud, ten to twenty times, "I will dream about my Quest, and I will recall my dreams."

Be prepared with your journal and a pen or tape recorder to capture your dream as soon as you awaken. If there is no dream, be receptive to your early morning insights. The important consideration in attempting to incubate a dream around a particular question is not necessarily whether you are given such a dream. Most people can incubate a dream only on occasion, if at all. Here, and in all the dream incubation instructions that follow, the primary intent is to have you invite insights from the deeper realms of your psyche and remain alert for what comes through in any form—fantasies, sudden insights, early morning thoughts, or nighttime dreams.

Also, do not be concerned if the relationship between a dream you recall and the question you asked is not readily apparent. Often, you will find as you examine the dream that it did touch upon your question in ways that were not obvious at first glance. You may use structured dream interpretation techniques, such as those presented in Appendix B, to gain a deeper understanding of the dream's meaning. Meg recorded the following dream in her journal:

> I am at a beach. The dry sand is white and deep, but slopes steeply to the shore. It is a clear day and the tide is low. My husband is asleep on the blanket beside me and our baby is exploring the water edge. I look up and see a line of huge swells coming in—the tide has changed abruptly. There is no way I will be fast enough to race down the shore and save my baby. I scream to Ron to wake up! Wake up NOW! He does and races toward the baby. I'm still screaming for him to hurry when I wake up, my heart pounding.

Meg used the creative projection technique to explore several of the elements from her dream:

> After I woke up, I remembered that the dream had come in answer to my meditations on the Quest portion of my Shield, with its words, *Freedom, Strength, Good, Competent,* and all morning I've sensed that there is a relationship between these words and the images in the dream . . .
>
> "I am the baby boy. I'm heedless and curious, exploring my world under the watchful eyes of my mother. I have never been

hurt and I have no sense of danger. I have no sense of my own limitations or mortality—I am fresh and alive. I am *freedom.*"

"I am the rising tide. I'm irresistible and subject to the laws of physics. I am moving forward, bound to follow my own destiny, subject to the pull of moon and sun, remote from human concerns. I am Nature—unsentimental, life-giving, life-extinguishing, harmonious, primal. I am *strong* and swift."

"I'm Ron—I've been ripped from relaxed sleep to complete mobilization—I have the speed and determination to save my son from the sea. I am mortal, but I'm rising to the challenge as if I had no limits. I will be successful, because to do otherwise is to lose what matters most to me—my sense of continuity and purpose. I am the essence of *goodness.*"

"I am Meg. I'm acutely aware of my senses on this beautiful beach and of my blessings, as I look at my beloved husband and beautiful child. My contentment is shattered by the annihilating danger approaching and I am suddenly suffused with terror—I feel the heaviness of my legs, my lack of agility, and know my competence to protect my innocent child is compromised. My child will die if I can't mobilize Ron to extraordinary effort. I am faced with the mortality of all that I love and of myself. My own *competence* depends upon recognizing the power of the natural forces that surround me. I must find my place in Nature and not foolishly decide that my mind makes me immune from the changing of the tide."

Meg elaborately linked her dream symbols with the four words that were on the "Quest" portion of her shield. Usually, such connections are not this direct, nor is it necessary that they be spelled out so literally. Yet just as Meg's initial creative projection with the four words on the "Quest" portion of her Shield revealed that each word contained its antithesis, this exploration of her dream also deepened her understanding of these four qualities in her life.

Personal Ritual: Your Shield as Autobiography

If you are working with a partner or with a group, present a brief (about 10 minutes) autobiography by describing the significant events of your psychological development as they are associated with the symbols on your Shield. If you have been working alone, it may be useful to share this experience with another person. Alternatively, speak your story into a tape recorder or write it in your journal. Before you begin, review the identifications you made with the symbols from your Shield during the previous ritual.

Meg wrote her story directly into her journal. While space does not allow for her entire account to be reported, the following excerpt, which focuses on the hypodermic syringe from the Paradise Lost portion of her Shield, illustrates the process:

> I feel very young when I think of the syringe. I remember my mother vomiting and crying out to my poor father for an injection, "Please, Ben, just one shot." She was in withdrawal from morphine that had been medically prescribed. The cycle seemed endless. She would choke herself to unconsciousness with her asthma, be revived with adrenaline, become hyperactive, be brought down with morphine, and instantly become addicted.
>
> I have plenty of feelings for the little kid, cowering in bed, uncomforted, who heard this every month for years. I have even more empathy for the kid who learned to give an injection at age nine. The crowning horror of my childhood was the time I came home from third grade and found my mother, at 3:30 in the afternoon, sprawled across the kitchen table with her fingers in a cup of cold coffee. I did as I had been instructed, filling the syringe with adrenaline to the 5cc mark, pressing the plunger carefully to release any air bubbles, and then dealing with her as best I could remember. That was the hardest part. She was unconscious and although she was not a large woman, I was only nine.
>
> I pushed her back in the chair and opened her robe. I had never seen my mother's breasts before. When I was instructed what to do in an emergency, they showed me on my own bony chest, demonstrating how to count the ribs and how to find the place beside the sternum to push the needle. They had me practice on a lemon. I found that pushing the needle into her body was infinitely harder than into the lemon—at one point I was afraid that the needle would bend or break. But I did as I had been told. Within a few minutes she revived enough to lie on the couch. Within an hour or so Dad was there, and he called the doctor, who came over to help my mother as best he could.
>
> Later, Dad told me I had been a "brave little soldier" and that I had done well. I don't think I ever cried about this incident until I was an adult. I've tried, most of my life, to be a "brave little soldier," not to cry but to take care of business. I also have had an unspoken, nearly unconscious, contempt for people who are

> chronically ill, seeing them as exploitive and treacherous. I'm basically a squeamish person. I've been able to take care of my kids when they were sick, and to handle emergencies and birthing situations, but I'm secretly sickened by illness. I've *hated* myself when I've been ill, associating it with my mother and her wretched helplessness that (unintentionally, of course) distorted my childhood and my father's life with her constant need for nursing, until she died the month I turned twelve.

The "brave little soldier" theme persisted as Meg grew up. It came to both serve her and limit her, as is often the case with personal myths that were initially developed to resolve specific dilemmas during childhood.

Your Shield symbolizes, in a highly condensed manner, many aspects of your personal history and unique mythology. You may wish to display it in a special place where you can see it frequently. It will be a companion as you go through the remaining personal rituals in this book, and you will be shown how to use it as an instrument for emotional protection as you move into uncharted areas of your personal unconscious. You may also, from time to time, wish to add a new symbol to your Shield or to examine existing symbolism further by using the creative projection technique. In chapter 5 you will complete the section of the Shield labeled "A Renewed Vision." Meanwhile, you may find your Shield taking on greater meaning as you proceed through the following chapters.

IDENTIFYING UNDERLYING MYTHIC CONFLICT

Your Shield and its symbolism provides a broad survey of the events that have shaped your personal mythology. Here the program shifts to concentrate on areas of your mythology that are no longer serving as allies in your development or adjustment to circumstances. As your understanding of yourself and your world increases, your myths are continually challenged and revised. By the end of this chapter, you will have identified at least one guiding myth that is causing difficulty for you.

The areas of your mythology that are the most primed for change are likely to be marked by personal conflict. Confusion over what is important to you or where you should direct your efforts may bring your attention to personal myths that are limiting you. Irrational fears, self-defeating behavior patterns, disturbing dreams, or inconsistencies between word and deed may also reflect parts of your mythology that need attention.

If, for instance, you find yourself frequently complaining about how busy you are but keep overscheduling every opportunity for free time, the personal myth with which you consciously identify may have little to do with your actual behavior. At the same time this myth is directing you to slow down and smell the flowers, a different myth, serving purposes that are outside of your awareness, may be governing your choices. Such unrecognized mythic conflict can keep you enmeshed in dysfunctional patterns of thought and behavior. When you bring the conflict into focus, however, the opposing myths can be recognized and a constructive resolution becomes feasible.

The continual search for approval, for instance, may be linked to a self-defeating personal myth in which you require validation from authority figures who, at an unconscious level, stand in for your father. If you are able to identify the myth that perpetuates the pattern, you have a chance to make changes in it. Perhaps you longed so much for affirmation from a remote father that you made every attempt to mold yourself into the image of who you thought your father wanted you to be. Even as you grew up and your father was no longer an active character in your life, you might have continued to make monumental efforts to gain approval from symbolic substitutes who remained cold and distant. Psychoanalysts use the term *repetition compulsion* to speak of "the blind impulse to repeat earlier experiences and situations quite irrespective of any advantage that doing so might bring from a pleasure-pain point of view."[11] By systematically working with your personal mythology, you will become less compelled to repeat destructive patterns that are maintained by outdated or conflicting personal myths.

Personal Ritual: Assessing Your Conflicts

In this ritual, you will create a broad summary of the points of conflict in your life. Write the words *Conflict Survey* at the top of a fresh page in your journal and divide the page into three columns. Label them "Self-Defeating Behaviors," "Troublesome Feelings," and "Symbols of Conflict."

Look at the first column and think about patterns of behavior that consistently fail to get you what you need or want. Identify recurring habits you seem unable to change, mistakes you seem destined to repeat, or decisions you seem unable to make. Describe these self-defeating behavior patterns in the first column of your Conflict Survey.

Then turn to the second column and think about emotional patterns that are difficult for you, such as unrealistic fears, inexplicable anxiety, unwarranted dissatisfaction, persistent ambivalence, or inappropriate discomfort. Describe these troublesome feelings in the second column.

In the third column, Symbols of Conflict, describe or draw any images from your dreams, fantasies, or artistic creations, such as your Shield, that seem to represent conflict in your personal mythology. We also suggest that you consider stress-related symptoms, such as shoulder tension or digestive problems, as symbols of possible conflict in your underlying mythology. Psychological conflict and stress are often implicated in ulcers, headaches, and hypertension, and there is increasing evidence of their involvement in other illnesses as well.[12]

Be speculative. Whenever you recognize an area of underlying conflict, you are taking a step toward participating more consciously in its resolution. We suggest that you carry your journal around with you for a few days and add new ideas or symbols as they occur to you.

Here is a sampling from Meg's chart of conflicts:

1. Self-Defeating Behaviors:
   - I seem fated to be stupid in money management.
   - Sometimes I really should back down on a stand I've taken, and I don't know how to without feeling like a jackass.
   - I become overly defensive when I think someone is putting something over on me or talking over my head.
   - When I'm sick, I either whine or withdraw.

2. Troublesome Feelings:
   - I think, too often, of dying as an escape from sometimes rather mild discomfort.
   - I become deeply anxious when a pretty woman pays attention to my husband, even though I know it is to his advantage to have these needed affirmations.

- I often have a desire to lie or conceal any unpleasant truth about myself, not trusting others to have generous judgments about me.
- I'm uncomfortable in the company of well-groomed, middle-aged women who have "paid their dues" and are satisfied with their conventional lives.
- I see the effects of the aging process on my body and I am ashamed, as if I had committed a great crime.
- I'm horribly selfish and possessive, unless it's easy to be gracious.

3. Symbols of Conflict:
   - In a dream, I have a hidden treasure. I don't know what it is, how to protect it, or who the enemy is.
   - The hypodermic needle from my Shield.
   - I feel like a fraud when identifying with anything beautiful, like the abalone shell or the yin-yang symbol.
   - My back problem. When I am overloaded or feel I must perform, I have characteristically stiffened my spine and by now have structurally damaged myself.

The survey identifies an assortment of conflicts and provocative issues in Meg's life. Most people can readily list several conflicts or concerns. If you are having difficulty finding areas that fit for you, ask for a dream or consult your Inner Shaman. Find a setting in which you can become deeply relaxed, and again draw upon the technique your Shaman instructed you to use when you wish to make a visit. Ask your Shaman to help you recognize behaviors or patterns of emotional response that are self-defeating.

When you have completed your list of conflicts, put a star next to the items you consider particularly problematic. By the end of this chapter, you will have settled on a single concern. The following dream suggestions and personal rituals will assist you in bringing it into focus.

Dream Focus: A Conflict to Resolve

Scan your dream journal to see if you can identify any recent dreams that symbolize an area of conflict for you. Examine any such dreams using a structured dream exploration technique (such as those presented in Appendix B). If you wish to incubate a dream that highlights areas of conflict that might be calling for your attention, review your Conflict Survey before you go to sleep. Then ask yourself for a dream that reveals an area of conflict that would be a particularly useful focus for you in this program. Repeat ten to twenty times before falling asleep a statement such as "I will recall a dream that shows me an area of my personal mythology that is ripe for exploration." Have your journal or tape recorder nearby. Use at least one dream exploration method with any dream you recall, even if you are not initially sure it relates in any way to an area of conflict. Remember also that, whether or not you recall a dream, you may awaken with fresh insights about your question.

Personal Ritual: Finding a Symbol for Your Conflict

This guided imagery ritual is designed to transform the feelings you have been generating about your conflicts into a single symbol. If you are already fairly certain about the conflict on which you wish to concentrate, the ritual will add to your understanding of its meaning in your life. If you have not yet settled on a conflict, it will enlist your unconscious mind to help you choose. Begin by finding a comfortable position, closing your eyes, taking several deep breaths, and starting to relax:

As you settle into this safe, secure spot, focus on your breathing. Begin to release any areas of tension in your body. [Pause] Listen for and feel each in-breath and each out-breath. [Pause] Notice your belly and chest rising and falling. [Pause] Your breathing becomes slow and deep as you relax more and more completely with each of your next five breaths—ONE, TWO, THREE, FOUR, FIVE.

Think about the areas of conflict you have been surveying. [Pause] One or two will be of particular concern. Feel your body's response in your breathing, muscles, and temperature. Trace with your fingertips or in your mind the shape of the part of your body that responds the most strongly. Note its color. Explore its texture. [30-second pause] In a moment you will see or sense a symbol emerging out of the shapes and colors.

Watch as a symbol appears that represents an inner conflict that is pressing for resolution. [Pause] You may actually see the symbol take form, or you may simply sense what it is. [Pause] It will further evolve over the next few moments. Relax as it becomes increasingly clear. You intuitively recognize the meaning of your symbol. Trust that further exploration of the symbol's significance will be valuable.

Prepare to return to your waking consciousness. Counting from five back to one, you will be able to recall all you need of this experience. When you hear the number 1, you will feel alert, relaxed, and refreshed, as if waking from a wonderful nap. FIVE, move your fingers and toes. FOUR, stretch your shoulders, neck, and face muscles. THREE, take a deep breath. TWO, bring your attention back into the room. ONE, open your eyes, feeling refreshed, alert, and fully competent to meet the requirements of your day.

Draw or describe the symbol in your journal. Record any insights or ideas you may have about its meaning. You also might find it valuable to use the creative projection technique to explore the meaning of your symbol further. The image that came to Meg was faulty scuba equipment that threatened her life in a dream. Frank, the investment counselor, wrote:

> Thinking about my conflict brings me to the pain of not living with more passion. The bodily sensation was a tight oblong black area, starting in my neck where it was the widest, and going down the center of the front of my body, perhaps 2 inches wide in most places. When it became a picture, it was a giant jaw and a little version of me was caught in its grip, not harmed by its teeth, but totally pinned. That image mirrors the feelings of being stifled and inhibited that I so long to be free of.

Personal Ritual: Finding the Roots of Mythic Conflict in Your Past

Up to this point, you have created an overview of your personal history by means of your Shield, surveyed areas of conflict in your life, and found a symbol for an area of mythic conflict that invites attention. You may or may not be clear about just how that conflict manifests itself in your life. This personal ritual will deepen your understanding about the conflict that is coming into focus. In it, you will be guided back in time to an early experience that is related to current difficulties in your life. By connecting present feelings to past experiences, you will gain a greater appreciation of the source of underlying conflict in your mythology. Start by finding a comfortable position, closing your eyes, and taking several deep breaths.

As you settle into this safe, secure spot, focus on your breathing. Begin to release any areas of tension in your body. [Pause] Listen for and feel each in-breath and each out-breath. [Pause] Notice your belly and chest rising and falling. [Pause] Allow your breathing to become slow and deep as you relax more completely with each of your next five breaths—ONE, TWO, THREE, FOUR, FIVE.

Recall your symbol from the previous ritual, or if you have a different way of thinking about the conflict you wish to explore, bring it to mind. Notice your feelings about this symbol or thought. [Pause] If there is more than one feeling, concentrate on the feeling that is the most dominant or uncomfortable. [Pause] If you are having difficulty tuning into a conflict, focus on any persistent troubling feeling.

Keep in your awareness the feeling you have identified and notice the part of your body in which you experience it the most fully. Bring your attention to that part of your body. [Pause] If the feeling is vague, imagine yourself breathing into it and intensifying it. If the feeling is so strong that it is distracting, imagine that your next few exhalations are breathing out some of the intensity. As this feeling absorbs your attention, observe the way your body reacts to it. Feel your body's response in your breathing, your muscles, and your temperature. [Pause] Find a word that describes the feeling.

You will use this feeling to lead you back to an earlier period of your life. Notice the flow of sensations that make up the feeling. Now create the image of a river as you continue to focus on your feeling. Think of your feeling as the river. Imagine yourself in a boat on that river. The river floats you back in time, safely and comfortably, to one of the first occasions on which you experienced the feeling you just identified.

On the bank of the river you see, as if on a stage, yourself experiencing the same feeling, but in a scene that occurred very early in your life. [Pause] Enter the scene.

How old are you in this scene? What are you doing? Where your memory does not offer answers, your imagination will. What do you look like? What are you wearing? Who, if anyone, is with you? Where are you? What are the surroundings? What sights, sounds, tastes, or smells do you experience? What, specifically, brought about the feeling? Recall or imagine as many details of that earlier time as you can. [45-second pause]

Reflect on some of the decisions you might have made as a result of this experience and others like it. [Pause] What conclusions did you come to about yourself and your world? What rules or codes of conduct did you adopt? What attitudes toward other people began to emerge? What views of the world? What philosophy of life? [45-second pause]

Prepare to return to your waking consciousness. Counting from five back to one, you will be able to recall all you need of this experience. When you hear the number 1, you will feel alert, relaxed, and refreshed, as if waking from a wonderful nap. FIVE, move your fingers and toes. FOUR, stretch your shoulders, neck, and face muscles. THREE, take a deep breath. TWO, bring your attention back into the room. ONE, open your eyes, feeling refreshed, alert, and fully competent to meet the requirements of your day.

Summarize this experience in your journal and reflect on the following:

1. What was the conflict or symbol with which you started?
2. What was the negative emotion or unpleasant feeling it evoked in you?
3. Describe the scene you went back to in as much detail as you can recall.
4. What rules of behavior and codes of conduct did you adopt based on experiences such as the one to which you returned? In what ways might such experiences have influenced your sense of your own capabilities, limitations, and personal destiny?
5. How do these rules, attitudes, and philosophy affect your life at this time? How might they be related to your current conflicts? Have they become outdated for you?

The answers to these questions will reveal many qualities of a personal myth you might have developed early in your life. For example, some people follow the river back to memories of unpleasant experiences with one or both of their parents. As a result of those experiences, they might realize they decided never again to do anything that could possibly risk the loss of approval from one they love. Others, in the same circumstances, might have decided never again to trust their parents or other intimates.

Such attitudes and values can sometimes be condensed into brief phrases that represent underlying themes in the person's life, such as, "I am a weak and dependent person"; "I must make great sacrifices to earn love and attention"; or, "The world is a jungle and people cannot be trusted." It is quite probable that even if such premises protected you at one time or solved real problems, the decisions you identified during this particular ritual have become self-limiting. The mythology that was shaped by those decisions comprises one side of the underlying mythic conflict you will be exploring. On the other side, as you will see in the following chapter, is an emerging myth that you have been formulating, perhaps outside of your awareness, to address the problems and limitations caused by the myth you just identified.

Meg went back to a time that is also symbolized on her Shield, when she was nine and had to give her mother the shot of adrenaline. She reflected on the regulations and codes of conduct she adopted for herself as a result of that experience and others like it:

> I learned that I have to be cool, maintain myself, do that which is repugnant to me in order to justify my existence. I have to perform far beyond what is reasonable to expect from one equipped as I am equipped. But I learned that adopting this behavior could earn genuine heartfelt praise from the most important person on earth—my Dad—for being a "brave little soldier." I didn't know what to do with my panic, but I decided to hide it since it didn't fit the program of being a "brave little soldier."
>
> I have learned that performance justifies existence, and I have reached the conclusion that my own performance is always suspect, at best, and hypocritical at worst. I let people think I'm brave, while underneath there is really a scared, inadequate little kid ashamed to admit that she's mad as hell at being put in this position by her parents, by the doctor, and/or by God. It doesn't seem fair, but she can't admit her fears without giving up the pleasure of being seen as a "brave little soldier."
>
> Some part of me believes that everyone can look right in my eye and see that my facade of competence is constructed of words and gestures, not of substance. Another part of me vehemently disagrees because I am, authentically, a capable, good-hearted, decent

woman. I see my quest in life as someone who seeks to nurture, but God help anyone who doesn't appreciate and acknowledge my "selfless" giving. If people don't respond to me as a "brave little soldier," I deny them closeness and intimacy.

With these reflections, Meg was able to complete the first stage of the program by articulating a basic conflict that seemed to be calling for her attention. Her "brave little soldier" theme emphasized a strong performance in the world at the expense of tenderness and intimacy with those who might recognize her vulnerabilities and lend support. Just as she had helped her mother, she felt compelled to nurture those in need. But inside of her was still an "angry little girl" who wanted to be nurtured and, at the same time, wanted to be seen as a "brave little soldier."

We have found this "river back in time" technique[13] to be an effective way for connecting current difficulties with experiences from the past. People quite reliably go back to a time when they were forming attitudes, values, and codes of conduct that have come into conflict with more recent understandings. The decisions that shaped a myth which has become outdated can thus be identified. Regardless of how often you use it, the "river back" technique can continue to be a useful tool for uncovering the mythic roots of psychological conflict.

At this point, you may be wondering if you have identified the "right" conflict or outdated myth with which to work. If you have been straining to find *the* focal conflict in your life, we suggest that you relax, let go of the pressure, and know that there is no "wrong" way to do this. While the choice you make at this point will provide a focus for the work that is to follow, we have found that as people go along in the program, the issues they need to face tend to surface anyway.

We refer to this phenomenon as the "holographic principle" of personal mythology. Each part of a hologram contains information from every other part. In a similar manner, whatever personal myth you may be examining in some fundamental way embodies your entire mythic system. Working through one area may have repercussions on many areas. Therefore, it is far less important that you select what you *rationally* deduce to be the "ideal" conflict than that you select an area for which you have some *feeling.* Your work with that conflict will lead to insight into other areas of your mythology as well. Also keep in mind that the program can be carried out more than once, and you can focus on different issues each time.

Using Your Shield for Emotional Protection

Sometimes when you request a dream, initiate a fantasy, or attempt some other way of contacting the unconscious mind, you will experience unsettling feelings. In addition to the instructions offered in Appendix C for taking care of yourself if the program becomes disturbing, we recommend the method illustrated in the following case for using your Personal Shield as a resource in protecting yourself.

A woman in one of our workshops followed her conflict back in time to a long-suppressed childhood memory involving sexual molestation. It was very upsetting for her to have this memory break through, and she was not at all prepared to address it in the workshop. We asked her to find a symbol for the molestation experience, draw it on the Paradise Lost portion of her Shield, and imagine sending the intense emotions she was experiencing directly into the symbol, literally transferring the emotions from her body to the Shield. By "depositing" her feelings into the Shield for safekeeping until she was ready to work with them, she was neither denying the experience nor forcing herself to work with it before she was prepared.

You may use your Shield in this manner at any point where a dream or one of the rituals triggers an upsetting memory or any other feeling you do not wish to work with at the time. Although it will sometimes be necessary to draw a new symbol on your Shield, one of the symbols that is already on the Shield will often be suitable, and the feeling can be focused directly into it. First, draw or select the symbol in which you will store the unpleasant feeling until you are ready to work with it more directly. Second, hold the Shield in front of you at eye level. Third, allow yourself to experience the feeling, and envisage the energy of the emotion being transported from your body into your Shield. You can imagine doing this both through your gaze and by exhaling directly into the symbol, like a dragon snorting fire.

When you feel somewhat cleansed of the feeling (after perhaps a minute or two), set your Shield aside, tune into your feelings, and work with your journal. You might want to complete the process with the progressive relaxation procedure described in Appendix A or the stress release technique in Appendix C. You might also want to symbolically "shake out" any unwanted emotional residue with rapid free movements of your hands and body. Finally, you might consider taking a journey to visit your Inner Shaman to discuss the experience.

On to Stage Two

At this point, some people feel discouraged, believing that the negative behavior patterns they have just identified will be almost impossible to change. If you are feeling that way, remember that you have been giving yourself instructions that *invite* areas of conflict to reveal themselves. You are taking an active and courageous step toward improving your life. While it is never easy to delve into one's own dark side, the instructions have been formulated to elicit aspects of your personal mythology that you are ready to deal with productively. The process of making needed changes will be energizing and inspiring. And, if issues emerge that you are not ready to work with, use your Shield for protection as just described, or find other support as discussed in Appendix C.

Once you have identified an area of your mythology that is no longer serving as an ally, and have begun to understand its roots in your personal history, you have completed this first stage of our program. In the second stage, you will further crystallize the outdated prevailing myth, the emerging myth that is challenging it, and the conflict that simmers between them.

3

The Second Stage: Bringing the Roots of Mythic Conflict into Focus

The task is to go deeply as possible into the darkness, to name the pain that one finds there, and the truth of one's perceptions, and to emerge on the other side with permission to name one's reality from one's own point of view.

—ANTHEA FRANCINE[1]

When you come to recognize an area of your mythology that is failing you, as you have done in the first stage of the program, you also begin to sense that this particular myth is not the only way to organize your life. Sometimes the failure of a long-standing myth, and even the pain involved in that failure, opens us to glimpse the Larger Story. The myths we follow often are challenged by perceptions and realizations that grow out of greater maturity and more recent experiences. When an area of your personal mythology has become outdated for your circumstances or level of psychological development, your psyche is likely to generate alternative mythic images, which we speak of as "counter-myths."

Even before you consciously recognize the shortcomings of an old myth, your psyche is usually generating a counter-myth to compensate for its limitations. Freud believed that a function of dreaming is to gratify wishes we have been unable to satisfy in our waking life. Counter-myths also have a "wish-fulfillment" quality. They guide us toward meeting needs, fulfilling desires, and reaching toward possibilities where the old myth was ineffective. But like dreams, counter-myths are often removed from the requirements of the real world. The tension between an old myth, whose familiar but limited vision grew out of earlier life experiences, and a counter-myth that promises a more fertile but untried future, is a battle between the past and the possible that is waged within each of us.

Your task in this second stage is to distinguish in your awareness the old myth and the counter-myth that are at the basis of the mythic conflict you identified in the first stage. In the previous chapter, you began to describe the old myth in terms of attitudes, values, and codes of conduct. The personal rituals in this chapter will help you to further delineate the old myth and articulate the counter-myth. Because counter-myths are formed largely in reaction to the shortcomings of prevailing myths, they contain their own distortions, and it is inevitable that conflict will exist between the two. The counter-myth is, in fact, characterized by this intimate but oppositional relationship with the prevailing myth.

Sometimes when people first recognize a counter-myth, they adopt it abruptly. Nonbelievers may convert to a religious orthodoxy in moments; college students often renounce a lifetime of religious observance in the space of a semester. Adolescent rebellion, sexual experimentation, and impulsive divorce may each be the expression of an emerging counter-myth. In this program, you will be encouraged to recognize the strengths and the shortcomings in both the old myth and the counter-myth, and to patiently cultivate a third, new mythic vision that incorporates the most vital aspects of each.

In the final ritual of the previous chapter, you identified a personal myth that has lost its efficacy, and you traced its origins back to events from your past. Even as the old myth is losing its hold, the experience may have helped you to better understand the circumstances that brought you to adopt it. Such insight into the personal, family, and cultural forces that shaped the old myth permits you to more readily accept the psychological death that is involved as it gives way, and to appropriately mourn for it. It also allows you to work for change in a more self-affirming manner, rather than to become enmeshed in self-judgments about previous beliefs and choices. By patiently examining these processes, you engage your "inner witness" rather than a fault-finding attitude as you come to recognize the problems the old myth is generating.

Counter-myths may be modeled largely after the myths of others who have an influence on you, may be rooted in a developmental readiness to accept more advanced myths from your culture, or may be patterned after an intuitive perception of archetypal images. Prevailing myths are difficult to identify because they are the psychological medium in which we live, as imperceptible as water must be to a fish; counter-myths are difficult to identify because they do not enter awareness until they have attained a certain critical mass. Still, they may be governing our behavior before we are able to articulate them.

Bringing the Roots of Mythic Conflict into Focus

For example, a man who has been a dedicated husband and father has an affair with a woman half his age. When he later enters psychotherapy to try to piece together the shambles he has made of his life, he is likely to discover that he was, with little self-awareness, acting out a counter-myth that challenged the stifling effects of his preoccupation with achievement and responsibility. Counter-myths provide us with an impetus to expand ourselves beyond the limitations of the mythology we have been living. They can hasten our development or ravage our stability, depending upon the awareness and skill with which we receive them.

Although counter-myths often operate outside of awareness, they break into consciousness in dreams, daydreams, art, slips of the tongue, and other expressions of the unconscious mind. The counter-myth is often imaginative, inspiring, and forward-thrusting—yet lacking a practical realism that allows it to be lived out in the same form in which it emerges. By focusing your attention on it, you are able to be more readily aware of its influence and to participate in consciously developing and refining it. You will find that through the use of guided imagery, story, and focused contemplation, the personal rituals that follow will sharpen your understanding of emerging directions in your life.

STORIES THAT CONNECT US WITH THE MYTHIC

Sam Keen and Anne Valley Fox have observed:

> So long as human beings change and make history, so long as children are born and old people die, there will be tales to explain why sorrow darkens the day and stars fill the night. We invent stories about the origin and conclusion of life because . . . they help us find our way, our place at the heart of the mystery.[2]

Parables and fairy tales are stories from which moral or spiritual truths can be drawn. Many cultural myths are expressed as stories that offer people guidance through imagery and metaphor. Sufi stories, Hassidic tales, biblical parables, and other spiritual literatures are the bearers of mythological insight into the human condition.

Today, with the intricacies of individual identity and the myriad role options allowed by complex societies, we need guidance that is highly personal to our unique circumstances. Discussing how modern men and women have developed the capacity to form identities separate from those prescribed by the tribe or nation, Anthea Francine observed that the "revelations of the Divine . . . we once found revealed only in the form of myth and fairy tale, we must now seek also in the story of our own lives."[3] Weaving your memories into a meaningful sequence of stories about your past can deepen your relationship with your own mythology and place your self-understanding in a richer context.

Psychiatrist Richard Gardner has developed an approach that applies the power of storytelling for helping troubled children.[4] He asks the child to tell him a story that has a beginning, middle, end, and a moral. As Gardner listens for the psychological themes that run through the story, elements of unresolved conflict are revealed. Gardner, in turn, tells a story to the child that also has a beginning, middle, end, and a moral. His story is built around the psychological tensions that were portrayed in the child's story. In retelling the story, however, Gardner has the characters find better ways to handle the core conflicts. By speaking to the child at this mythic level, Gardner creates an opportunity for the child to adopt a new personal myth that may be more effective than the one that has been operating.

Gardner describes a story told by Martin, a withdrawn seven-year-old, with a bitter, self-indulgent mother who was sometimes warm and loving, but at other times openly expressed her dislike for her son. Martin's story was about a bear who was trying in vain to get honey from a beehive without being stung. In his response, Gardner's story also featured a bear who craved honey. Gardner's bear knew that bees were sometimes friendly and would give him a little bit of honey, and he also knew that at times they were unfriendly and would sting him. At these times, Gardner's bear would go to another part of the forest where he could obtain maple syrup from the maple trees. In this story, Gardner offered Martin a mythology for acquiring love from his mother without provoking her hostilities, and for discovering alternative sources of affection to compensate for his mother's deficiencies.

In this chapter you will learn to tell your own story and, in so doing, to identify critical points in the development of your personal myths. You will anticipate directions that may be emerging, and recognize areas of darkness that need to be more fully understood and perhaps healed. Viewing yourself as the heroine or hero in your own personal parable allows you—unlike Narcissus captivated with the reflection of his own surfaces—to peer more deeply into your nature and to appreciate more fully the wonder of the human drama as it manifests in your personal story.

Periodically reviewing your actions and decisions in terms of their mythic dimensions makes it possible for you to grasp the pattern of the story and effect changes in its plot. Casting the development of your own life in the form of a fairy tale is one of the primary devices used in this chapter to help you bring into focus the prevailing myth and the emerging counter-myth that are at the root of your conflict.

MEG'S NEXT STEP

This second stage of the program will be illustrated by returning to Meg's experiences as she brings her prevailing myth and an emerging counter-myth into sharper focus. From this point onward, Meg's experiences are presented toward the beginning of each chapter to provide an overview of the personal rituals composing that stage of the work. Following the instructions for each personal ritual, a second person's journal entries will illustrate that particular ritual.

The second stage of the program begins with the creation of Part One of a three-part personal Fairy Tale. Meg reviewed her Shield and then created this story:

> Once upon a time there was an island separated from a continent by a wild strait, impassable by boat or swimstroke. A little girl, Juanita Margaret, lived upon the island. She was busy from dawn to dark with her tasks. Two times a day she went to watch the tides change below the cliffs. She checked the quails' nests for eggs and new chicks. She monitored the polliwogs as they magically became frogs, and she gasped in wonder as the butterfly emerged from the cocoon and unfolded its wings. She spent time in gathering sour grass bouquets and driftwood dragons. She ate loquats and mulberries that grew on the trees, and she gathered seaweed and mussels from the rocks by the sea.
>
> She kept an orphaned ground squirrel, a lame coyote, and a nest of swallows in her cave. The squirrel taught her about seeds, thrift, industry, foresight, and planting. The coyote showed her the value of patience, stealth, and suppleness. From the swallows she learned of delight, nesting, and freedom. At night she slept in a hollow she'd made in the notch of a cliff, facing the sunset, at the edge of the sea. The moon and the storms were her nighttime companions.
>
> Juanita Margaret did not know that she was in exile, a creature to be pitied, remarkable, in an embarrassing way, to the people on the mainland. They were busy, too, in hurrying from this place to that place, talking about property and assets, arranging their

clothes and their expressions, actively meeting one another in a continuing process of confrontation, seduction, deception, denial, torment, and illusion. Her wholesomeness offended them.

No one remembered exactly who had put Juanita Margaret on the island, but the truth was that they had been glad to get rid of her. They were uncomfortable when they saw that she would rather climb the cyprus tree than try on a new dress. They became upset when they saw that she was loud, demanding, curious, and unhampered. They were annoyed with her coarse, naturalistic behavior. They kept sending her outside to play so that they could read their newspapers and magazines in peace. One morning she climbed into an old boat to play; a storm came up, carried her away, and she was washed ashore on the island. When she never came back, everyone seemed relieved.

One day, a man on the mainland took a telescope and looked at Juanita Margaret's island. He saw how many wonderful fruit trees grew on the island, and how clear the water was on the narrow beaches below the cliffs. He thought, "I could put a resort there and make a million dollars." Before long, engineers studied the strait between the mainland and the island. They put in a bridge and a highway. They took out the loquat and mulberry trees to build the Orchard Motel. They put a single loquat and a lonely mulberry tree into pots in the lobby. They cut stairs into the cliffs and made them as permanent as possible with cement and steel handrails. The trash cans overflowed.

Some men came and saw Juanita Margaret sitting behind the bushes in the parking lot, eating scrap food from bags thrown out of cars. She didn't go with them willingly at first, but they offered her warm socks and cinnamon rolls and, in the end, she agreed to return to the mainland.

Juanita Margaret went to school, leaving her squirrel, coyote, and swallow friends to save themselves if they could, because she didn't know what else to do. She was just a little girl. Inside, she was furious at the changes that had come into her life, and at the people bossing her around without asking her opinion. Now she had to sleep in a bed, wash in a tub rather than the ocean, speak softly, be respectful, make everyone proud, and live up to her potential. She was told that "some things aren't nice to talk about" and "your temper will be the death of you." The worst insult for a bungled job or sloppy workmanship was to call it "womanish." She was learning the ways of becoming a proper young lady.

Meg explored her reactions to various aspects of her story. When she examined her bodily response to the way Juanita Margaret was pitied, in exile, and embarrassing to the people on the mainland, she noted:

> My face feels flushed, exposing my sense of inadequacy. My eyes want to look defiantly or challenging. I feel resentment in my mouth: tight lips, set jaw, controlled breathing. I can identify a smugness too, a sort of superiority. I sense these feelings in my upper lip, with a kind of a sneer pulling at my face.

She reflected on the personal significance of these feelings:

> I have always resented, intensely, any hint of mockery or patronizing. I am very quick to jump to the conclusion that I am being made fun of, and I am ruthless in defending myself. I've always had a tendency to create scapegoats, generalize, and to reject anyone or any group whom I saw as having the wherewithal to put me down. I've been absolutely unwilling to be vulnerable to such groups. I've been a dismal failure whenever circumstances have put me into positions where it would have been politic for me to ask permission, give unwarranted strokes, belittle myself, or conform to stupid bureaucratic rules, protocols, and standards.

When Meg considered the way Juanita Margaret was always being "sent outside to play" because she was loud, curious, and unhampered, she noticed that

> my stomach is tense, not upset, but muscularly tight. My breathing is conscious, controlled, and slow. I feel rock-hard and unmovable, rigid, unyielding, and violent in my determination to hold my ground. I feel an "I won't" in my neck, jaw, and eyes.

The personal meanings she attributed to these observations included:

> I never learned to give in gracefully. I've fantasized murder, vandalism, and mutilations. I've collapsed. I've gone down fighting. I've slammed doors. I've nearly suicided. I have learned how to say "I'm sorry" sincerely, but not how to back down from a stand I see as one of principle. I can compromise and be a team player or partner as long as I don't feel put down or am asked to yield a

principle. I've been hypersensitive to insult, expecting it and often soliciting it. What a distasteful realization! What a losing way of doing business!

We see from these comments, and from the first segment of her Fairy Tale, that Meg is on a highly individualistic Quest. Recall that in her original vision of Paradise, she had been alone. You will see that her vision of returning to Paradise Regained is also an isolated Quest. While she does want to nurture and love, it must be on her own terms.

Her alter ego, Juanita Margaret, did quite well when she could nurse wounded animals and homeless birds. When placed in a social context, however, she scavenges food from the hotel trash cans, and meanders through life without peers, playmates, or friends. Once off her island, there is a rebelliousness in Juanita Margaret that seems to be dissonant with the "earth child" who had befriended the creatures of nature.

After having created and examined Part One of your Fairy Tale, you will explore experiences from your past that might be important as you create Part Two. Part Two of the Fairy Tale is to represent an idealized Quest for a return to the Paradise Lost of Part One. One of the rituals you will use in preparing yourself to create Part Two is to initiate the healing of an early emotional wound whose effects may still be interfering with your life. You will focus on an area of your old myth that you find particularly difficult to consider giving up, even though you may see flaws in its guidance. You will be instructed on how to identify sensations in your body that you associate with this aspect of your mythology, and you will go back in your memory until you identify an incident that seems related to those sensations. You will call upon your Inner Shaman to assist you. Meg began:

I find myself with a very tight neck, so tight that I cannot turn my head. I can only look straight ahead. To look sideways farther than my eyes will roll, I must shift my whole body. My neck hurts!

I remember my grandfather's hard fingers digging into the back of my neck, hurrying me along faster than my three-year-old legs will carry me. I stumble and he saves me from falling by tightening his grip on my neck. The pain is terrible. I cry and am cuffed in the face for making a racket. I can hear his voice listing my sins: I have left a mess while playing with wood chips and sawdust in his carpenter shop; I have lied about being there; I am disobedient and insolent. It is clear, I deserve what I am getting because I'm so

> inadequate and slovenly. I had better not cry because that will just compound my sins by showing me to be a contemptible female weakling.

Meg brought her Inner Shaman into her imagery:

> My Inner Shaman touches my neck with fingers so soft and warm they feel like a warm washcloth laid on the contracted tissue. He tells me I am a normal, curious little girl; that I haven't yet learned the difference between imagination and lying; and that my natural and spirited reactions to abuse and accusation are not sins, but misjudgments about my accuser. I feel worthwhile, after all, and I notice that there is much less tension in my neck.

After appealing to your Inner Shaman for an emotional healing, you will take another imagery journey to the past. But this time, rather than beginning with the unpleasant feelings you associate with your conflict, you will begin by imagining the feelings you would have if the conflict were magically resolved. Meg generated these feelings by imagining the exact opposite of the emotions she associated with her conflict:

> The opposite of anger is serenity and the opposite of defiance is acceptance. When I thought of serenity, I saw an image of my abalone shell. I returned to the cliffs, explored the tidepools, felt myself vigorous and reckless, unaware of my own mortality. The sounds around me are of the water, wind, bird cries, and my own breathing. I feel no fear, no need to achieve or compete, only to be wholly present. I savor the feeling of discovery and freedom. I like the sense that I am alone and there is no limit to the number of marvels I shall experience. I have no sense of limitation.

Meg reflected upon the attitudes, beliefs, and codes of conduct that seemed related to this memory and others like it:

> It seems to me that I have sought that sense of freedom and discovery all my life. I have been intolerant of pedestrian thinking in myself or others, uncompromising about making my own decisions (while longing for a wiser teacher). I hate to be coerced. I love the naturally occurring things—shells, gnarled wood, sand pat-

> terns, clouds, bodies. I've resisted contrivances, strictures, conventions. I do not feel at home in crowds, board meetings, political gatherings, cocktail parties, or PTA meetings. I do feel at home out of doors, with books, and with intimate groups of like-minded souls. I have had to compromise all my life and I've been in a state of continual rebellion. I have not been graceful in accommodating myself to the world. I've thumbed my nose and had it pushed into my own eye. I wonder *how* one learns to be graceful in accommodating to stultifying reality?

Meg drew upon this experience as she wrote Part Two of her Fairy Tale. Part Two will reveal new solutions to the dilemmas encountered by the hero or heroine of your Fairy Tale in Part One:

> Juanita Margaret was sitting on the mainland beach one day, looking across the raging straits that separated her from her ruined island. She saw the harsh bridge, made of iron and asphalt, bristling with cars like busy ants on their hill. She was wearing a lovely pink ruffled dress, but she had soiled it by playing with puppies, and there were paw marks blemishing the ruffles. Imagine her surprise when a porpoise swam up the shallow surf and called out to her, "Juanita Margaret! I've come to rescue you! Mount my back, and I will take you on a great journey."
>
> He was smiling at her and his voice was as vibrant as the ruby throat of a hummingbird. She went, of course, and climbed up on his gray-blue back, grasping his ribs with her legs and clinging to his dorsal fin for balance. He moved across the water in jubilant leaps, arching his back and singing joyously as he traveled. Juanita Margaret forgot that she was odd and foreign, riding a porpoise across the waters wearing her dainty pink dress.
>
> "You are learning a great lesson, Juanita Margaret, in the way you learn best—by doing. Do not forget this lesson: Take time in your life to be spontaneous in nature, without agenda, without time constraints, and you will be wrested from your complaints. I am taking you now to visit some other teachers. Fear not that harm will come to you when I dive beneath the surface. You are equipped for survival and your faith will protect you even in an alien environment."
>
> So saying, the porpoise arched high into the air and dove beneath the surface, Juanita Margaret safe upon his back. The world beneath the sea was shimmering with green and golden light, the

white sand lay in gentle mounds, and a tall forest of kelp grew from black rocks. The porpoise swam into the forest of waving plants, each moving independently in the currents. "You see the flexibility of these stems and leaves, responsive to the moving waters? When mighty storms come through this part of the ocean, the kelp forest is whipped from side to side, scourged with driven sand, tested to its limit. Only the weary, old, or poorly rooted plants are torn loose to be cast on the shore. The plants that have gripped the stones with their roots, and that have put their growth into sturdy trunks, are secure and even invigorated by the storm. You see it is possible to be firm and still move with the currents, whether energetic or gentle." She thought she understood what he was talking about.

He took her to a submerged reef, and she saw that it was encrusted with abalone. The shells were as black as the reef, domed like oval cups and covered with volcano barnacles, hermit crabs, and sea lettuce. If she hadn't seen them long ago, when she had her island to herself, she would have thought they were just bumps on the rock. The porpoise told her to speak to the largest abalone in the cluster. "Hello," she said, tentatively.

"Hello, yourself," answered the abalone in a slow and draggy voice. "What brings you here today?"

"I think you're supposed to teach me something."

"Do you have any idea what it is?" The abalone sounded puzzled and a little resentful.

"Maybe if you described yourself and your life, I might get a clue. Right now I just think you're pretty much a dull and surly fellow." Juanita Margaret had the habit of saying what she thought without much consideration of how it might feel to the person she was talking to.

The abalone was silent and the bubbles coming from his vent holes nearly stopped. When at last he spoke, it was with a distant air, as if he didn't much want to have anything to do with her but felt obliged to answer. "I am, as you say, dull. I have been on this spot for many years. It is a good spot because the current sweeps a lot of plankton my way and I have flourished. It is true that I am not a scintillating personality, that I am politically isolated, that I am drab and lack a rapier wit. I have captured no prizes and have never been to war. My body is muscular, my personality is a yawn, and my attitude is tenacious. I fear only the marauding starfish who is both tenacious and mobile, able to pry me off the rock and eat me.

"I have a secret, though, Juanita Margaret. Under my drab and unprepossessing exterior, I am a great artist. I go nowhere, engage in no social activities, even family reunions, because I am at work on the most beautiful sculpture-painting-architecture imaginable. I am preparing the inside of my shell, hidden from sight, as a permanent memorial to God. To learn from me, you must be less concerned with your everyday outer shell and put your care into making the inside as beautiful as possible. With me, my secret beauty will be concealed until my death. With you, who knows?" With that the abalone let loose a long spout of bubbles and Juanita Margaret knew he had said what he had to say.

As if in a trance, Juanita Margaret pondered what she had learned from the porpoise, kelp, and abalone. She promised herself she would take time from her duties to find herself in Nature like the porpoise, to flex in the currents of life while maintaining her roots, like the kelp, and to be unbothered by the plainness of her exterior while privately, without fanfare, enriching her interior, like the abalone. The porpoise delivered her to shore, and she found she had a great deal to think about and even more to do.

Part Two of Meg's Fairy Tale contains the wish-fulfilling motifs of an androgynous Peter Pan character, who refuses to adopt a gender role or to grow up socially, and of a "naughty little girl" who dislikes the thought of interacting with humans for fear of being forced to behave like a "good little soldier." If the Fairy Tale ended with Juanita Margaret and her porpoise sailing gleefully into the sunset, it might have had the ring of happily-ever-after, but it would do Meg a disservice, for there is still much for her to learn, as you will see later in Part Three of her Fairy Tale.

CRYSTALLIZING YOUR OLD MYTH AND YOUR EMERGING MYTH

We can see how Meg was able, through this series of personal rituals, to clearly identify opposing myths competing within her, and how she gained a perspective on the place of each in her life. Your goal in this second stage of the program also is to articulate both sides of the mythic conflict you identified in the previous chapter and to deepen your understanding about each.

Personal Ritual: Part One of Your Fairy Tale

You have already worked with many of the raw materials that you will be weaving into your Fairy Tale. Part One will symbolize your very personal Fall from Paradise, the way you dealt with that sudden or progressive loss, the vision you adopted of Paradise Regained, and the beginnings of your Quest toward it. In addition to your Shield, features of Part One may be patterned after the early rules of conduct and philosophy of life you identified on your journey back in time or conflicts that have appeared in your dreams. You might want to pause here and review your journal entries describing your Shield, conflict symbols, dreams, and journey back in time.

The setting of your Fairy Tale can be an ancient kingdom, a futuristic city, a far-away galaxy, a land of elves and gnomes, a family of deer, chipmunks, chimpanzees, or sea otters, a primitive culture, a period of history, or any other context that might occur to you. Label a page of your journal "Fairy Tale—Part One." Compose Part One of your Fairy Tale using one of the following approaches: Find a comfortable setting and allow the story to emerge in your imagination; tell the story to another person as you are creating it; or talk it into a tape recorder. Record or summarize the story in your journal. Before you begin, take time to center yourself on the aims of Part One: to metaphorically portray an innocent and hopeful time from your childhood, its loss, and how you set out to make up for that loss.

We suggest you start with the words "Once upon a time" and continue to talk or write, allowing the saga to unfold. It is not necessary to rehearse. Let your spontaneity take the story wherever it will go; editing and interpretation can come later. At this point, do not judge what emerges. You may be surprised at unexpected twists in the plot or at new characters that may suddenly appear on the scene. We will follow Frank, the investment counselor, as he progresses through the remainder of the program. Part One of Frank's Fairy Tale read:

> Once upon a time, long long ago, in a land far away, was a Prince who lived in a beautiful castle with his mother, the Queen, and his father, the King, and all the members of his family and the Royal Court. The King and Queen dearly loved their son, Prince Francisco, and spent all their free time playing with him and indulging him. He was the most fun-loving boy in the Kingdom. He felt very safe and deeply loved. One day the Queen told the Prince

that something very wonderful was about to happen to him, for he was going to begin school. This made him very happy because there were no other boys or girls his age living in the castle, and he had always had to play by himself when the King and Queen were off taking care of the Kingdom.

The first day that his mother escorted him to school, Prince Francisco was quite excited, until in one terrible moment he realized that the Queen was not going to stay with him, but was going to leave him in this strange and foreign place. There he was left, and with more children of his own age than he had ever seen. And that day he found out a most upsetting thing—every one of these children had Kings and Queens for parents. If everyone was a King or a Queen, then "King" or "Queen" must not be very important; it must be kind of ordinary.

But what was even worse was that the teacher would tell the class what to do and everyone would begin to do it except him. He would hang his head in shame and confusion, for he never seemed to understand anything the teacher said to the class unless she also explained it specially to him. Not surprisingly, the other children in his class began to make fun of him and stay away from him. So he had to realize that he was just an ordinary boy on this first day of school, and he had to suffer the humiliation of not even being very good at being an ordinary boy. The other children wouldn't even address him in the Royal Tone that made him know he was Prince Francisco. They just called him Frankie, if they used his name at all. The worst shock was the next morning, when he found out that he had to return to this waking nightmare called school, and that he would have to return day after day after day. He was sure some evil spirit had placed a terrible curse upon him.

Frankie returned to the school, and every day he was met with mockery, criticism, and failure, until his spirit was beaten to a pulp. Finally, when he could stand it no longer, a deep stirring in his soul caused him to clench his teeth, control his breathing, grip his hands, and muster every ounce of energy and courage so he could learn the things that he must to please his teachers, impress his peers, and most of all, to be accepted. He decided he would break the curse through sheer power of will. While far from the most naturally talented kid in his class, he became the most industrious—developing himself socially, athletically, and academically. And, to his enormous relief, he did begin to find acceptance—labored, joyless, and stilted, but still, acceptance.

As you see, Part One begins in a Paradisiacal setting, portrays Paradise Lost within the contour of a single incident, and reveals the code of conduct that governed an unsuccessful Quest toward Paradise Regained. Part One depicts a trauma, betrayal, or other tragedy that darkens the life of the main character, and it reflects some of the decisions he or she made to cope with these difficult conditions.

Once you have written Part One in your journal (or spoken it and later entered it), reread it. Make whatever revisions seem necessary, but for the most part stay with your first impulses in developing its plot. Then reflect upon the meaning that Part One of your Fairy Tale holds for you.

Frank used a technique called "focusing"[5] to reflect upon his most vivid reaction to the story—the ridicule he felt when the children made fun of him for not understanding the teacher's directions. In focusing, you direct your attention to your bodily reactions about an experience and then begin to sense their meaning.

> My initial sensation was of a heaviness in my throat and in my eyes, which I associated with tears and sadness. I also noticed how I had tightened my body and was controlling my breathing. I stayed with this awareness, and as I continued to scan my bodily sensations, I had a sense of pressure and recoil in the front of my body, as if I'd bumped into an invisible wall and had the wind knocked out of me. The feelings I felt were of bewilderment and a painful emotional thud that caused me to want to put on my brakes, pull in, hold back.
>
> My first impulse was to call this cowardice. Then I realized that the caution seems to have become built into my body. I automatically hold back. It's like I've lost the choice of opening myself. With that realization, I had the thought that maybe I could change this, and there was an immediate, noticeable decrease in the pressure on my chest.
>
> I think it means that I never completely got over the shock of being plopped out of my safe home into the terrifying jungle of kindergarten. When I bumped so hard against that invisible wall, I pulled into myself with all my strength because it was so dangerous to be out there in this new world. I do not believe I ever again let myself be vulnerable to the degree I was when I walked into that classroom—and I've held myself back ever since, trying to control things instead of just allowing them to be. Although the "curse" from my Fairy Tale seemed to have lifted by my late teens, I continue to step cautiously as if the evil spirit may be there waiting when I turn the next corner.

But however hard I would try to be in control of my life, I had an ingrained conviction that I couldn't influence things, and no faith that I could make it, regardless of my determination. So, as hard as I tried, my efforts weren't supported by any confidence, and therefore a good deal of my strength was not available to me, even when I was putting out my very best. Still, I saw no alternative but to keep trying—harder and harder.

When you reflect on this or any of the personal rituals, we encourage you to also begin by focusing upon your strongest feelings about the experience and taking cues from your bodily responses as you explore its meaning.

Personal Ritual: Healing an Ancient Wound

Old myths that have become dysfunctional often have their roots in early attempts to compensate for traumatic, humiliating, or other painful conditions from childhood. We may continue to follow the old myth's guidance, even though it limits us, in order to uphold an unconscious covenant that it will protect us from feeling the pain of early emotional wounds. "If I fully devote myself to my work, no one will ever again think of me as a 'no-good, lazy kid.' " It is sometimes possible to heal an old wound by creating a supportive and constructive situation where you can reexperience the circumstances in which the wound occurred. Such a healing can reduce the emotional charge that keeps you attached to the old myth and open the way for a more beneficial counter-myth. Initiating a healing of this nature is the purpose of this personal ritual.

Stuart, an avocado farmer and photographer whose parents both died during his adolescence, developed and shouldered a personal myth that he too was destined to die before his own children were fully grown. The untimely deaths of his parents were the last of a long string of terror-inducing experiences from his childhood, and imagining his own early death somehow helped him to live with his unresolved grief and unnamed terrors. If he knew he would die young, he did not have to worry about the uncertainty of when death would come. But after he had children of his own, he bargained with God to allow him to see his children reach maturity; he would then willingly die whenever fate decreed. As his children approached the age that he had been when his parents died, however, he began to feel terrified about having made this pact. Although only in his mid-forties and newly remarried to a woman who wanted to have a child with him, he felt that to have another child just as the term of his bargain was coming to a close would be a show of arrogance and an irrefutable invitation to death before the child was grown. All the positive thinking in the world was no match for his pervasive anxiety. Changing a myth of this magnitude, so deeply entrenched in one's posture in the world, requires what therapists call a "working through" of emotional wounds that are yet unhealed. This ritual will help you to identify an area from your past that is ready for further "working through," and it will get you started in the process.

There are several ways that the transformation of an old myth into a more fulfilling one may be impeded by emotional trauma that has not been worked through. Unhealed emotional wounds tend to shape our perceptions when there is an analogue between a situation we encounter and the circumstances that wounded us. We will focus more on the dangers, miss the opportunities, and be weighed down by the emotional load we are carrying from the wound. Unhealed wounds also tend to inhibit us from taking further emotional risks, and abandoning a familiar though failing myth for an untried though promising myth is almost always an emotional risk.

In Stuart's case, he needed to work through not only the trauma of his parents' deaths, but also other insecurities that traced back to his childhood. Opening yourself to the pain of your past can lead to a healing that transforms your mythology. When the pain is overwhelming, the process may best be assisted by outside resources. Stuart entered psychotherapy as he began to sense how much he was still living according to a mythology that had been built around raw emotional wounds. Announcing to his wife that he would like to have a child with her was a milestone as that mythology changed.

But even without outside interventions, your psyche is continually dealing with and attempting to heal old wounds that are interfering with your current functioning. Dreams can provide a window on this process. You can also, with intention, direct your energies toward healing old emotional wounds. Although the healing process may require a long period of time, the act of initiating the process can open you to a more creative and hope-inspiring mythology.

The following personal ritual will help you identify an emotional wound from your past that is interfering with the resolution of your mythic conflict, and it will show you how to bring your psychological resources to serve in its healing. You will need one extra prop for this ritual, a "huggable" pillow.

Begin by reflecting on this question: Are there aspects of your old myth that you believe will be difficult to change although their shortcomings are evident? Frank identified the following areas:

> I'm not willing to part with my insistence that I give a consistently optimal performance in my job, even though these standards are very costly for my personal life and I could get away with a great deal less.
>
> I have no reason to trust that passion and playfulness would suddenly appear were I to slow down and make room for them, so I'd wind up not only without my high work standards, but also demoralized and bored.
>
> I am afraid that if I were to get more into my passion and to let it show, I would be obvious and boorish and would become the object of painful teasing to my face as well as behind my back.
>
> If I allow myself to have more time to relax and play, I'm afraid that my motivation to be productive would begin to erode, the quality of my output would deteriorate with it, and I'd start to hate having to work.

Once you have identified a few areas of continued conflict or impasse, record them in your journal. Then find a comfortable position with your pillow, take a few deep breaths, close your eyes, and relax as you allow the following instructions to guide you:

As you settle into this safe, secure spot, focus on your breathing. Begin to release any areas of tension in your body. [Pause] Listen for and feel each in-breath and each out-breath. [Pause] Notice your belly and chest rising and falling. [Pause] Your breathing becomes slow and deep as you relax more and more completely with each of your next five breaths—ONE, TWO, THREE, FOUR, FIVE.

Bring to mind the areas of your mythology that you believe would be difficult to modify. [Pause] Focus upon one issue which you cannot imagine changing or strongly resist changing. [Pause] Experience a place in your body that represents this area of your life. Explore the sensations. [Pause] Identify its boundaries and draw an outline of the area with your finger or in your mind. [Pause] Discover the weight, size, color, and temperature of your feeling. [Pause] Breathe consciously and deeply into this taut area.

You will use this feeling to lead you back to an earlier period of your life. Notice the flow of sensations that make up the feeling. Now create the image of a river as you continue to focus on your feeling.

Think of your feeling as the river. Imagine yourself in a boat on that river. The river floats you back in time, safely and comfortably, to one of the first occasions in which you experienced the feeling you just identified. At the source of your feeling was an early emotional trauma or other difficulty. The river takes you back to this source. On the bank of the river you see, as if on a stage, the circumstances that created a wound—an experience that involved loss, betrayal, rejection, or other emotional injury. It may be the same scene you went to in the previous journey back in time or an entirely different one. Enter the scene.

In this scene are the origins of a wound that is still affecting your life. Notice who is there and what you are doing. Where your memory does not offer details, your imagination will. All the colors and sounds of people, surroundings, and actions are present. What do you smell? What are you wearing? How old are you in this remembered or imagined scene? [45-second pause]

As you recall the circumstances that caused this trauma, take the pillow and hold it close to you, positioning it so it has some contact with your wound. Feel the changing sensations in your wound as you give it this contact and attention. Imagine that this pillow now becomes the you of an earlier time, back when you were experiencing this memory. Hug the pillow and give comfort. Experience this connection with the child within you for the next several minutes as you reconstruct the details and reexperience the event. [If you are reading these instructions into a tape, add: "Turn off the tape and take all the time you need."]

Still holding this younger you represented by your pillow, imagine that your Inner Shaman has heard about your suffering and has come out of the depths to help you. Look at this being, taking in his or her stature, posture, facial qualities, and expressions. [20-second pause] This old soul is a powerful healer of body, mind, emotions, and spirit. Feel the power of your Shaman's eyes as she or he looks at you with great caring and understanding. [Pause] Notice that there is a glow about your Shaman's head and hands. Watch this glow as it attracts shimmering rays of energy from the atmosphere until you are also surrounded by and bathed in a tranquil, radiant, healing, crystal light.

Your Shaman is making contact with you, placing one radiant, healing hand directly on the child where the pain is greatest and the other hand on your back. Feel the healing forces of the universe being channeled from these hands and directly into your wound. [Pause] Feel this soothing warmth entering your body as your Shaman's breathing keeps a perfect rhythm with your breathing. Sense how with each inhalation a fresh charge of healing light enters your body. [Pause] With each exhalation, be aware that you are releasing stale energy and other residues as your wound begins to heal. [Pause] Remain aware of the hands over your wound with each inhalation and each exhalation as the healing process continues. [If you are reading these instructions into a tape, add: "Turn off the tape and take all the time you need."]

Now your Shaman has some counsel for you. Listen as you are told how to better protect yourself and avoid reinjuring your wound. [60-second pause] Once more, your Shaman lays a hand over your wound, giving you another dose of this creative healing power. [Pause] If you have any further questions, ask them now, and listen for the answers. [30-second pause] When you are ready, say good-bye to your Shaman for now.

Bring your attention to the pillow you have been holding, and give affection and courage to the child or infant you once were. Tenderly comfort the child with your touch and adult experience. Give your thoughts and kindness generously to turn hurt to useful experience. Be the adult you wish had been there for you. [60-second pause]

Again see and feel this younger version of your self, hug it tightly, and shower it with all the love you have. You may even cry together. [Pause] As you continue this embrace, feel the child merging back into you, returning into your present body and mind. Be aware of the ways that healing has taken place and also feel the gifts—childish glee, enthusiasm, creativity, anticipation—this child has for you. [Pause] You have given your younger self the love and best advice you have to offer. Now feel that love and wisdom come back to you as your younger self reintegrates into your being.

With your next deep breath, come forward in time to your current age. [Pause] Attune yourself to the part of your body that you associated with your emotional wound. Have the sensations changed? [Pause] Know that you may repeat this healing ritual or any part of it as many times as you would like. Make a commitment to yourself to check in on your wound from time to time so you may provide it with all the healing energy it needs.

Prepare to return to your waking consciousness. Counting from five back to one, you will be able to recall all you need of this experience. When you hear the number 1, you will feel alert, relaxed, and refreshed, as if waking from a wonderful nap. FIVE, move your fingers and toes. FOUR, stretch your shoulders, neck, and face muscles. THREE, take a deep breath. TWO, bring your attention back into the room. ONE, open your eyes, feeling refreshed, alert, and fully competent to meet the requirements of your day.

Summarize this experience in your journal, and reflect upon its meaning. Frank recorded the following passages in his journal:

> As I thought about my strict adherence to high standards in my work, regardless of the personal cost, I noticed that my neck felt extremely tight and constricted. As I focused on these sensations, my attention moved up to my jaw, which felt hard and brittle, teeming with heavy, taut sensations that reminded me of a bicycle inner tube that is being stretched. The closest description I could find for the emotion I associated with these sensations was "burning determination." I had trouble getting back to an earlier experience—I even had to turn the tape off because it got ahead of me—but once the images came, they were very powerful.
>
> I know that in the first weeks of my life I suffered from slight malnutrition because my mother was determined to breast-feed me but could not produce enough milk. After that, I was fed according to a schedule and even held on schedule, as was the custom of the times. My parents have reported to me how agonizing it was to hear me scream for hours at the top of my lungs and feel they could not go in and comfort me. I have no recollection of these times, but in this fantasy, my imagination took me back to them in a reasonably vivid manner. There I was in the crib, just screaming and screaming my little jaw off. Finally, in utter exhaustion I quit screaming and set my jaw to scream no more, and to contain the pain and neediness within me.
>
> As I hug the pillow, which is touching my jaw, the hardness starts to melt and the tightness releases, and I begin to feel warm, pulsating sensations through my jaw. I have the thought that if I were still in that crib and my jaw were free like this again, I would once more scream out with terror and with rage. But now, troubled by neither hunger nor fear, it is only pleasant to be feeling the warm sensations radiating through my jaw. As I hold the pillow, it feels shaky, so I squeeze it all the more tightly, trying to give it comfort.
>
> This time my Inner Shaman looked like a cross between Father Time and George Burns. His advice went something like: "You approach the world leading with your hard jaw the way an insect leads with its antennae. The very hardness that protects you in this world also barricades you from receiving the satisfactions

you most desire. Your perfectionism is a slick shell that keeps your inner softness from touching the world or from being touched by it.

"I proclaim on this day that you have developed many strengths well, and the brittleness in your jaw and in your standards are no longer required for your protection. I invite you to beckon me to come to you every day this week. I will come and I will focus the strength of my healing power upon your jaw while you massage and soothe it, bringing yourself, through the magical powers of your imagination, back to the very crib in which your jaw and your joy first began to harden. After seven such meetings, we shall decide what further treatment is required. Do you accept this offer?" As I hedged about being too busy, he sent me an amused, knowing glance and I capitulated.

After extending my farewells to the Inner Shaman, I told the little infant something like this: "I see that your first lesson in life was that if things just take their natural course, you will not get what you need. As a result, you will grow up with tremendous determination to marshal all the powers at your command to ensure that your needs *will* be met. You will develop a refined capacity for impressing others through the excellence of your work. In some ways this will serve you well, but it also will blind you to the simple joys and satisfactions of life. You are so certain these will not come easily that you will not perceive them as possibilities and you will miss them. I want you to know that the survival abilities you *will* develop will be more than adequate. You may rest with assurance about that. It is my wish that you allow yourself to relax into the simpler joys that will come your way with no effort, if only you let them be."

There are several ways in which you may extend this ritual. You can repeat it as often as you wish or invent variations or further rituals, as Frank's Inner Shaman suggested. Sometimes this process brings other traumatic memories to mind, and you may carry out the same instructions to attend to whatever wounds those events may have caused.

If, however, this experience opens old wounds that continue to plague you even after you have completed the ritual and reflected upon it in your journal, refer to the section toward the end of the previous chapter that describes how to use your Shield to protect yourself. Use that technique or any of the other suggestions provided in Appendix C to work with the emotions you have uncovered.

Personal Ritual: Finding the Roots of Mythic Renewal in Your Past

Your old myth helped you adjust to the Paradise Lost of separations, betrayal, or other trauma. Yet glimmers of earlier, more innocent times remain in your unconscious mind, and they provide a prototype for the hopeful new directions represented by counter-myths. The following personal ritual will renew your connection with experiences from your past that gave you a reason to hope that your aspirations can bring you into a better world.

The instructions here are similar to the previous journeys back into time. Here, however, instead of starting with an uncomfortable experience associated with a conflict, you will begin by focusing on a positive feeling. You will follow this feeling back to events from your past that serve as underlying models when you envision more promising new directions. Have the instructions read to you; read them into a tape and let the tape guide you; or familiarize yourself with them enough to be able to lead yourself through the exercise. Find a comfortable position, close your eyes, and take several deep breaths:

As you settle into this safe, secure spot, focus on your breathing. Begin to release any areas of tension in your body. [Pause] Listen for and feel each in-breath and each out-breath. [Pause] Notice your belly and chest rising and falling. [Pause] Your breathing becomes slow and deep as you relax more and more completely with each of your next five breaths—ONE, TWO, THREE, FOUR, FIVE.

Magically, the dilemmas of Part One of your Fairy Tale have been resolved. You no longer feel the confusion and pain of that time. Instead you are optimistic and refreshed. Your body is suffused with energy and a particular good feeling that delights you.

Bask in these good feelings. Discover their colors, textures, taste, and scent. Find a name for your feelings. Your imagination and mind are working in perfect harmony to fix this wonderful experience in your body and memory. You feel revitalized. [60-second pause]

You will use these feelings to lead you back to an earlier period of your life. Notice the flow of sensations that make up the feelings. Now create the image of a river as you continue to focus on the feeling. Think of your feeling as the river. Imagine yourself in a boat on that river. The river floats you back in time, safely and comfortably, to one of the first occasions on which you experienced this affirming feeling.

On the bank of the river you see, as if on a stage, yourself enjoying the same feeling, but in a scene that occurred very early in your life. Enter the scene.

How old are you in this scene? What are you doing? Where your memory does not offer answers, your imagination will. What do you look like? What are you wearing? Who, if anyone, is with you? Where are you? What are the surroundings? What sights, sounds, tastes, or smells do you experience? What, specifically, brought about the feeling? Recall or imagine as many details of that earlier time as you can. [45-second pause]

Now reflect on some of the decisions you might have made as a result of this experience and others like it. [Pause] What conclusions did you come to about yourself and your world? [Pause] What rules, ethics, or codes of conduct did you adopt? [Pause] What attitudes toward other people began to emerge? [Pause] What views of the world? [Pause] What philosophy of life? [30-second pause]

Prepare to return to your waking consciousness. Counting from five back to one, you will be able to recall all you need of this experience. When you hear the number 1, you will feel alert, relaxed, and refreshed, as if waking from a wonderful nap. FIVE, move your fingers and your toes. FOUR, stretch your shoulders, neck, and face muscles. THREE, take a deep breath. TWO, bring your attention back into the room. ONE, open your eyes, feeling refreshed, alert, and fully competent to meet the requirements of your day.

Having completed this process, open your journal and summarize your experience, addressing the following:

1. What was the positive feeling with which you started?
2. Describe the scene you went back to in as much detail as you can recall.
3. What rules of behavior and ethical codes did you adopt based on experiences like the one to which you returned?
4. What sense did you have of your destiny, capacities, and limitations?
5. How are these codes and attitudes affecting your life?

By contrasting this ritual with the previous experiments in "time travel," you can see how some experiences set the stage for maintaining myths that are self-limiting and others provide a foundation for more imaginative and self-affirming myths. Frank wrote that if the problems associated with his old myth were suddenly resolved,

> I would feel the passion I've been wanting to develop, a sense of aliveness and tingling radiating out from my heart and filling my body with an enthusiasm for living.
>
> I went back to age eight. It was the first time I'd ever excelled at anything. I'd been taking piano lessons for about a year, and coinciding with my best week ever, the school happened to sponsor an unannounced contest where the winner was the person who had mastered the greatest number of pieces that week. I came in with five new pieces and the next person came in with three, so I was treated in front of the whole group of some 120 young musicians with a Snickers bar for each piece and a lavishness of praise that had me glowing with warmth and pride.
>
> Where I had always felt inadequate around my peers, the single experience of standing there in front of that large group and being praised for something I had achieved left an indelible mark. I felt worthy. As I think about it, however, I'm not sure this experience provides the basis for the new myth I want to develop. My conclusion from this episode was that if you work very very hard, fortune will eventually smile on you, so I further mobilized my passion for hard work. The experience helped me feel worthy for my accomplishments but not simply for being who I am.

Dream Focus: A Renewed Image of Paradise Regained

When you were asked to identify or incubate a dream of Paradise in the previous chapter, you were instructed to ask for a dream that showed how things might once have been. This time you will be looking for a dream that shows you how things might become. The dream may portend the blossoming of your highest potentials and the best possible future. It may reveal new solutions for the problems inherent in your conflict. It may point the way for you to transcend the dilemmas faced by the main character in Part One of your Fairy Tale. And it may renew your Quest toward Paradise Regained.

You will be looking for an ideal solution to the problems caused by the old myth. This solution does not need to be realistic. In fact, it should be extravagant, even a return to a matured image of Paradise. The dream need not offer practical instruction, only an imaginative fantasy of a more satisfying future.

Scan your journal for any recent dreams that suggest positive directions. To incubate such a dream, bring to mind the Paradise Regained symbol from your Shield, or a positively charged image from the previous guided fantasy, or another hopeful image you might generate in the moment. Allow the feelings you associate with this image to permeate your body. Before going to sleep, repeat to yourself ten to twenty times instructions similar to the following: "I request a dream that shows me a creative response to [describe the old myth or the problems associated with it]. I will recall my dream as soon as I awake."

Immediately upon awakening, record any dreams you do recall. If you do not remember a dream, stay attuned to your early morning thoughts, insights, and fantasies. Use techniques such as those in Appendix B to examine any dreams you incubate or select from your journal. After requesting a vision of Paradise Regained on several consecutive evenings, but having no dream memories, Frank recalled the following:

> The setting of my dream resembled ancient Greece, and I was an Olympic wrestler. I recall my strength, my sweat, my confidence, my focus on the opponent's every move, my respect for him, my joy in being in this event, my catlike readiness and speed. I felt very powerful, as if all my muscles were developed to their full and natural capacity. I felt so alive and strong that I imagined a glow must be radiating from me. I don't even recall how the match ended, although there was no question that I won, and suddenly I was carrying the Olympic Torch around this massive stadium with my gaze and energy unabashedly meeting the massive, cheering crowd.
>
> When I woke up, I remembered several things about the dream that seemed related to Paradise Regained. First, I was outgoing, enjoying getting involved with others, intimate with everything—trees, people, everything. I wasn't my usual shy, retiring, scared self. In addition, a wonderful energy, a *joie de vivre,* was surging through me. Whatever that dream was about, I wish I could package it. It offered me a deliciously lavish image of where I want to be headed.

Personal Ritual: Part Two of Your Fairy Tale

In Part Two of your Fairy Tale, the hero or heroine from Part One will go on a magical journey that reveals the creative promise of your counter-myth. Part Two is not bound by the "reality principle." You may draw upon your unbridled creativity in finding the solutions to the dilemma faced in Part One. This second part of your Fairy Tale will, like some dreams, probably be a blend of the plausible and of your uncurbed imagination.

Part Two will reveal a new direction. The journey back in time that you just completed may have opened you to an intuitive sense of new possibilities for yourself. This second segment of your Fairy Tale will suggest an ideal resolution to the difficulties that emerged in the first segment. The solution may be in an exaggerated and extravagant form. That is appropriate for this ritual. The key ingredients are that a new solution to the dilemmas of Part One will be revealed, and instructions on how to achieve it will be offered. While Part One probably paralleled events as they actually occurred in your life, you will not be following your actual history in Part Two. Instead, you will be using your ingenuity to discover an inventive solution to the original problem.

Part Two will have the same central character seeking to solve the problems that were introduced in Part One. In Part Two, however, the action will occur as a drama within a drama. Rather than happening directly within the main character's life, he or she may have a dream, reverie, or vision, be in a play or read a story, meet a teacher, encounter the Inner Shaman, or speak with an animal, plant, or object. This device gives you maximum poetic license. Meg took a magical ride on her porpoise. Frank's Part Two, as you will see, unfolded while he gazed into a crystal ball.

Read any sections of your journal that you want to review. Take time to center yourself on the aims of Part Two: to reveal to the hero or heroine of your Fairy Tale a fresh solution to the dilemma that emerged in Part One and to provide instruction on how to reach that solution. Then compose the second part of your Fairy Tale. Find a comfortable setting and allow the story to emerge in your imagination; tell the story to another person as you are creating it; or speak it into a tape recorder. Record or summarize the story in your journal. This was Frank's Part Two:

> As Frankie learned to please others and meet their expectations, he forgot how much he enjoyed playing in the towers of the castle

and swimming in the giant lake and getting all muddy on its shores. He had no time for such foolishness. He had become a very intense, stern, and serious, though increasingly successful, young chap. He grew bigger, stronger, and more confident. But he had ceased to be the fun-loving boy he once had been.

One day, in homage to dim memories of those early days from once upon a time, he was drawn to a traveling minstrel troupe that was passing through the Kingdom. With them was a wise and kind old Wizard who had a crystal ball. Whoever would look in the crystal ball could see "the future of their heart's desire." Frankie never thought much about the future because he was always trying so hard to get ahead in the present. But he became so curious to look into the future of his heart's desire that he gave the Wizard a silver token he had earned that week polishing his teacher's gilt-edged boots.

When Frankie looked into the crystal ball, he saw himself many years hence as King Francisco. King Francisco carried himself with all the confidence and dignity that might be expected of one of royal blood. He was respected throughout the land for his competence in ruling the Kingdom. But he was an unusual King. He was the most childlike person in the entire Kingdom. He was alert to the miracles of life no matter where he was or who he was with. He approached every situation with curiosity and a freshness of spirit that made each moment alive and brought much laughter from the belly. Where there were obstacles, he was moved to elevate the problem into an intriguing challenge. As a result, other people loved to be with him.

Frankie loved the images he saw, but he became very despondent with the realization that he was growing up to be a very different man from the King he saw in the crystal ball.

Whereas Meg's porpoise ride brought her to teachers who were very explicit in the lessons they had for her, Frank's crystal ball provided an image of a better future but little other instruction. Review Part Two of your own Fairy Tale and reflect upon its meaning by reading it slowly and immersing yourself in the story. Note where your reactions are the strongest, and focus on your bodily sensations at those points. Consider the meaning of these feelings and describe your reflections in your journal. Frank had a strong reaction to his Fairy Tale:

My physical sensations while imagining the scenes in the crystal ball included an openness and tingling in my chest, almost an exuberance, and a sense of my breath having become very deep and full. This feels like power. It feels like I have a lot of energy available. I also feel anticipation, a readiness to meet the world. What does it all mean? If I can be feeling so much passion by just imagining a situation, then I must have a larger reservoir of passion than I've been able to reach. My tendency has always been to pull back because that feels much more comfortable. But the King put himself right out there, he engaged life, and seeing him led to wonderful sensations, leaving me feeling stronger, more energized, and more sure of myself.

Personal Ritual: A Body Metaphor of Your Conflict

Mythic conflicts are expressed in people's thoughts, feelings, and behavior, and they are also often somaticized—that is, symbolized by conditions or events in the body. You may feel full of zest if you have just fallen in love, but may be stricken with the flu or worse after a significant loss or disappointment. In the following rituals, you will be shown how to use your body to better understand a conflict that you have already identified.

We remind you one final time that in this and in all subsequent personal rituals that include guided imagery, you may speak the instructions into a tape and let that lead you, or you may have a partner read the instructions to guide you through the exercise, or you may make yourself familiar enough with the instructions that you can lead yourself through the ritual unassisted. To begin, sit or recline comfortably and start to relax.

Close your eyes and take a few deep breaths as you settle into this position. Feel yourself relaxing more completely with your next five breaths: ONE, TWO, THREE, FOUR, FIVE. Place your hands in front of you, extending your arms as if you were reaching out. Keeping your palms facing each other and your hands about two feet apart, let your elbows bend so you can relax your arms into a more comfortable position. With your hands still facing each other, reflect for a moment upon the myth that is guiding the main character of Part One. [Pause] Imagine that this myth is being placed in one of your hands. Which hand more correctly represents that myth? What does the myth feel like in this hand? Is it hot or cold? Heavy or light? Rough or smooth? What color might it be? What other sensations do you notice? Take a few moments to explore the ways you experience this myth from Part One of your Fairy Tale as you represent it in your hand.

Now reflect on the myth that is guiding the main character of Part Two. [Pause] Imagine that this myth is placed in your other hand. What does this myth feel like? Is it hot or cold? Heavy or light? Rough or smooth? What color might it be? What other sensations do you notice? Take a few moments to explore the ways you experience this myth as it is represented by your hand.

Now begin to notice the differences in your hands. Focus on the skin and muscles of each hand as you attend to these differences. Which myth is harder to hold? Which myth is easier to hold? Which myth has a more pleasant feel? Is one harder and the other softer? Are there differences in weight? Is one more buoyant?

Now hold your hands so they face each other and explore the space between them. Be aware of any attraction, any repulsion, or any tension. [Pause] When you have completed exploring the relationship between the two myths as symbolized by your hands, take a deep breath, and slowly count yourself back from five to one.

In your journal, summarize the sensations you experienced, and reflect on their significance. If one myth was harder to hold, did that mean it is too difficult to manage, or is it so new that it will take a while to get accustomed to? If one myth was rougher, does that mean it is causing you trouble, or that it is trying to get you to abandon attitudes that are soft or disempowering? If one myth was heavier, does that mean it involves more problems or that it is more important? If one myth was more buoyant, does that mean it is more inspirational or that it is impossible to achieve?

Next, consider how you experienced the space between the two myths. Did they repel each other? Was there an attraction between them? Did one seem to overwhelm the other with its weight or its power? When there is a conflict between myths, sometimes one of them has so much force that it appears invincible. Sometimes the two myths are so equal in strength and clash so strongly that the two hands repel each other. In other instances, each has qualities the other needs and the hands are magnetically drawn together. Frank reflected in his journal:

My left arm *became* the old myth. Represented this way, I saw the old myth as keeping me restricted and weak and likely to stay that way because it didn't give me any confidence or impetus to push into new frontiers. That insight came when I noticed a parallel between my under-used left hand and the way my old myth keeps me from developing. My left arm is not nearly so developed as my right arm because whenever I have a choice between hands, I don't use my left hand. That's kind of how the old myth operates. The old myth keeps me weak by not having me use all of myself, putting great effort into things I already do well to the exclusion of those parts of me that call for new tricks. I don't take many emotional risks, and then I wonder why my passion is dampened.

On the other hand, so to speak, my right arm felt strong and sure of itself. It had no question of its competence. But, as I put the counter-myth into my right hand, it did not feel right. While the sureness and strength in my right hand accurately represented the passionate qualities of the counter-myth, I was also aware that the myth itself was not well developed like my right arm. The old myth seemed to match the weakness of my left arm perfectly, but the counter-myth was not confident and well developed like my right arm. So, I was having two opposing and confusing feelings about representing the counter-myth this way. In its content, the myth is strong like my right arm; in its development, it is still weak and immature.

It boiled down to a paradox: The old myth, which is very strong within me, was keeping me weak; the counter-myth, which is very weak within me, promised to make me stronger. I tried to make the two myths merge by bringing my hands together, but I couldn't get it to happen. The old myth stayed with my left hand just fine, but the counter-myth kept jumping away whenever the two hands would come close to each other. I guess that tentative passionate part of me doesn't want to have much to do with the long-standing restricted part.

On to Stage Three

Besides the structured approaches you have been using in this chapter to cultivate a productive counter-myth, other experiences also may point you in new directions. A version of the myth that is emerging for you may, for instance, be found in some corner of your culture. You might be drawn toward a novel, movie, or play in which the characters are grappling with an issue similar to yours. You may find that discussing the issue with someone whom you feel has something to teach you reveals new possibilities. You may come upon some classics or inspirational writings that provide thoughtful guidance. Remain alert for such resources. The following chapter will help you begin to refine your counter-myth and to resolve its inevitable conflict with the myth that has prevailed until now.

4

The Third Stage: Conceiving a Unifying Mythic Vision

Positive images of the future are a powerful and magnetic force. . . . They draw us on and energize us, give us the courage and will to take important initiatives. Negative images of the future also have a magnetism. They pull the spirit downward in the path of despair [and] impotence.
—WILLIAM JAMES

The personal myths that guide us as we are growing up usually do not prove adequate against the realities and demands we face as adults. Sometimes those myths become transformed, perhaps through experiences that contradict their premises, and they may evolve enough that they continue to provide valid guidance. In other cases, experiences that contradict a myth may make it more rigid, and its capacity to offer effective direction is further compromised. In any realm of life that requires important decisions—from our behavior in relationships to our career development to our spiritual aspirations—both the tendency to find comfort in familiar myths and the impetus to discover fresh ways of understanding are in continuous play. From this dynamic tension, we adjust and we grow.

Where your myths are rigid or outdated, your ability to adjust to changing circumstances and to progress in your psychological development is diminished. By formulating counter-myths, alternative mythic structures that attempt to make better sense of the world and help you cope in it more effectively, your unconscious mind compensates for such liabilities in your mythology. The prevailing myth and the counter-myth support partial and seemingly incompatible directions for your growth. They inevitably come into conflict with each other.

The process, however, can ultimately serve to expand the boundaries of your sense of who you are and the options your world offers. In depth psychology, tension between competing aspects of the psyche is seen as a natural and unavoidable aspect of personality development. Such tension stimulates the psyche's energies and regulates the personality. As you work with a mythic conflict, you become increasingly capable of embracing a larger view that integrates both of its sides. Depth psychologists believe that symbols are a primary vehicle for helping the psyche reconcile opposing tendencies that reside within. Jung referred to this property of symbols as their "transcendent function." Meg's symbol of the abalone shell helped her to reconcile the part of her represented by the shell's drab and ordinary exterior with the part of her represented by its iridescent interior. The shell served as a symbol of integration for these opposing aspects of her personality.

Counter-myths embody the novelty of imagination, the inspiration of the fresh view, and the appeal of promised solutions to enduring problems. Like a desert reservoir whose life-sustaining waters push against a dam, the emerging counter-myth may finally break into consciousness and flood parched psychological terrain with lush symbols that reveal rich possibilities and offer new hope. Life does not, however, flourish in either a desert or a deluge.

The personal rituals in this chapter are designed to guide you toward achieving a balance. Your attention will be directed toward integrating the old myth symbolized in Part One of your Fairy Tale and the counter-myth symbolized in Part Two into a single myth that inventively incorporates what is vital and beneficial from each of them. Without such balance, the promise of the counter-myth sometimes ignites an individual into making a radical change—quitting a job, leaving a marriage, moving to a new town, joining a cult—which, in the long view of his or her life, proves to have been a self-defeating choice. Changes that are rooted in an integration between the lifelong values embodied in the old myth and the inspiration of the counter-myth are made from a larger perspective. They are better attuned to the meaning of the decision and its long-term consequences.

Many people report the experience of having left a dysfunctional marriage only to select another partner with whom they created a painfully similar relationship. At the core of the mythology keeping the person locked in this kind of relationship may be unresolved issues with a parent. While a counter-myth may have emerged with enough strength to make it untenable to stay in the marriage, the old mythology still prevailed in the selection of the next mate. When your mythology is being challenged by a counter-myth, the possible outcomes range from living out the conflict unconsciously, and repeatedly, to working it through and moving on to other developmental tasks.

The conflict between a prevailing myth and a counter-myth was poignantly evident in Philip, a successful young executive who sought counseling because, in his words, "I am failing as a husband and I am afraid that my marriage is not going to survive." Philip's highly religious parents had placed heavy emphasis on family loyalty, and his father, whom he admired greatly, was almost a television caricature of the 1950s "family man"—a dedicated, trustworthy, and quietly self-sacrificing provider. The son not only attempted to emulate his father in his own marriage, but upped the ante by selecting a woman who was so insecure and demanding that no matter how hard he tried, he continually fell short in his attempts to satisfy her. She expected his unwavering attention during every free moment he had away from work, and she was prone to terrible psychosomatic illnesses when he would balk at her excessive demands. Given the structure of the personal mythology that was defining Philip's role as a husband, he could only sympathize with her illnesses, take extra special care of her while she was sick, and amid great guilt and self-recrimination, pledge himself to show greater devotion the next time so he would in no way disappoint her. But, of course, she was always disappointed. He was giving her exactly the opposite of what she needed if she was ever going to develop beyond the dependency-engendering mythology to which the marriage helped her cling.

As is often the case, when Philip came for help, he was scrutinizing the problem through the lens of the old myth. He believed that the marital difficulties were caused primarily by his failure to live up to the image he held of his father, whom he saw as being so patient and giving that he could make anyone happy. Just beyond his awareness, however, another vision of the role of a marriage partner was being kindled, and it was fanned as he witnessed successful relationships through the media and the lives of acquaintances. In attempting to make sense of the contradiction that although he was trying so hard to fulfill the role of husband as his mythology dictated, his wife was still unhappy and resentful, he began at some level to generate another view of what was required in a marriage. This counter-myth held that both partners are equally responsible in making a marriage work, and it gave credence to his needs as an individual, separate from the marriage. But these ideas seemed extremely self-indulgent to him, and he rejected them as unworthy of serious consideration.

Conceiving a Unifying Mythic Vision

The inclination to attend more to his own needs, however, and to expect more from his wife kept cropping up in subtle ways and became increasingly difficult for him to ignore. While this emerging myth was at first outside of his conscious awareness, it was reflected in his growing anger and resentment. Sometimes, after feeling quite satisfied with the marriage, Philip would suddenly swing pendulum-like to an extreme of the usually repressed counter-myth, behaving spitefully and with an emphatic dose of selfishness. Then, as if the counter-myth were eclipsed by a revival of the old myth, he would again find himself in the grips of guilt and remorse. When he discussed his marriage during a therapy session, shades of anger, of which he was unaware, were conveyed through his voice and facial expressions. After seeing a videotape of a session that made these deeper feelings visible, he began to probe his anger. Philip was challenged to find a larger mythic vision that would retain the wholesome family values from his old mythology while supporting a more vital personal life for himself and a more realistic relationship with his wife.

The personal myths you hold are continually being challenged as you are exposed to new information and experiences. When your experiences are incompatible with the mythology you have been living out, you will at some level feel tension. The inconsistency becomes a disturbing element in your psyche, and stress is created. Two basic outcomes are possible. Your mythology may itself be modified to incorporate the new information, or the new information may become distorted so it can be force-fit into the existing mythic structure. If you believe yourself to be an effective sales manager and are fired from your job, and then turned away after each of eight promising job interviews, your self-image may be challenged, or you may blame your string of misfortunes on bad luck, incompetent interviewers, or an impossible job market. While personal myths are capable of ongoing adjustments to new circumstances, you can also unconsciously ignore or distort disagreeable experiences in order to retain the familiar myth. Some people have hardly adjusted their mythologies for decades.

However dysfunctional a long-standing myth may have become, to abandon it is often a difficult transition from the familiar into the unknown. When young children lose a parent, they go through several predictable stages. First they protest, then despair, and finally, if the parent does not return, the child will take a defensive stance against the pain of future longing and feelings of abandonment.[1] The protest stage is analogous to the way we sometimes cling desperately to the familiarity of a failing myth. The despair is akin to the uncertainty we feel when we are between myths—when the one we have been living out has undeniably proven its unworthiness but a new one to replace it has not emerged. The defensive stance resembles the way we may finally reject everything we can about the old myth. Ken Wilber has spoken of *the supreme law of mythological development:* in each newly achieved stage of consciousness, the distinguishing features of the previous stage, which were once worshipped and revered, are "now looked upon as something to struggle against, to subdue, even to scorn."[2]

Extreme fluctuations are inevitably painful, and they often result in a defensive and self-limiting posture. One way to make the fluctuations less extreme is by bringing your awareness to the process. If you can grasp the bigger picture, the mythic proportions of your discomfort, you are less likely to cling so hard to the old myth. Then you do not later have to vehemently reject it to distinguish yourself from it. According to Wilber, each stage in the evolution of consciousness "goes beyond its predecessors but must nevertheless include and integrate them into its own higher order."[3] By dealing with the transition in a more conscious manner, you increase the likelihood that the experience will lead you toward more flexible and effective guiding myths.

Mythological development proceeds as a dialectic in which the old myth is the thesis, the counter-myth is the antithesis, and a new myth that represents the resolution of the two is the synthesis. As a counter-myth develops, it competes with the prevailing myth to dominate perceptions and to guide behavior. Their dialectical struggle may resemble a sort of "natural selection" within the psyche, a "survival of the fittest" elements of each myth for optimal growth and adjustment. This may be a confusing period. You might think that you could just climb out of the old myth and into a new one. But the new one is limited in ways you have not yet encountered, and the old one still tugs at you with its familiar rules and promises. We all are embedded in our old myths. Before we make lasting changes in fundamental beliefs, there usually is an inner struggle between those beliefs and new directions we have envisioned but that have yet to go through the mill of our experience.

Many techniques are available for bringing about a more conscious and constructive resolution of this conflict. Before you go through this chapter, however, we want to emphasize that a dialectic between your competing myths occurs naturally, whether you assist or not. The psyche thinks in myth, and as "mythical thought moves from an awareness of contradictions towards their resolution, [it attempts] to mediate opposites and resolve them."[4] The choice facing us is whether or not to engage consciously and willfully in the process. The consequences of that decision may be immense. In William Blake's analysis, we have the option to fight mentally within ourselves or physically between ourselves.[5] In this chapter, you will facilitate a creative interchange between your old myth and the emerging counter-myth.

To summarize, sacrificing the familiarity, self-understanding, and world view associated with a prevailing though outdated myth can be so painful that we fight dearly to reject the emerging myth. On the other hand, we may be so distressed with the problems the old myth creates for us that we attempt to sever ourselves from it and clutch at the counter-myth. But the counter-myth, which was in part developed to compensate for the old myth, will have its own distortions and limitations. Understanding these polarities can help you achieve a balance when you find yourself on a seesaw between the old and the emerging. Paradoxically, in order to grow beyond an old myth, it is often necessary to accept the role it played in your life, understand the reasons you at one time needed it, and appreciate the valid messages it still holds. The old myth and the emerging myth will naturally, and often outside of your awareness, engage in a dialectical process as they compete to influence the way you make sense of your world. By focusing your awareness on the inner struggle in this third stage of the program, you will be increasing the likelihood of a more constructive outcome. We once again follow Meg as she moves through this stage of her work.

MEG'S NEXT STEP

In the opening ritual of this chapter, you will be asked to create a chart that contrasts the old myth and the counter-myth and that lists a motto for each. Meg reflected on her contrasting mottoes:

> Old Myth Motto: *Adult life is a spoiler.* I think I discovered when I was called to help my mother in her illnesses that much of life was distasteful and difficult. The only reward that seemed worth having was the approval of my father, who saw me in terms of being a "brave little soldier." This was not only defeminizing, but put an expectation of stalwart courage and ability to rise to tasks both frightening and inappropriate. I think that my Paradise was so lovely because I was part of something unspoiled, healthy, natural, free of demands, rich in discovery. Paradise was lost with outside

demands, standards, requirements, coercion. Beauty was sacrificed to expediency.

Counter-myth Motto: *Life is juicy all the way through.* By translating the lessons from nature into a self-appropriated set of standards and values, a sense of purpose emerges and guides. Hope, action, and discovery make an internal life of value and purity a worthy goal, devoid of excess concern for outside validation.

What seems to be needed in my life is tempering the delight, freedom, and exploration of Paradise with an adaptability that permits me to yield, understand, and adjust to the requirements of everyday life. Defiance has served me poorly, and I'm ready to test out flexibility and acceptance of my place in the world.

Next, you will personify your conflicting myths, giving each a character, a posture, and a voice. After reviewing the contrasting mottoes that summarized her mythic conflict ("Adult life is a spoiler" versus "Life is juicy all the way through"), Meg chose the name "Proper Young Lady" for the character who represented her old myth and "Born-Again Child" for her emerging myth. She had the two characters engage in a dialogue and later transcribed for us a tape of their conversation:

Proper Young Lady (scolding, shaking finger)*:* Look at yourself! You're a disgrace to me and everyone around you.

Born-Again Child (puzzled)*:* What are you talking about?

Proper Young Lady (pointing)*:* Your clothes are worn, and they have stains and loose buttons. Your hair is unkempt, and (condemning, censuring tone) you're barefooted.

Born-Again Child (defensively)*:* I'm playing.

Proper Young Lady (sighing with exasperation, shaking head, tightening mouth)*:* Yes, I know. You play entirely too much. Life is serious; life is demanding. And you are missing the point.

Born-Again Child (on the attack)*:* You just want me to be like you . . . neat, tidy, and emotionally constipated. Never a hair out of place or an original thought. Your idea of an adventure is to ride the city bus. You've got too many rules, too many resented duties, too little imagination. You're scared of making mistakes.

Proper Young Lady (shocked and insulted)*:* How dare you! You who won't do a moment's work unless you're having fun doing it! You who have no responsibilities! You who have no sense of history or future! You *dare* to mock me? I've lived and I've suffered. I know ten times as much about life as you. Do you *dare* reject what I have to say?

Born-Again Child (rolling down a long hill slope, getting grass stains on her jeans)*:* Yep. I don't need what you've got to teach.

Proper Young Lady (frustrated)*:* Sit down and listen to me. It's not polite to talk back to your betters. And look at how disheveled you've gotten yourself!

Born-Again Child (laughing)*:* I'm never going to be polite. I'm going to be honest instead. I'll say what I think and feel and I'll do what feels good. Like this (throws an imaginary water-balloon at the conservatively dressed Proper Young Lady).

Proper Young Lady (drenched and acting outraged)*:* You miserable brat! You self-indulgent, inconsiderate, rotten child! I'll show you (starts toward Born-Again Child, who skips away, just out of reach).

As you see, this dialogue allowed Meg to externalize her mythic conflict and also to have some fun with it. In her journal, she reflected:

> I had a good time with this one. People sometimes comment that I am "strong" or "sure of myself," and they are accurate to a degree. I often, however, feel stuck in the nonconforming posture of the child—as if that stance were a mold of its own and I were not truly free. And I choose my ground carefully, avoiding social settings where I will be in contact with traditional, conservative, establishment types because I feel so unequipped to deal on that level. I do kind of wish I could "pass" as a normal person when I want to, just as black people who were light-skinned used to try to "pass" as whites. But that never worked very well, and I don't suppose it would work for me. Maybe what I need to do is accept myself as a slightly out-of-step person, be grateful for the love I get as an eccentric, and stop worrying about making myself fit in.

The next task is to identify a personal quality that is hindering a resolution between the competing characters. You will call upon your Inner Shaman to perform a ritual transformation of this trait. The ritual is designed to reveal the quality's underlying virtues and to help you embrace its virtues while transforming its liabilities. Meg performed this ritual twice, first focusing on the self-righteousness of the

Proper Young Lady and then on the defiance of the Born-Again Child. With these rituals, she had the experience of seeing her self-righteousness begin to shed its rigidity and her defiance begin to lose its anger. Later, reflecting on these two qualities in her journal, she noted: "They seem like perversions of two *positive* aspects of my personality—self-assurance and individualism."

In the next personal ritual, you will again use a body metaphor to represent your conflict, and you will transform the bodily imagery into other symbolism as you examine the conflict further. Meg reported:

> I imagined my left hand (Born-Again Child) playing with my dog (Gud Dawg), fooling around with his muzzle, letting him mouth my hand with his potentially destructive but oh-so-gentle jaw and teeth, feeling his glove-leather ears, scratching under his chin. The energy between us was just lovely.
>
> My right hand (Proper Young Lady) held a leash attached to a collar. It was smooth and strong, with a pivot attachment and a heavy hand grip. My hand felt occupied and useful but limited.
>
> It's laughably simple to see the symbolism in this fantasy. Gud Dawg is utterly trusting, has great yet gentle strength, and is the epitome of innocence and charm. He is also lacking in judgment in the ways of the world and would quickly be hurt or killed without the limits I put on his freedom. I love him and in many ways he is a teacher for me, but I must look out for his in-the-world welfare, providing him with proper food, shelter, and fences in order to keep him safe. In return he shows me pure joy, forgiveness, generosity of spirit, and nobility of character.
>
> The leash is an instrument that limits the activities and distance Gud Dawg can move. While it is effective and life-preserving, any time I can, in my responsible judgment, leave it off him, I do. I let him run freely in the forest. I restrict him in the city. I could punish him by use of the leash and sometimes he reacts as if I had. It is important that I keep it clear in my mind what my motive is when I use it—if I am controlling for the sake of control, that's wrong and an insult to his character. If I use it to protect him from pain or confusion, then I am justified, whether he understands or not.

Next, you will work toward finding a single image of the old myth, a single image of the emerging myth, and you will create a fantasy or daydream that symbolizes an integration of the two. Meg wrote:

Image of the Old Myth: An Italian leather leash with a heavy braided hand grip.

Image of the Counter-myth: Gud Dawg romping on the beach, free and joyous.

Integration Fantasy: I am skipping and turning, running in broken circles on the beach. Gud Dawg is leaping and frolicking beside me. The wind is crisp but without chill, the waves are beautiful, not stormy. He takes the leash I'm carrying and tugs on it with his mouth, inciting me to pull back, to whip him around before he drags the leather out of my hand. I have a good grip and know he can't take it from me, but neither can I pull the other end out of his mouth. We are both enjoying the contest.

It occurs to me that if I can use the leash playfully and responsibly, it will become a valuable part of my life, saving me endless grief and difficulty. The innocent part of me needs the experienced part, and vice versa—I'm not so much at war as I was.

In reviewing Meg's development, we can appreciate her efforts to break loose from her earlier conditioning. This struggle has been private and individualistic for Meg, perhaps because she lacked sensitive understanding and support from other people as she grew up. But missing from Meg's mythology are images that help her to incorporate significant relationships with other people and with social institutions into her own process. One of the purposes of classical mythology is to keep people attuned to the Larger Story as they move through their personal developmental crises—which you see Meg reaching toward in an exemplary manner. But another purpose is to facilitate relationships with social institutions and other members of society. Up to now, Meg's journey has been decidedly solitary.

TOWARD A RESOLUTION OF YOUR MYTHIC CONFLICT

In the following personal rituals, you will be directing your efforts toward resolving the struggle between the old myth and the counter-myth. If you can work the conflict through in your inner life, you will be less compelled to play it out in your outer life. In addition, by applying the methods offered here, you will increase the chances of coming to a resolution that embodies the best qualities of both of these prevailing and emerging aspects of your personal mythology.

Personal Ritual: Charting the Effects of Your Conflicting Myths

In this ritual, you will create a chart of the thoughts, feelings, and behaviors that are consistent with the old myth and with the counter-myth. From this understanding of how the old myth and the counter-myth operate in your life, you will be more able to recognize when each is dominating in a given situation. You will continue to refer to this chart as you work toward resolving your mythic conflict.

1. Review your journal to crystallize your understanding of the prevailing myth and the counter-myth.
2. Draw a line down the center of a blank sheet of your journal so that there are two columns. Label these columns "Old Myth" and "Counter-myth."
3. (Optional). You may wish to take a journey to your Inner Shaman at this point in order to request that new light be shed upon your understanding of the old myth or the counter-myth. Use the method you were given in chapter 1 to begin your visit. Bring with you any questions about your old myth or counter-myth that you might wish your Shaman to consider.
4. Write a motto that characterizes the old myth toward the top of the first column and a motto that characterizes the emerging counter-myth in the other column. You may create your mottoes on the spot or adapt a phrase from a piece of literature, a song, a proverb, or your Fairy Tale. If the motto for one or the other does not come to you easily, remain alert for it as you proceed with the instructions that follow.
5. Reflect upon your actions, thoughts, and feelings during the past several hours. In the appropriate column, record which feelings, statements, or behaviors were guided primarily by one or the other of these myths. Next, reflect upon the past couple of days. Then consider patterns of thought, feeling, or behavior that characterize the past year or two.

Some people find it quite difficult to make these connections. If the connections between your experiences and your myths do not readily appear to you, don't press yourself after giving it a fair try. Instead, carry your journal with you for two or three days, making new entries as they occur to you, or reflecting each evening on your actions during that day.

Your chart will describe specific thoughts, feelings, and actions that are connected with long-standing as well as emerging patterns in your life. One woman sadly had to admit that the motto of her old myth could have been the Country and Western lyric, "If You Won't Leave Me, I'll Find Somebody Who Will." A middle-aged minister chose as his counter-myth motto, "We shall be called to account for all pleasures we failed to enjoy." The motto of Frank's old myth was "Be careful, try hard, look out." In its column he described his fears, his uncertainties, and his cautious approach to life. The motto of his counter-myth was "Follow the Scent," and in its column he described the feelings and actions he associated with passion. He closed with the following thought:

> Every situation in my life is an opportunity to feel and express more passion than I might have. I've become more aware of when I'm holding back or distracting myself with nonessential, spirit-deadening pursuits. Even if I still hold back, just being aware of it changes the experience. And when I do smell excitement, I will allow myself to follow that scent.

Personal Ritual: Bringing Your Conflicting Myths into Dialogue

This ritual involves an enactment in which you will create a dialogue similar to Meg's for examining the two sides of your mythic conflict. Characters personifying old myths or counter-myths can be thought of as *subpersonalities.*[6] A subpersonality is an aspect of the self that is governed by a particular personal myth. Choose a name for the subpersonality that is associated with the prevailing myth and a name for the subpersonality associated with the counter-myth, as Meg did with "Proper Young Lady" and "Born-Again Child." Todd, a forty-four-year-old community college instructor, named his old myth "Altar Boy" and his counter-myth "Pioneer." A twenty-eight-year-old computer engineer used the names "Robot-Woman" and "Flash Dancer." Allow yourself to participate fully in this exercise, using appropriate gestures, and wholeheartedly dramatizing the dialogue.

This will engage not only your intellect but also your intuition and your feelings about these competing myths. It also will attune you to relevant "body memories" and other physical aspects of the prevailing and emerging mythic themes. Draw upon your sense of humor in emphasizing and appreciating the differences between the characters.

If you are not working with a partner, use a tape recorder both for leading you through the instructions, and also as a sort of witness. New insights about the relationship between the opposing myths often emerge from reviewing the exchange. You will need a blank tape, as well as a tape on which you have recorded the instructions. The instructions will indicate when to use the blank tape.

Find a physical posture that portrays your old myth. What facial appearance is most fitting? Should you smile, grimace, scowl, laugh, frown, stare, twitch? What kind of gestures would be most appropriate for this character? Will you point? Put your hands in your pocket? Hug yourself? Shake nervously? Dance? Applaud? Jump? Pray? Crawl? [60-second pause]

Once having found this first posture, step out of that spot, face the "person," and assume a posture that represents your counter-myth. You might start by finding the posture and gestures that are the opposite *of your old myth. Give yourself enough time to work your way into this role. Try out a few different postures so you may feel your way into the one best suited for this subpersonality. Note what is happening to your muscles and your sense of balance. Once you have found the postures and facial expressions that best represent each character, go back and forth a few times between them, and have each one begin to look at and size up the other. Either figure may evolve beyond its initial identity. This can be a valuable development—just keep the character consistent with the myth it represents. [2-minute pause]*

Begin the dialogue. One of the parts of you speaks to the other. Alternate. In each role, assume the characteristic posture and say the words that express your feelings and thoughts while looking at and reacting to the other character. You are conscious of using a fitting tone of voice. As is appropriate for your character, your speech may be smooth or raspy, loud or soft, high or low, rapid or slow, guttural or nasal, fluid or stuttering.

After one of the characters offers some initial comments, move over to the other character's spot, assume the appropriate posture, and answer. Again find a fitting voice quality. Continue to move physically between the two characters as you let the dialogue develop.

As these characters encounter each other, allow the words to flow out. Keep the dialogue going without long pauses or planning. Be spontaneous. Simply move into one of the positions and assume the appropriate posture as that character is speaking, and move out of that position and into a facing position whenever the second character responds. Keep your facial expressions, posture, gestures, and tones appropriate to the character you are portraying.

In the early part of the dialogue, the emphasis is to be on the conflict and to establish the differences between the two sides. As you continue the discussion, however, bring the focus toward establishing improved communication between the characters. A good way to start, or to proceed from any point where the dialogue gets bogged down, is to have one side ask the other, "What do you want from me?" [If you are taping these instructions, add: "Now stop this tape, replace it with a blank tape, set the machine to 'record,' and proceed with the dialogue."]

After completing the dialogue, re-create or summarize it in your journal. As you reflect in your journal, consider how the old myth and the counter-myth were expressed. Were some feelings or ideas disclosed that you did not know you held? Because it engages you at bodily as well as verbal levels, this exercise often reveals aspects of the conflict that were previously outside of awareness. Besides having a special name for each character, you also may want to draw simple figures that portray these subpersonalities and can remind you of the qualities each represents in your inner life.

Frank used the names "Earnest" and "Jolly Green Giant." Here is an excerpt from his dialogue:

Earnest: If you're not careful, you're going to get both of us hurt.

Jolly Green Giant: You little wimp! If I was as careful as you, we'd never get out of bed! You work so hard on the dumbest things so that you don't ever have to risk that there'd be a moment you might have to enjoy. It would make you feel too guilty!

Earnest: You are going to get us in a lot of trouble. Consider the industrious ant who builds a giant hill despite his tiny size.

Jolly Green Giant: That's terrific if building anthills is your mission in life. Besides, if we go at your pace, rigor mortis will set in by April.

Earnest: Well, what do you want me to do?

Jolly Green Giant: You might try smilin' sometimes. Or laughin'. Or playin'. Maybe just start with breathing fully, you constricted little worm!

Earnest (haughtily)*:* Fiddlesticks! All that nonsense is hardly necessary for a *mature* person.

Jolly Green Giant: That's the funniest thing I've ever heard! Your image of "maturity" is of a dried-up, convoluted, scared old bullfrog. The reason for life is to *live!* And with *zest* and *vigor* and *joy.*

Earnest: I'd be embarrassed to be as audacious and brazen and vain as you, exuding all over the place.

Jolly Green Giant: Embarrassed, eh? I think you have exposed the chains that are binding you to your dreary, colorless existence.

Earnest: Well, it's not just embarrassment. What people think matters for many reasons. It even holds consequences for my profession.

Jolly Green Giant: It's your profession you're worrying about? Let me tell you somethin' about what your profession's doin' for you. It's not only making you dead while you're still alive; it's gonna have you dead before the retirement years for which you think you're living.

Earnest (befuddled)*:* So you're trying to tell me that if I stop worrying about being embarrassed, I'm going to live longer?

Jolly Green Giant: Why, Earnest, I believe I finally have your attention.

Earnest: Well, I'm not sure I believe you, but I must admit I've been feeling less than sensational lately. Maybe there is something to what you're saying.

Jolly Green Giant: Less than sensational, eh? You do flatter yourself with understatement. Listen, pal, you come along with me on my path. You're gonna like walking the first mile so well that you're never gonna wanna go back to your old ways.

Earnest: Did you say come with you on your path? You, sir, are out of your mind! You are of the vulgar and unrefined sort whose sensibilities are barbaric. You'd zip me along into your uncouth ways so fast and blatantly that I'd be humiliated in a thousand ways. Besides, I'd be so terrified that I wouldn't enjoy a thing. Forget it!

As is evident, Earnest and the Giant still have some distance to cover before a constructive resolution is likely to occur. The remaining rituals in this chapter are designed to further such synthesis. We suggest that, as you proceed through the chapter, you have your characters engage in additional dialogue. You may find that after each of the rituals, their ability to communicate has been somewhat enhanced. Use the physical posturings as you extend the dialogue during at least two 10-minute sessions over the next few days. Record the highlights in your journal.

Dream Focus: Identifying Obstacles to Resolution

In the same way that you have focused on specific dream themes in previous chapters, scan your journal or incubate a dream that gives you insight into the roadblocks that lie on the path toward resolution. Such a dream would serve to help you identify obstacles that prevent an integration between the old myth and the counter-myth. To request such a dream, reflect on where the two characters in your dialogue continued to disagree and, before going to sleep, picture them walking down separate paths that are destined to meet at a common point. Imagine the roadblocks each encounters on this path toward resolution. Before falling asleep, and while keeping in touch with this fantasy, ask several times for a dream that reveals the obstacles that are keeping you from reaching greater resolution between these opposing aspects of your inner life.

Personal Ritual: Transforming Obstacles into Opportunities

The procedures that medieval alchemists used for attempting to transform base metals into gold have been studied in the past century by such thinkers as Carl Jung and Mircea Eliade. These methods have been recognized as the outer expression of a profoundly sophisticated transformative spiritual discipline. According to Ralph Metzner, "chemical experimentation was like tantric yoga ritual: slow, deliberate, with a maximum of empathic awareness and sensitivity to the changes in matter. . . . The science of consciousness transformation was practiced simultaneously and synchronistically with the science of metallic or chemical transmutation."[7]

Part of the challenge in this third stage of working with your own personal mythology involves transforming the base qualities of the old myth into the gold of new energy and resources. In this ritual, you will identify an obstacle to the resolution of your mythic conflict and attempt to transform it into a condition that promotes your development.

Most of us have certain personal qualities that we feel are liabilities—perhaps an oversensitivity to criticism, a fear of authority, or a tendency to intellectualize. Such qualities are usually supported, at least in part, by old mythic structures. If you have been shy all of your life, your mythology may justify or rationalize solitude. Often, such qualities, rooted in the old myth, interfere with the expression of the emerging myth. If your counter-myth requires that you become more socially involved, you may have to conclude that your shyness is holding you back. Frank identified his drivenness as a quality that was interfering with a more dynamic relationship with his passion.

Often the elements that people like least about themselves, or repress completely, contain qualities that must be recognized and embraced for mature personality development. Discussing the Jungian concept of the shadow, Erich Neumann observed: "At first, the figure of the shadow is experienced externally as an alien and an enemy, but in the course of its progressive realization in consciousness it is . . . recognized as a component of one's own personality."[8] The shadow is "the paradoxical secret of transformation itself, since it is in fact in and through the shadow that the lead is transformed into its gold."[9] A disowned element of an individual's psychological makeup may push for expression, fiercely disrupting all equilibrium.

But the shadow can also be incorporated into the person's mythology in a way that results in an expanded self-identity, as we see in the following case:

> Mary Beth was forty-six when her husband died, suddenly and tragically. Their youngest child had left home a year earlier, and they were looking forward to peaceful years of retirement. Mary Beth had been an exemplary mother and homemaker, but she had never developed skills that could earn an income. She had enough savings and insurance benefits to carry her for about a year. After that, she would have to figure out how to support herself. About six months after her husband died, just as she was starting to panic about her financial predicament, she had the first of a series of dreams.
>
> She dreamed she was at home sleeping in bed. It wasn't her actual home, yet she felt she was at home. She dreamed she was awakened by the sound of pounding. She was petrified. Suddenly, a masked man jumped through the window. He was a burglar with a burglar's sack. When he saw her in bed, he approached her ominously. She woke up screaming as he began to mercilessly rape her.
>
> Mary Beth had difficulty sleeping after this dream. Her sleeplessness led her into psychotherapy. About that time, she also came to a decision about how she would support herself. She enrolled in an intensive 10-week course that taught basic secretarial skills. She did well in the course and easily found a job in a small law firm. To her great relief, she was not fired during her probationary period. In fact, she had a sense that she was well liked. And she loved cashing her paycheck.
>
> About then, Mary Beth had a second dream. She was again in the same bed in the same room, sleeping. This time, she was awakened by a knocking on the door. She timidly opened the door, and the same masked man pushed his way in. This time, however, she did not sense that he meant to harm her. He did not. He seduced her. She woke up with a sense of excitement.
>
> About four months later, she had her final dream in this series. She had been flourishing in her work. Not only were her basic secretarial skills more than adequate, she found that underneath her shy, self-effacing public self was a witty, good-natured woman who was able to understand others extremely well, and to convey both empathy and good advice. To her amazement, she was made office manager. In that position, she started to enjoy a kind of power that she had never even conceived of, and she was gaining increasing respect from the staff. In the third dream, she was in the

same bed and the same room. But this time she had left the door ajar for her lover. In he comes . . . the same masked man, now with flowers and charm. She embraces him. As they begin to make passionate love, she looks at his mask, grabs it, and peels it off. There she sees her own face looking back at her.

The last dream is a vivid illustration of what we mean by an "integration dream" (see the next dream focus instruction). The dream series shows how undeveloped qualities may demand expression, particularly when circumstances beckon to them. Until these latent potentials are acknowledged, they are more likely to be detrimental. This is especially evident with powerful emotions like anger and resentment, but we see here with Mary Beth that even characteristics that might seem quite positive may, unacknowledged, play havoc in your inner life. Her identity was so removed from the competencies and independence that her society associated with the male role (Jung referred to this constellation of qualities as the "animus") that radical adjustments had to occur if she were going to mobilize herself to become a breadwinner.

In this ritual, you will identify a quality in yourself that you believe interferes with the resolution of your mythic conflict, and you will call upon your Inner Shaman to help you transform that obstacle into an asset.

Select a personal quality that you feel may be keeping you trapped in your conflict. Perhaps your impulsiveness prevents you from creating a more stable life-style, your compulsiveness prevents you from enjoying the stable life-style you have established, your fearfulness interferes with your ability to take risks that are required for professional success, or your insecurity causes you to push away relationships by clinging to them. Meg went through the ritual twice, once focusing on the self-righteousness of the Proper Young Lady and a second time on the defiance of the Born-Again Child. Frank, as you will see, worked with his compulsion to achieve. Choose a quality you wish to transform.

In the following instructions, you will be doing a ritual dance with your Inner Shaman to transform this quality into a resource. You may physically do the dance, which we recommend, or simply do it as a fantasy. You will need a single sunflower seed, almond, or similar food. Leave the seed where you can reach it easily. During the part of the ritual where you are doing the dance, you also may wish to have tribal music with drumming playing in the background. A fast, steady beat is best.

Standing where you have some room to move, take a few deep breaths, plant your feet on the ground, and prepare to invite your Shaman to visit you in the Outer World. Recall what your Shaman looks like. [Pause] Now, watch as, standing before you, your Shaman starts to materialize. [Pause] You will be able to sense your Shaman's presence, and in your mind's eye you may even be able to see shades of your Shaman standing before you.

As you look at your Shaman, sense how you feel about offering up the quality you wish to transform. [Pause] An imaginary bundle appears before you, and you begin to hold it with both your hands. You know that the quality you wish to change is inside the bundle. Examine the bundle. What color is it? Is it heavy? Does it have an odor? Are there sounds coming from within it? [Pause] Present the bundle to your Shaman. Explain the quality. Maintain your self-respect by describing the quality with dignity and compassion for yourself. Establish what it is about the quality that is not working for you. [60-second pause] Now consider the ways in which you hope to transform the quality. Stubbornness may become a balanced determination. A quick temper may provide the zest for passionate involvement. Laziness may be the safeguard against frenzied overinvolvement. Find in the quality you wish to transform the kernels of a quality you would like to acquire. Once you have described the change you are requesting, listen for your Shaman's response. [60-second pause]

Your Shaman faces you and places his or her hands on the bundle. The bundle is between you, and both of you are holding it. Now your Shaman starts to move. You realize that you are to move in synch as you both hold the bundle. Begin to move, keeping a harmony with your Shaman. [Pause] The movement begins to gain speed. [Pause] The rhythms change. [Pause] Soon it is a free form of dance with the bundle held between you. Your Shaman begins to chant: "Let the change begin!" You chant along. [Pause] Now you notice that the bundle is surrounded by a luminescent color, a bright light that almost obscures it. You begin to feel that a change is indeed occurring. You continue to chant. The movement becomes centered on the luminescent bundle you are both holding. You begin moving it high and low, to and fro. [Pause] It becomes brighter with each additional motion. The dance continues and works up to a frenzy. You are chanting as fast as you can now: "Let the change begin!" [60-second pause]

Finally, you stop and look your Shaman in the eye. Both of you still have your hands on the bundle, which continues to glow. Your Shaman tells you that the quality in the bundle is being transformed, just as you requested. You are told to place the bundle onto the spot where you have stored your seed. As you do so, the bundle suddenly disappears, and your Shaman tells you that all the energy of its bright light has gone into the seed. As you look at the seed, you begin to sense more deeply just what this new quality is and how you would feel if it were fully developed within you. The Shaman tells you to pick up the seed and slowly chew and swallow it. Put the seed into your mouth and slowly begin to chew. With each bite and each swallow, you feel yourself ingesting the new quality that has been transformed from the old. You recall the color from before, and you begin to feel the energy of that color filling your body with each motion of your mouth. You know that the quality you had asked for is contained in the energy of this seed and that you are now taking it into yourself.

As you finish this sacred morsel, you savor the taste and you savor the knowledge that a seed has just been planted for an important change in your life. [Pause] You realize that from this moment on, whenever the old quality might get in your way, you can have access to the feeling you received from the seed. By evoking this feeling, you will begin to take actions that are in concert with the transformed quality, and as you do, that quality will gain strength within you.

This ritual marks a turn in your path. While the changes may not be immediate or radical, the shift in direction at this point will make an increasing difference as you go further down the road. Say good-bye to your Shaman, and watch as he or she fades back into the Other World.

Frank wanted to identify what was making it so difficult for him to do something as simple as being more relaxed and peaceful. "Surely it couldn't be my persistence and willingness to try hard? I've always thought those were virtues." The problem, he realized, was that he applied his diligence to areas of his life that gave him external rewards and the satisfaction of achievement, but not much happiness. It was his compulsion to achieve that was keeping his life out of balance. This was what he offered to his Inner Shaman.

> I told the Shaman that I want to transform my compulsion to achieve into confidence that I don't have to worry about achievement. I explained that I already get things done so habitually and effectively that my internal push to do more and better, which costs me my tranquility, is really just so much overkill. I have reason to feel confident that my world isn't going to fall down around me if

I were to take a nap, but I am driven mercilessly from within. I speculated that if this burden were lifted, I could relax into my true nature. The Shaman replied: "You have chosen well. A former compulsion in a given realm of life can indeed be transformed into confidence within that realm. Making that transformation will truly free you."

I thought all the gestures and dancing were a bit silly, but I did get up and do them. At first I felt like I was just going through the motions, but it suddenly hit me that I could sense a blue energy around the "bundle." With that, I really got into it. We were dancing all over the room chanting, "Let the change begin!" When we finally stopped, I felt an immediate sense of peace, and by God, I believed the quality in that bundle had gone through some real transformative process. When the Shaman condensed the energy into a seed, I believed that the seed had real power. I hadn't bothered to get a seed or nut, and I regretted that I didn't have one at that moment because the ritual was feeling so real to me. Still, when I ate the seed in my imagination, I could sense an energy of confidence coming into me.

At any point when you notice the old quality getting in your way, you may, in your imagination, again take the seed into your mouth, and as you ingest it, feel the energy of the transformed quality infused into your being. Because Meg had selected two qualities that she wished to transform, she performed the ritual twice. Consider for a moment if you, too, wish to repeat this ritual, concentrating on another characteristic. The transformation of such obstacles is a step toward the integration of your old myth and your counter-myth. The remaining three rituals in this chapter, and the dream focus instructions, are oriented toward furthering that resolution.

Personal Ritual: A Resolution Fantasy

Having earlier represented the mythic conflict in your body, you will now create a fantasy—a symbolic journey—whose purpose is to further the integration between the old myth and the counter-myth. You will seek a unifying symbol that assists in resolving their discord. Many depth psychologists see such symbols as powerful allies. Liliane Frey-Rohn noted: "Inasmuch as *the conscious experience of life* demanded an always new balance of opposites, a constantly renewed bridging of the powers of drive and spirit, the unifying symbol really had a creative function in guiding the individual to a deeper psychological truth."[10] To begin, find a comfortable position and start to relax.

Close your eyes and take a few deep breaths as you settle into this position. Feel yourself relaxing more completely with your next five breaths: ONE, TWO, THREE, FOUR, FIVE. Recall the feelings you were having as you explored the different sensations in your hands. Starting with the hand that represented the old myth, bring back the experience of these sensations. [Pause] Now, re-create the sensations in your other hand.

Tune into the energy and sensations of the hand that represents the old myth. [Pause] An inner image of this hand develops—perhaps it is only vague and shadowy or perhaps it is rich with color and distinct shapes. As you watch this image, you have an increasingly certain sense of a symbol that represents your old myth. [30-second pause] Once this symbol has become clear to you, tune into the energy and sensations of the hand that represents the counter-myth. [Pause] An inner image of this hand develops. This image becomes a symbol that represents your counter-myth. [30-second pause]

Now you have identified the two symbols and can imagine a setting. The light, colors, textures, and forms become vividly clear. [Pause] Next, place the two symbols into the setting. [Pause] The two symbols are about to become animated. They are going to be the characters in a fantasy. This fantasy will have a beginning, a middle, and an end. The fantasy will bring the symbols closer to each other. Their relationship and their understanding of each other will have improved. The fantasy will lead to an integration, a blending of the two sides.

Begin your fantasy now. Watch as the two symbols begin to interact. Allow their interactions to unfold into a story or dialogue that dramatizes a settling of their differences. [60-second pause] When you have completed your fantasy, count yourself back from five to one, take a deep breath, and open your eyes.

Immediately record the fantasy in your journal. Do not at this point analyze or judge it. Then, again assuming a relaxed position, move directly into the following instructions:

Take a few moments to relax again, breathing deeply. [Pause] You will be taking your fantasy a step further now. Begin by replaying it in your imagination, once more experiencing the symbols and the setting, and going through the sequence of events. This time, however, stop the action at points where your fantasy starts to resolve your conflict, where the old and the emerging are the most integrated, where there is the greatest synthesis between them.

Make a "still photograph" in your mind or a short "film clip" of such scenes. Do not be concerned if your fantasy tries to take a slightly different direction during this rerun; simply follow its lead. Begin now to reexperience your fantasy, this time stopping where there is the most integration or resolution. [60-second pause] When you have reached the end of your fantasy, extend it. Add a final scene that carries it further and in the direction of even greater resolution or integration. [30-second pause] When you are ready, count yourself back from five to one, take a deep breath, and open your eyes.

Once you have completed this experience, draw or describe the scenes you mentally photographed in your journal, and record your associations to them. From Frank's journal:

> This time, as if to show how confused I am about which myth is stronger, my right arm became the old myth. I see it as a massive, cold stone wall. My left arm is also a wall. But this wall seems ethereal and is very fragile. Next, I see a knight on a horse. The knight has incredible muscles, kind of like the strong man in a circus. I see him reaching across so he is touching both walls, and he is going to pull them together. I see him struggling to pull them closer together, but something is stopping him. It seems he is realizing that the fragile wall will just crumble when it meets the stone wall, and that is not what he wants. So he builds a latticework structure into it so that even if it does crumble, it will still retain its character. And then, through some magic spell, he brings heat to the other wall, and it begins to soften. It becomes transformed from cold blocks of stone into mounds of some warm, inviting, doughlike substance. Then, as he pulls the two sides together, the fragile wall does indeed crumble, but that's okay because the latticework and the ethereal quality remain. When the two walls have merged, the lattice framework brings a magnificent sculpted form to the dough, which remains warm and soft. It was like I was being shown that for my two myths to come together, I have to soften the structure of the old myth and give more structure to the new myth.
>
> When I took the fantasy further, the new wall came to life and became animated. It actually became like a cartoon character of a mammoth elephant with the lattice becoming its skeletal structure

and the doughlike substance its massive flesh. It started to walk around and do little dance steps and sing and play. The creature was very funny as it hobbled around, but then it caught my eye and knowingly winked at me, and it suddenly struck me that this colossal, playful creature was somehow very wise.

Dream Focus: An Integration Dream

If you felt that your resolution fantasy did not go far enough, did not adequately point the way toward resolving the conflict, or if you simply want to request further inner instruction about resolving your conflict, you may find it valuable to scan your journal for a dream that pointed toward resolution or to ask for an integration dream. To incubate such a dream, bring to mind the points in your fantasy of greatest integration between the two myths. If there were none, reflect again on the conflict and ask for a dream that provides further guidance about finding a resolution to it. Immediately upon waking, record any dreams or insights you may recall. Explore the dream using the technique you used with your resolution fantasy, where you recreated the fantasy to explore it. Redream your dream in your imagination and find the points of maximum integration.

Personal Ritual: A Body Metaphor of Resolution

This chapter closes with a ritual for further deepening the integration you have already attained between the old myth and the counter-myth. Just as you've seen how your body may be a battlefield for the conflicts in your personal mythology, it may also be a temple for the resolution of those conflicts. It is possible to use bodily imagery to help resolve the discord. You have already been identifying your old myth with one hand and your counter-myth with the other hand as a way of symbolizing the conflict. In the following ritual, you will also begin by representing your mythic conflict with your hands, but this time you will wind up with a feeling in your body that serves as a sensation-based symbol of resolution.

Begin by reviewing the entries in your journal that describe the resolution symbols, fantasies, or dreams emerging from the last several sets of instructions. Next, find a comfortable position and begin to relax.

Close your eyes and take a few deep breaths as you settle into this position. Feel yourself relaxing more completely with your next five breaths: ONE, TWO, THREE, FOUR, FIVE. Sense one more time which hand you associate more with the old myth and which hand you associate with the counter-myth. [Pause] Are these myths still represented on the same sides as they were earlier? Focus now on the hand that represents the old myth. Notice the sensations in this side of your body. [Pause] Now focus on the other side of your body and notice the sensations. [Pause] Is one side warmer than the other? Lighter? Heavier? Darker? [Pause] Notice where the two sides meet. Is that line jagged or straight? Do the energies of the two myths repel each other along this boundary line? Do the energies blend? Is one side reaching or pushing over into the other side?

Mentally communicate with both sides, telling them that just as they are each part of the same body, it is in the best interest of your total being that they learn to live together in harmony, or even to integrate with each other.

Again place your hands so your palms face each other, about two feet apart, and let your elbows bend so you can relax your arms in a comfortable position. First explore the hand that represents the old myth. [Pause] Now focus on the hand that represents the counter-myth. [Pause] Can you feel any sensations in the space between your hands? Just as opposites attract, sense that there is an energy pulling your hands together. This energy increases with every breath. [20-second pause] Slowly, allow your hands to be drawn together. Know that the instant they touch, you will feel a merging of the energies between the two sides and a single, unified feeling will encompass your hands and permeate your body. [30-second pause]

As the energies of your hands and the two sides of your body blend and integrate with one another, feelings of harmony fill you. [Pause] Sense the spirit of the old myth and the counter-myth mingling, synthesizing, integrating, becoming a single energy that retains the most vital qualities of both. Merge the old myth and the counter-myth with every breath.

As the mingling of the two myths permeates your body, you have stronger and stronger feelings of resolution and of a new direction. Reflect on any thoughts or images that come to you in the next few moments which might represent a new direction for you as the integration between the old myth and the counter-myth deepens. [30-second pause]

Find an image, phrase, or thought that for you represents this integration. It becomes vivid and memorable. [20-second pause] You may affirm this feeling of integration any time you wish by taking three deep breaths, bringing your hands together, and squeezing them as you recall this image, phrase, or thought. Do this now. Lower your hands. Take three deep breaths as you recall your image, phrase, or thought. [30-second pause] Bring your hands together and squeeze them. [Pause] Sense the charge of integration and wholeness shoot through your body. You may repeat this sequence any time you wish.

Now, as you count yourself back from five to one, the feelings of resolution completely permeate your body and your spirit. FIVE, coming back now. FOUR. THREE. TWO. And ONE. Eyes open, relaxed, and refreshed.

Describe this experience in your journal. In what ways did you feel an integration between the two sides? Of what obstacles were you aware? What new directions seemed to emerge for you? What was your image, phrase, or thought? Be sure to describe the steps you can take (three breaths, bring hands together, and squeeze while recalling the image, phrase, or thought) any time you need to deepen the integration between your conflicting myths. This procedure can serve you much like the action of a positive posthypnotic suggestion. When Frank's hands met,

> the ethereal wall started to move in ripples and kind of undulate against the hard wall, almost as if it were massaging it. It was quite enticing in its slithery, snakelike, almost sexual dance. Its ardor and playfulness were trying to have some effect on the brittle wall, and my sense was that they were going to.

Continuing the Dialogue

At this point, Frank returned to the dialogue between the characters representing the two sides of his mythic conflict. The personal rituals from this chapter opened a few doors of communication for them, and we invite you at this point to extend your dialogue as well.

> ***Jolly Green Giant*** (responding to Earnest's last outburst after the invitation that he try Giant's path)*:* Calm down, little man. I

can understand that you're scared. Maybe we can find a pace that will keep me feelin' like we're still alive without scarin' you to death.

Earnest: Well, you talk like I wouldn't have anything to offer even if I wanted to do something with you.

Jolly Green Giant: One thing you certainly know how to do is to apply yourself, although you generally have the imagination of a goldfish in the choices you make for those precious efforts. I propose that you apply yourself to some of the things I might get a kick out of too.

Earnest: Such as?

Jolly Green Giant: I thought we might try downhill skiing this month and white-water rafting in the summer.

Earnest: That does it! You go your way and I'll go mine. I find your proposed endeavors totally terrifying, and I find you, sir, to be an insensitive, reckless boor.

Jolly Green Giant: Your oversensitivity certainly balances any insensitivity in me, but I guess I can understand your fears. What if we start with your takin' some time off to go cross-country skiing? You enjoy that, much as you hate to admit it.

Earnest: But before we can go off on this wildly irresponsible odyssey of passion and flight, we must be sure that someone is minding the store.

Jolly Green Giant: I don't mind bein' sure the store is minded, but if we must be certain that no speck of dust that lands may light in its resting place for more than seventeen seconds, such as is your custom, we shall have precious little time for anything else.

Earnest: But if I do not attend to the store in the exquisite manner to which I, along with anyone with any class, am accustomed, two complications may be foreseen. First, all our excess and idle time might soon become dreadfully boring unless your program is quite magnificent. Second, I would surely lose the opportunity of being this year's recipient of the National Broom Society's Best Kept Shop Award. If I am to forgo that honor, then this trip had better, pardon the expression, be damned good.

Jolly Green Giant: Trust me, Earnest. Take a deep breath, lean back, and enjoy the ride.

Earnest: I think this is rather insane, but I shall retain an open mind about your idiotic scheme.

If you have not yet had the two characters from your dialogue meet for a second or third encounter, do so now, creating another "face-to-face" dramatization, and summarizing the dialogue in your journal.

On to Stage Four

It is entirely possible that rather than leading to resolution, your imagery and dialogues showed that the two myths are not yet ripe for integration. Some people find this very frustrating and want to push toward a resolution for which they are not ready. Regardless of the obstacles you may be encountering, you will be able to adapt the remaining personal rituals to your own pace and readiness. Even if you were unable to attain any sense of resolution in the exercises to this point, the following chapter will show you ways to draw on the careful and penetrating work you have been doing in order to create a closing to your Fairy Tale that points toward constructive new directions in your life.

5

The Fourth Stage: From Vision to Commitment

Like a lure-casting fisherman, man seems to cast a fantasy far in front of him and then slowly reel himself into it.

—WILLIAM IRWIN THOMPSON[1]

The rituals presented in this chapter are designed to further the integration between your old myth and your counter-myth. As the resolution of their conflict becomes more complete, you will be able to articulate and examine a new direction, and you will be drawn toward committing yourself to it.

Where there is conflict in your personal mythology, several scenarios are possible. Consciously or unconsciously, you may: (1) identify primarily with the old myth, (2) identify primarily with the counter-myth, (3) become increasingly torn or confused, or (4) work out a compromise that sacrifices some desirable elements of each. Or, as the inner resolution becomes more complete, a new myth may emerge that incorporates the best qualities of both. Further directing your efforts toward this last prospect is the goal of this chapter.

While it is necessary to allow certain conflicts to take their course, there is truth in the ancient proverb, "If you don't change your direction, you may wind up where you are headed." Outmoded myths distract you from the "path with heart." The conflicts they cause are painful. But that pain also shows you where your mythology is ready for change. As Marcel Proust tartly observed, "Illness is the most heeded of doctors: to goodness and wisdom we only make promises; we obey pain." Formulating the most worthwhile mythic guidance within your reach, and committing yourself to it, is a way of heeding the call of goodness and wisdom before pain demands your attention.

In this fourth stage of the program, you will envision a new direction for your life, conceived of the creative tension between your old myth and counter-myth. The personal rituals will guide you toward a single mythic image which holds enough promise that you will be moved, in the final stage of the program, to commit yourself toward weaving it into your life.

Innovative possibilities may already be occurring to you. Experiences that bring you outside the normal realms of space and time can generate further insight. The rituals in this chapter are designed to lead you into such altered states of consciousness. They will bring you within listening range of the voice of your innermost wisdom as you take this next step in formulating a creative resolution of your mythic conflict.

MEG'S NEXT STEP

In the personal ritual that introduces this stage of the program, you will return to the dialogue between the characters representing your old myth and your counter-myth, but this time you will ask your Inner Shaman to mediate. Meg taped her dialogue and later transcribed it for us:

> ***Proper Young Lady*** (yelling to Born-Again Child who has just gotten away)***:*** Your obstinacy is going to keep you from becoming a mature and responsible adult!
>
> ***Born-Again Child:*** Seems to me that the people who you call "mature and responsible" are just bored, and they are certainly *boring.* They think that now that they are mature, everything is all settled, finished, with nothing new to learn. I am happy that I'm always growing and learning new things.
>
> ***Proper Young Lady:*** Well, I was taught all I need to know by my parents and my Sunday School teachers. But sometimes I do ask if I'm being the full person I was meant to be.
>
> ***Inner Shaman:*** Good question. I want to congratulate you on asking one of the seminal questions of all time.
>
> ***Born-Again Child:*** Hey, I can ask that same question! I'm the most curious of the lot.
>
> ***Proper Young Lady:*** I never thought I'd hear you admit to being anything but completely satisfied with your total self-indulgence.

Born-Again Child: I hate giving in to the stuffy likes of you, but the fact is I am somewhat attracted to pretty clothes and would like to learn how to earn a living. I would even like it, I think, if someone courted me.

Proper Young Lady: Fat chance.

Inner Shaman: Now, now . . . see what you can do to behave like loving sisters. Otherwise, you are each always going to feel incomplete.

Born-Again Child: Oh my! I don't want that.

Proper Young Lady: Me neither! Let me, since I'm the more mature, make the first concession. I would like you to teach me to build a sandcastle. Some I've seen are very pretty.

Born-Again Child: You'd get all sandy and feel like you'd lowered yourself . . .

Inner Shaman: You must give each other the benefit of the doubt. If you do that, you are much more likely to be believed yourself.

Born-Again Child (enthusiastically)*:* You're really willing to learn from me, Proper Young Lady? No kidding? Wow! I do much better when I'm treated like an equal rather than a defective piece of machinery.

Proper Young Lady (looking old and tired)*:* I need you because maybe you can help me to feel alive, robust, excited. Without you, I get caught up in competition, sickness in my spirit and my body. I bog down, feel heavy, on the brink of death. Can you teach me to play again?

Born-Again Child: I will teach you all about sandcastles *and* dams! How's that?

Proper Young Lady: And I will give you the pink dress with the lace collar I've seen you looking at enviously. I'll even throw in some satin hair ribbons. But you're sure you can teach me how to play?

Born-Again Child (taking her hand)*:* Hey, it's just like riding a bicycle. Come on, I've got a golden retriever puppy I want you to meet.

Inner Shaman: I'm pleased with both of you. I think it is time now to consider how you are going to work out living together.

From Vision to Commitment

Proper Young Lady: I think it makes sense for me to be in charge during the school and business day. Maybe when we're out in public, too. And I hope you, Born-Again Child, will be in charge of our free time when we can have sensations, be loud, ask questions, and be free of constraints.

Born-Again Child: You bet. Good plan. Could I wear your eyelet petticoat with the pink dress, too?

In the next ritual, you will find an object from nature and reflect upon it as you consider several questions related to your mythic conflict. Meg chose a geode (a stone that has a cavity lined with crystals), which she had treasured for a long time. From her journal reflections:

My power object is my geode. It has been cut in half and the cut surface has been polished. The outside is rough and looks unpromising. The cut surface has many shades of cream, gold, and honey in frozen rings. At the center is a literal heart of crystal. The crystal catches and refracts the light with its tiny prisms. The whole thing is wonderfully complex and beautiful.

I see that it took a major change—cutting the geode in half—to expose the magnificent center. I realize that the process must have been violent and intrusive to the raw stone. I see that the polishing has exposed remarkable intricacy and subtle beauty. I imagine that the crystal center is grateful to be exposed, after millennia, to the light.

I think the lesson for me is that I can trust that if I move deeper, beyond my mundane surface, I will expose the valuable and pleasing potentials hidden within me.

Based on the variety of resolution experiences that grew out of your work in the previous chapter, and your explorations in this chapter, you will next write Part Three of your Fairy Tale. This task calls upon you to symbolically formulate a mythic image to cast toward the future. Part Three of Meg's Fairy Tale reads:

After the porpoise delivered Juanita Margaret to shore, the first thing she saw was a broken Annie Green Springs wine bottle bouncing in the surf. The second thing to happen was that her caretaker, Prudent, was appalled at the condition of her clothes and hair. The third thing was that her schoolteacher, Rational, heaped contempt upon her wild story that she had ridden a porpoise to the depths of the sea.

Juanita Margaret decided that the first lesson she could practice was retreat to Nature, and this she did until her head and heart settled down and even ceased to ache. "Ah ha," she thought. "It works! When I am hassled, a retreat to a peaceful, timeless space is indeed healing. I will remember that."

Being as flexible as the kelp had never been easy for her. She was undoubtedly a stubborn, even rigid child, in that she usually could see only one way to accomplish anything. That lesson came one day when she, a devoted health-food nut, was offered a hot chocolate fudge sundae with whipped cream, three cherries, chopped pecans, and a little American flag on the summit. Her conflict was truly epic. "I want it! I want it! I want it!" cried her impulsive, reckless part, with visions of sweet shudders passing through her mouth and limbs. "Oh no, never ever under any circumstances!" proclaimed her righteous, rigid self, snapping her mouth closed, tight as an abalone on the reef. Fortunately, at that moment a vision of the flexible kelp came to Juanita Margaret. "I will stay rooted in my beliefs, but I do think I will eat this sundae. After all, it's only six weeks until my birthday!"

Being secret about her good works had never been Juanita Margaret's way. Keeping silent about her talents was not her strong suit. It is true that she often did genuinely good things for high motives. She had many skills and assets. But there is just no nice way to deny that she was a big mouth, often blowing her own horn in the town square. It wasn't so much that she was full of herself; it was more that she was actually rather empty inside, having been sent out to play so often. One day, while she was caroling her own virtues, she saw someone yawn. "Oh my," thought Juanita Margaret, "I am becoming the worst sort of a bore. Even I am bored. Boredom is a dreadful sign; it means I am sick of my own company. What to do?" She thought of the abalone with his boring exterior and palace of lights interior. She thought, "I believe I should pay attention. It seems to me that if I save some of my good stuff, my very best good stuff, and keep it inside, silently, it may serve me better. I will have to wait for someone to notice me to have the attention I love so much, but I can be occupied with adding lovely nacre designs to my interior canvas. I believe I will try this as a cure for boredom." It worked so well that no one ever yawned in her face again, and the people she invited in to see her mother-of-pearl and rainbow painting came to love her deeply.

Next, you will project your new myth five years into the future. Meg wrote:

> I'm sitting at my word processor, writing a book, smiling. No one is with me physically, but I am very conscious that loved ones are within reach. I take time out every day to go out of my house, into the woods, to be in the forest and by the creek. I have found the theme and the method to communicate my ideas about Nature and life effectively, and I feel useful and competent. I'm very aware of a growing edge of freshness and novelty and discovery in my life. But I'm not so subject to the storms and the emotional violence that once plagued me constantly. My relationships with people are deep and real and enduring. I'm contented with the direction of my growth and my changes, and I don't see any end to them.

In the next personal ritual, you will beckon the most highly spiritual feelings you can attain. After invoking that state, Meg summarized her new myth in a single, guiding sentence: "Serenity is gained through loving, thoughtful action." She described the essence of the myth as: "I am part of Creation. I, and all my relationships, are, just like Creation, continually evolving and growing more interconnected through the forces of Love." As Meg comes to identify herself with larger spheres than her isolated inner world, we sense that the self-centeredness that characterized her earlier mythology (partially the product of needing so early to be self-reliant, and partially a product of being an only child) is changing. Up to now, the collective "other" had seemed so oppressive to Meg that she could only come as far as allowing it to serve as an *object* of her love, with little room for the intermingling of the other's wants, needs, and myths with her own. Now, as she is beginning to integrate opposing elements of her inner being, she seems better able and more willing to engage in the give and take of interpersonal relationships as well. She also is beginning to appreciate that her need to be alone in nature provides a balance to social life rather than only an escape from it.

When, in the early part of the program, you constructed your Personal Shield, the last section, "A Renewed Vision," was left blank. Your final task in this fourth stage of the program will be to complete that section, drawing upon all your experiences since first constructing your Shield. Guided imagery instructions designed to help you find a renewed, more matured image of Paradise Regained will be offered.

For Meg, the abalone shell from her first Paradise Regained image returned as an element of her new image. But, rather than an isolated piece, it became part of a delicate, butterfly-shaped necklace made of silver and abalone shell, hanging from a fine chain. She drew this necklace on the final section of her Personal shield, and she reflected, "I can always quietly carry this totem of my great teacher."

CULTIVATING A RENEWED MYTHIC VISION

To this point, you have been tilling the symbolic soil of your inner life, finding the roots of existing mythic images, cultivating new imagery, and experimenting with novel combinations. Through the following personal rituals, you will attempt to reap a single guiding vision that points you in a new and more fulfilling direction—toward a meeting of your highest possibilities and the opportunities your world presents.

Personal Ritual: Extending Your Dialogue with Your Shaman's Support

The subpersonality representing your old myth will again meet with the subpersonality representing your counter-myth so they may further discuss their areas of disagreement. This time, however, you also will be calling upon your Inner Shaman to help you find creative solutions to the problems that are still of concern to each side. His or her aid may be of special value here, as it is particularly important at this point to reach the greatest amount of resolution possible.

In previous rituals, you have seen your Shaman's power as a healer, combining the strength of understanding, empathy, and love. You sensed his or her gentleness and wisdom. Your Shaman is also rugged and disciplined, fully recognizing that at times difficult decisions, compromises, and sacrifices *must* be made, strength *must* be developed, and in certain circumstances that strength *must* be creatively but forcefully applied. You can expect your Shaman to be a fair but tough moderator in this next dialogue. As in the previous dialogues, you may wish to have a blank tape available so you can record the encounter.

Begin by once more finding the stance, posture, and facial expressions of the figure who represents the old myth. [Pause] Then step back, face that character, and find the stance, posture, and facial expressions of the figure who represents the counter-myth. [Pause]

Now step out of that role and move into the position of your Inner Shaman, forming a triangle as you face the other two figures.

Create in yourself the sense of confidence and compassion your Shaman exudes. [Pause] You have time to find the stance, posture, and facial expressions that fit these feelings. [30-second pause] Make any further adjustments so that your stance accurately portrays your Inner Shaman. [Pause] Now, as the Shaman, ask the other two figures: "Where are you not in agreement?"

The figures representing your mythic conflict engage in a dialogue about this question and continue until they reach an agreement or an impasse. Whenever they reach an agreement, you will return to the position of the Shaman, comment on the resolution they reached, and ask: "Are there any other areas in which I may help you?"

When the two figures come to an impasse, return to the position of the Inner Shaman, consider the desires of each and the needs of each, and address one or both of them. Then allow them to engage each other in further dialogue, until they reach some level of agreement or need further shamanic intervention.

Continue by moving into all three of the positions as needed, until the most important issues have been addressed and the highest degree of resolution possible for the three of you, combining your resources, has been achieved. [If you are taping these instructions, add: "Now stop this tape, replace it with a blank tape, and record the dialogue. When you have taken the dialogue as far as you are able, reinsert this tape and continue with its instructions."]

Much has been accomplished in understanding and resolution. Return to the position of the Inner Shaman. You are rich with compassion and wisdom and are pleased to share with both figures, answering their questions, sensing their concerns. When you are finished, invite each figure to contact you, through imagination or through another enactment like this one, whenever he or she needs your help.

Re-create or summarize this discussion in your journal. At the end of Frank's last dialogue, the two figures had reached a tense agreement about taking time off to go cross-country skiing. This segment of the dialogue begins with Earnest having second thoughts:

Inner Shaman: With what disagreements may I help you?

Earnest (to Jolly Green Giant)***:*** I've been reconsidering the prudence of our pact. I believe you want me to all but drop out of my work and all my responsibilities. I do not believe you have seen to all the details to ensure that *everything* will be kept in Proper Condition.

Jolly Green Giant: If we wait until your good time to start enjoyin' ourselves, we'll still be in the office at midnight on New Year's Eve in the year 2020! I'm *tired* of waitin' for you, and if you won't make some major changes right now, I'm goin' to quit cooperatin' with you at all. You need me in ways you don't know about. If I weren't taggin' along in the dreary life you have carved out for us, you'd have dried up and died years ago.

Earnest: You always want to move so fast! How about if we take off to play one time this year to see if we like it? An experiment. If we like it, maybe we'll do it again next year.

Jolly Green Giant: One time this year—perhaps again next year! My, you are gutsy! I don't think this discussion is goin' anywhere except to bog us down in your characteristically obsessional and boring ways. I appeal to our wise old friend here to get us out of this endless rut you keep draggin' us into.

Inner Shaman: I have comforting news for you, Earnest. You truly can afford to relax. You have my assurance that you are not going to be so powerfully swept away that you cannot return to the ways with which you are so familiar and comfortable. Should you stumble, you need only stand up. You can take many more risks than you have ever imagined would be within the limits of conscientiousness.

And, Giant, you must be much more appreciative of the steps Earnest does take. Rather than continually pointing out to him how much farther he has to go, you can relax too, and immerse yourself in the small new freedoms that are offered by the changes he has sincerely begun to make. He will blossom only if you reward him for what he does correctly rather than to continually criticize and ridicule him for not doing enough. I ask each of you to alter your attitudes in these ways, and you will reap the gifts you have for each other more fully. You will each find the other to be less of an enemy and more of a friend.

Earnest: Okay, Giant, I will trust you to lead me to take *small* steps. That much of an invitation, I offer. But if you *dare* to force me to go too fast, or say another *word* about downhill skiing or white-water rafting unless *I* bring up these horrific subjects, it will be seven years and seven days before I will even discuss so much as a vacation with you again.

Jolly Green Giant: Okay, Earnest, that is fair. And I do appreciate the efforts you are makin' to increase the enjoyment each of us has in his life, however cautious they may be.

Inner Shaman: Watch that sarcasm, Giant.

Jolly Green Giant: Okay, okay. I know that each step you take into my territory is frightening for you, and I will acknowledge your efforts, and yes, even your courage for takin' them.

Inner Shaman: That's better.

Jolly Green Giant: Well, I guess that's about as much fun as we can hope to have for today. Let's shake on it.

Earnest (extending his hand, playfully)*:* Aren't you getting to be the gentleman!

Inner Shaman: This is a good beginning. I must warn you not to expect too much from each other. Each of you will make mistakes in learning the ways of your until-now distant counterpart. I encourage you to treat what you have agreed upon as an experiment, to approach it with goodwill, and when you have difficulties, to return to me and to continue our deliberations.

You can see that, with his Shaman's help, Frank's competing subpersonalities each began to recognize the strengths of the other's position and to find within itself more room to experiment with ways that had seemed foreign. Use your Inner Shaman to teach the figures representing your conflict to cooperate in a way that makes the resources of each more available to you.

Personal Ritual: Your Power Object

The natural environment is rich in metaphors that can instruct you on attaining greater rapport with your inner nature. In this ritual, you will use a natural object as an ally to teach you about harmonies and balance as you envision your new personal myth. Go outdoors and find a Power Object—a stone, a flower, a milkweed pod, a piece of wood, a leaf—that draws you to itself, or select something you already possess. One man found a stone near his driveway that was smooth on one side and rough on the other side. Meg chose her geode. People often select something that grows. After you have selected your Power Object, find a quiet space where you will not be interrupted. Become comfortable and begin to relax.

Sink into the stillness and concentrate on your Power Object. It will answer questions for you about your life and about your personal mythology. This object from nature is a teacher, a guide, a gentle witness about life. Look closely at your Power Object and get to know it: touch it, feel it, smell it, taste it if you like. Get to know it well, receiving information about it from all your senses. [60-second pause]

Ask, "What do you have to teach me about myself?" Allow the answer to bubble up in your mind while you are touching or gazing at it. Perhaps you and the object are similar in some ways. Or maybe the object holds certain qualities that you are trying to attain. Maybe the Power Object can tell you how to overcome certain obstacles. Discover what your Power Object has to teach you about yourself. [2-minute pause]

Changing the focus of your question, ask your Power Object what it has to teach you about formulating a new myth that resolves the conflict between your old myth and your counter-myth. [2-minute pause]

Now ask your Power Object what it has to teach you about life. It will show you much about living with more vitality as you approach the perplexities and promises of existence. [2-minute pause]

When you have examined your Power Object and learned something of what it has to teach you about yourself, your mythology, and your life, turn to your journal and record any further reflections.

Frank's Power Object was an intricately layered piece of bark that came from a fire-scorched tree.

> My first observation when I asked what it had to teach me about myself was that wherever the dead bark had fallen away, the bark underneath it was more beautiful. This suggested to me the importance of letting go of past restrictions and of trusting that my deeper parts will have more vitality than my outer "bark."

When I asked what it had to teach me about my new mythology, I received the same basic message. Parts of me through which I once made contact with the world, such as my dedication to my work, have now become veils. I must learn to drop away what is dead, what does not enhance life, and to trust that what is beneath it will serve me better. I also noticed that beneath the top layer, which the tree was so freely discarding (there were chips all over the floor), fresh healthy bark was hidden. So when the dead bark dropped away, new strength and beauty appeared. This suggested that I keep cultivating the inner parts I want to develop, rather than to get too bogged down with trying to peel off the dead bark (my hardness and drivenness) which will fall away on its own.

When I asked the bark what it had to teach me about life, I saw how much that death is part of life, natural and inevitable. But I am oriented to fight death, not just with my terror when I think of dying, but in my fear of losing whatever I have. If I am willing to risk the death of certain habits and patterns that are very familiar to me and very comfortable, other vital but latent inner parts will have room to flourish.

When you have finished asking these questions of your Power Object, keep it in a special place, perhaps near your Personal Shield, where you may easily consult it for further guidance. Native Americans often construct special areas for their Power Objects or put them in a position of honor in their homes. If their Power Object is perishable or fragile, they may gently return it to the earth where it can rejoin the cycle of change.

Dream Focus: Dreaming Your New Myth

Review your dream journal for any dreams that provide a glimpse into a new myth that synthesizes the most functional parts of your old myth and of your counter-myth. Use one or more dream techniques to work with any dreams that you identify. If you wish to incubate such a dream, before you go to sleep, ask for a new myth that resolves your original conflict. Such a myth would incorporate the best of your old myth with the best of your counter-myth. Before falling asleep, take a few deep breaths, think about your conflict, tune into your desire for such new direction, and repeat ten to twenty times a statement such as "I request a dream that reveals to me a new, more wholesome, guiding image." Immediately upon waking, record and work with your dreams or insights.

Personal Ritual: Part Three of Your Fairy Tale

Creating Part Three of your Fairy Tale is the next step in consciously and deliberately laying out a metaphorical image that you may then "reel yourself into." Prepare yourself to create Part Three by reviewing the two sections of your Fairy Tale that are already completed. Consider the contrasting ways each part suggests for approaching the problems life has presented. Also review the subsequent work you have done toward resolving the conflict between the myths that govern these differing life postures.

Approach Part Three using the techniques that were most valuable for you in creating the first two parts of your Fairy Tale. Regardless of which methods you use, begin with the following instructions:

Take several deep breaths and let your breathing become slow and deep. [30-second pause] Reflect on Part One of your Fairy Tale. [20-second pause] Find which side of your body best represents this segment of your story and the old myth whose roots it describes. [Pause] What are the sensations in this part of your body?

Reflect on Part Two of your Fairy Tale. [20-second pause] Feel how the other side of your body may represent this segment of your story and the emerging myth that it depicts. [Pause] What are the sensations in this part of your body?

As before, have your palms face each other and slowly bring them together. When they touch, the sensations in the two sides of your body will begin to mingle. As these sensations come into contact, notice how they blend and merge. [30-second pause] Allow these energies to swirl around one another, until a single feeling remains that contains the best, the most vital, the most life-affirming aspects of each. [Pause] With every breath, allow this new, unified sense to move throughout your body and intensify.

Remaining attuned to this feeling of wholeness, you will create Part Three of your Fairy Tale, extending the journey of the main character beyond the trials of Part One and the magical adventures of Part Two. A third segment will now emerge. Begin to develop that story in your imagination, or speak it into a tape, or write it in your journal, or share it with your partner. The story will end with a plausible resolution to the dilemmas that the main character faced in Part One, attained perhaps through the lessons or inspiration of Part Two. When you are finished, be sure that it has been adequately recorded in your journal.

Part Three of Frank's Fairy Tale read:

Frankie had learned by this time that he was not destined to be a King as he had once believed, and he had learned that to continue to wish he could be a King would bring him much unhappiness. On the other hand, he had reason to believe that if he could accept his own ordinariness, he would be successful as a citizen and could have much the kind of life that he wished. What surprised Frankie when he looked in the crystal ball was that he did not envy the King for his crown but for his vitality.

Frankie saw that he had made many choices that led him away from such vitality. He realized, for instance, that the only thing requiring him to do everything Just Right was his *belief* that he had to, no matter what the personal cost. He also knew he could succeed when he set his mind to something, and he decided that his desire to regain his spontaneity should be no exception. As he went about this, however, he found that in one sense this project was an exception. His style of persistently pushing toward a goal actually interfered with the goal of being free in the moment. Still, he harnessed his persistence even in learning how to let go.

By the time Frankie had become a grown man, he was comfortable living in an ordinary home in an ordinary village. He had an ordinary wife, ordinary children, and an ordinary job. But his favorite word was "extraordinary." Every day he would look in wonderment at his world. His children were miracles to him. He would spend hours playing with them, and he would delight in their curiosity and enthusiasm for life. He cherished his wife—so different from him, so mysterious, so exquisite, so lovable. They would look in each other's eyes for eons and make up poems about what they saw. He loved his work. He would become absorbed in the challenge of doing things a bit differently every day, always

> finding a creative twist. For this, he was appreciated by his colleagues and valued by his employer. He took great satisfaction in the job he did, *and* he did not confuse his work with his worth, so when he went home, his job responsibilities stayed at the office. Frankie did not grow up to be King, but he lived happily ever after with the wealth and power supplied by his rich inner life.

Here we see Frank adjusting what he values, what he will pursue, and how he will pursue it. While his insistence on relaxing and enjoying the moment may seem somewhat frivolous when you think of the profound life choices governed by personal myths, Frank's ability to relax and enjoy himself affects critical issues in his life. He was particularly concerned about chest pains that had been increasing in frequency in recent months, and he was allowing himself to feel his sadness that he had grown more distant from his wife over the years. While he was not certain that the obsessive style supported by his old myth was responsible for either of these problems, it had clearly dominated his life and eclipsed his vitality. He became determined to change it.

Your Fairy Tale will also suggest a new direction for you that draws upon the inspiration of your counter-myth in correcting at least some of the problems inherent in your old myth. The remainder of this chapter will provide opportunities to review this new segment of your Fairy Tale, make appropriate adjustments, and translate it into language that is directly applicable to your current life.

Dream Focus: Seeking Confirmation from Your Dreams

Mentally review this newest section of your Fairy Tale before going to sleep and ask for a dream that will in some way confirm its validity for you. Immediately upon waking, record any dreams, thoughts, or inspiration. Be prepared to edit and revise Part Three of your Fairy Tale to bring it in line with the insights that emerge. The above version of Frank's Part Three is actually his second rendition. After sleeping on his first attempt, he realized that he had become carried away with his literary creation and the power of authorship. He had gotten to "happily ever after" easily and quickly by giving Frankie a Kingdom of his own where he lived in pleasure and joy. He realized that his initial effort was really another counter-myth solution. It did not utilize what he had learned in Part Two to work out a practical approach for resolving the conflict. With this realization, revisions and innovations began to occur to him, such as how he could have Frankie discover that he can use his persistence as a strength, and he rewrote Part Three that evening.

Personal Ritual: The Sequel to Your Fairy Tale

A sequel is a literary work, complete in itself, but continuing a preceding work. In the Sequel you are about to create, the direction taken by your Fairy Tale will intersect with the anticipated direction of your life. Before you begin, review Part Three of your Fairy Tale. Then find a comfortable spot, settle in, and take a few deep breaths:

Close your eyes. Allow your breathing to become slow and deep. Feel yourself relaxing more completely with your next five breaths: ONE, TWO, THREE, FOUR, FIVE. Bring Part Three of your Fairy Tale back to mind. [Pause] Tune into the most dominant positive feeling. [Pause] Locate the part of your body in which you are most strongly aware of this emotion, and let your breathing intensify it. [30-second pause] Again experience the feeling as a river, and imagine yourself in a boat on that river. This time the river takes you forward five years into the future. [30-second pause] On the bank of the river you see, as if on a stage, a scene five years from now in which you are living according to the guidance of your new myth. Enter the scene. Notice the sights, sounds, and smells. Where are you? What are you doing? Who is with you? Observe the scene carefully and note what occurs. [60-second pause] When you are ready, count yourself back from five to one.

Under the heading "Fairy Tale—Sequel," record this story in your journal. Frank's Sequel read:

> The first thing I see on the shore is that there are children, playful and full of fresh energy. As I dock my boat, the children run up to me full of excitement and curiosity. I have no concern about

taking the time to speak with them and play with them. Nor am I stopped by any shyness. I know how to open my heart and let the energy flow. Later, I am in a hut transacting some business. The same openness and vigor are there in my dealings. I can play hard, and I can work playfully.

Suddenly Diane [his wife] is there. We have grown closer and have much more fun together. We take a walk in the woods. We have learned to see and deeply feel the miracles of life that teem in the forest. We show each other intricate root patterns and speculate on how they developed. She takes my hand and gently places it on some lush moss. I take my finger, wet now with dew, and moisten her lips. I'm very much in love.

Personal Ritual: Seeking Confirmation from the "Powers That Be"

When people reflect upon the most far-reaching powers that human consciousness can begin to conceive—the realm referred to by words such as *God, the Tao,* or *the Ground of Being*—they may relate most strongly to a picture, a concept, a voice, or even a sound (great musicians have been thought of as implements for the "signature of God"). Although it is beyond the human intellect to understand this realm, many rites, prayers, and meditations are designed to elevate our feelings to reach toward it.

In this ritual, you will be asked to open yourself to this realm—however you conceive of it—and to submit, for confirmation or adjustment, the new myth you have been formulating. Your Inner Shaman, who dwells close to this domain, will be your guide. To begin, find a comfortable spot, settle in, and take a few deep breaths:

Close your eyes. Allow your breathing to become slow and deep. Feel yourself relaxing more completely with your next five breaths: ONE, TWO, THREE, FOUR, FIVE. Carry out the method you have been using to visit your Inner Shaman. [30-second pause] After you have greeted your Shaman, let it be known that you wish to be transported into the Upper World. You want to enter a realm where you will be blessed by the presence of the Divine, or the "Powers That Be."

Your Shaman smiles and bids you to be seated. You are given a sacred herb. You ingest it, lie back, and relax. Soon you are entering a powerful state of spiritual awareness. You feel yourself entering the realm of the Divine, the Kingdom of God. [Pause] Your sense of a Divine presence intensifies as you continue to breathe deeply. [60-second pause]

You remember that you have a task to perform. You are to review your new myth. From this higher awareness, you are to consider the worthiness of the new myth that is expressed in your Fairy Tale and its Sequel. Sense that there are wise and benevolent forces around you, and they bring to your awareness the answers to your questions. Does this guiding myth call to the best and the highest that is within you? [Pause] Is the myth built on arrogance or grandiosity? [Pause] Does it lack in ambition? Is it limited by your fears and apprehensions? [Pause] Will it lead to problems in five years that you did not anticipate? [Pause] Is it simply more than you are ready to attempt to implement in your life at this time? [Pause] Should any adjustments be made before you set your will to changing your life in the image of this myth? [60-second pause]

Now state your new guiding myth. [Pause] Find a single sentence or short paragraph that contains its essence. Know that you are surrounded by sacred forces that will help you. Listen as this direct statement of your new myth enters your awareness. [60-second pause]

When you are finished, again bask in the high energies that surround you. Be open to other visions or insight. [30-second pause] Again find your Shaman. Describe your new myth to your Shaman. Listen for a response. [60-second pause] When you are ready, take leave of your Shaman and count yourself back from five to one.

Under the heading "My New Guiding Myth," describe your new myth, along with any other reflections on this experience. As Frank listened to the instructions, he was flooded with the feelings of awe and inspiration that had surprised and transported him to a sense of religious appreciation a dozen years earlier when he had visited a magnificent cathedral in Cologne. Describing his new myth, he wrote:

> My new myth instructs me to affirm all within me that is passionate and life-supporting—to appreciate it, attend to it, make room for it, and enjoy it as I move through life. I am to be particularly alert to my tendency to lock myself into unnecessary or high-paced activities that crowd out spontaneity and passion. And while I am taking the time to affirm what joy and creativity may be mine,

I am not to judge what is not there; I am not to focus a searchlight on every inner event and sit in judgment should it not live up to my hopes or expectations.

I am to use this principle both in work and play. I am to use it in looking backward and in looking forward. When I look back on events that have occurred, I am to immerse myself in what was life-affirming, and to align myself with such experiences. I am not to keep focusing upon times that were limited by my obsessions and deficiencies. Such analysis has been my pattern, based upon the belief that I can only learn from my mistakes, but beyond a point this has had only the effect of dragging me down. Looking in the forward direction, I am to project this same life-affirming emphasis into my future. The expectations I send out for myself are to be confident and encouraging. Specifically, my new myth assures me that I will activate the more vital and passionate ways of being I have been exploring throughout the program. I can see this; I can expect it; I know it will come to pass.

As you can see, this statement is expressed neither in the form of a story (as in his Fairy Tale) nor as a rule of conduct (as would be found in ethical systems such as the Ten Commandments), but simply as a reminder, in Frank's own language, of how he intends to monitor certain thoughts that affect his passion. Some people, such as Meg, use more poetic language in stating their new myth ("I am part of Creation. . . ."), and you are encouraged to make your statement in the language most fitting for you. You will see in the following chapter how even an abstract or poetic statement of your new mythic vision can be translated into concrete steps for living by its guidance.

Personal Ritual: Completing Your Shield

When you created your Personal Shield, you did not complete the fifth section, which is to symbolically represent your renewed vision of Paradise Regained. Your final task in this chapter will be to formulate an image for the Renewed Vision section of your Shield, based on all the work you have done to this point in the program. First, review the initial image of Paradise Regained from your Shield and any comments you made about it in your journal. That image represented an ideal you had been following before beginning the program. The work you have done to this point has probably challenged that image. Does a new symbol occur to you that captures the spirit of the new myth you formulated in the previous chapter? If one comes easily and spontaneously, or if one appeared to you during a dream or one of the previous rituals, simply draw it on your Shield and skip over this exercise. Otherwise, examine the original Paradise Lost and Paradise Regained portions of your Shield. Get a mental picture of these symbols that you will be able to recall as you listen to the following instructions. Find a comfortable spot, settle in, and take a few deep breaths:

Close your eyes. Allow your breathing to become slow and deep. Feel yourself relaxing more completely with your next five breaths: ONE, TWO, THREE, FOUR, FIVE. Imagine that you are in front of a great pyramid. [Pause] Place the symbol from your Shield that represents Paradise Lost at one corner of the base of this pyramid. [Pause] Place the Paradise Regained symbol from your Shield at the other corner. [Pause] Your symbols are about to rise along the sides of the pyramid. They begin to rise now, coming closer and closer together.

Know that when they meet at the tip of the pyramid, they will transform into a new symbol. This new image will symbolize an integration, a renewed image of Paradise Regained. It will account for the realities that are part of Paradise Lost, and it will reveal new possibilities. Allow the symbols to move up the sides of the pyramid at their own rate. When they reach the apex, watch how they merge into the new symbol. [60-second pause] If your symbol has not yet appeared, watch for it during the following moments.

Study your symbol, using the power of your imagination. [Pause] Step back and look at your symbol from another perspective. [Pause] Take the symbol off the pyramid and bring it closer. Touch it and explore it. [30-second pause] Finally, if you are willing, merge the symbol with your body. Incorporate it into your being. Sense its vitality as it becomes part of you. [Pause] When you are ready, count yourself back from five to one, take a deep breath, and open your eyes. Draw or describe the symbol on the "Renewed Vision" section of your Shield and reflect on it in your journal.

Here is Frank's description of his new Paradise Regained image:

> When the symbols touched, the background was all pink and I kind of slipped back in time to feelings from a very early age.

> Suddenly, there was this warm, pink, soft-plastic toy I haven't thought of since I was maybe two or three. I had deep, rich, warm feelings as I remembered this toy (I couldn't quite see the toy, I just remembered its pinkness and how good I felt playing with it). It seemed to represent a time in my life when my spontaneity was uninhibited, my appetites were honest and unrestrained, and my experience of the world was sensual and innocent. When I brought the image into my body, it suddenly *became* my heart, pulsating, pink, vibrant, alive. I felt myself reclaiming my childhood enthusiasm, happiness, and bubbling laughter, and this newly enlivened heart was the image I drew on my Shield.

On to Stage Five

The personal rituals you have carried out to this point have focused primarily on your inner life. The rituals in the final stage of the program will bring your attention to the relationship between your inner world and your environment. You will be challenged to translate your new mythic vision into practical guidance for your life.

6

The Fifth Stage: Weaving a Renewed Mythology into Daily Life

Carefully observe what way your heart draws you and then choose that way with all your strength. —HASSIDIC SAYING

The first four stages of the program have been an exercise in carefully observing "what way your heart draws you." This final stage is an exercise in choosing "that way with all your strength." You have been freeing yourself from limiting visions that trace back to your childhood and to your culture's mythology. But even implementing changes that are clearly desirable may require the full strength of your will. Behavioral patterns and habits of thought that grew out of an old myth, now consciously rejected, may tenaciously persist.

On the other hand, by bringing resolution to the mythic conflict you identified early in the program, and formulating a new mythic image, you have already brought fresh momentum and direction to your inner life. A number of additional steps can be useful for integrating into your world the renewed mythic guidance you have been developing. These steps call for both an inward focus and an outward focus. The inner focus involves additional changes in the images you "cast" in front of yourself and changes in what you say to yourself as you make your way through your daily experiences. The outer focus involves practical changes in your habits and priorities.

This final phase of the program draws particularly from techniques that have been developed by cognitive[1] and behavioral[2] psychotherapists for bringing about changes in thought patterns and behavior. You will, for instance, monitor your "self-talk"—the subvocal and often subconscious speech we direct toward ourselves—which might unwittingly promote the old myth. And you will formulate fresh "self-statements" that support the new myth.

You also will carry out "behavior rehearsals," role plays that allow you to experience acting upon the new myth under simulated conditions. You will transmute your new myth into a vivid thought form, and you will be using bodily postures and mental imagery to internalize it further. You will create "behavioral contracts" with another person or your Inner Shaman. These contracts will focus on changes needed in the areas of your life that still reinforce the myth you want to move beyond, as well as on possible changes that would reinforce the mythic image you want to pursue. You also will be invited to inaugurate your new myth formally in a ceremony with those who are intimate with you, to reinforce it with daily rituals that you will design, and to maintain ongoing contact with the deeper dimensions of your mythology. By the time you have performed the personal rituals presented in this chapter, you will have established a framework for understanding your life in a way that supports the myth you have so conscientiously been cultivating. And you will have taken deliberate steps to implement that new myth in your conduct and your daily routines.

MEG'S ONGOING JOURNEY

In the first ritual of this final stage of the program, you will experiment with feeling your new myth in your body and living it in your imagination. You will see yourself carrying out the new myth flawlessly. Meg used the image of her abalone necklace as a catalyst for calling up her new myth and experiencing it in her body. Staying with these feelings, she brought to mind a situation that she knew would be challenging:

> I have made an agreement with an acquaintance that he will do something for me. I have made several commitments and accommodations based on that understanding. Then he fails to follow through, and I am left in an awkward and compromised position. This always has elicited feelings of abandonment, betrayal, and anger on my part. I've tended to feel punished and punishing. I would withdraw to such a degree that the person would have absolutely no access to me. There would be no way he could ever have anything from me again. I would also feel like a fool that I was misled by the other person.
>
> Operating from my new myth, I see myself redirecting this energy, giving the best possible interpretation I can find for understanding the person's behavior. I don't take it as a personal affront. I stay rooted in my principles, but I also stay flexible like the kelp

and consider all that might have caused the other's actions and all the possible ways for me to respond other than withdrawal. I feel good as I imagine myself operating from this position.

Your next task will be to notice the kinds of self-statements that are maintaining your old myth, and to formulate self-statements that will support your new myth. Meg invoked her Inner Shaman to help her with this task. Among the inner vocalizations serving to maintain her old myth were:

If I'm pleasant to people who don't see things my way, I'm giving in to the codgers and the emotionally constipated.

If I restrain an impulse in a particular situation, I will be killing my spontaneity and my spirit.

If I carry out a task in the routine and established way, I will be inhibiting my self-expression and stifling my growth.

Inner vocalizations that could help implant her new myth included:

Understanding the other person's point of view will increase my effectiveness and equanimity.

Saying no to some impulses is in my interest and leaves energy to invest in other ways.

Moderation allows me the self-control to develop skills and understanding I once thought impossible.

She familiarized herself with both lists and began to recognize when the self-statements associated with the old myth were operating. She learned how to stop such thoughts and to replace them with self-statements that supported her new myth. After you have done this with your own self-statements, you will plan a series of action-oriented rituals that further establish your new myth.

Meg designed the following ritual, which served as a daily reminder of her new myth:

I will get a package of colorful balloons and choose one whose color matches a quality I want to develop. I will slowly blow it up until it is plump and pretty, and I will write on it the name of the quality. When there are several balloons, I will hang them carefully from my bathroom mirror until there is a wreath of words like *patience* (soft blue), *kindness* (warm pink), *humor* (red), *forgiveness* (deep blue), *learning* (green), and *honor* (white) surrounding

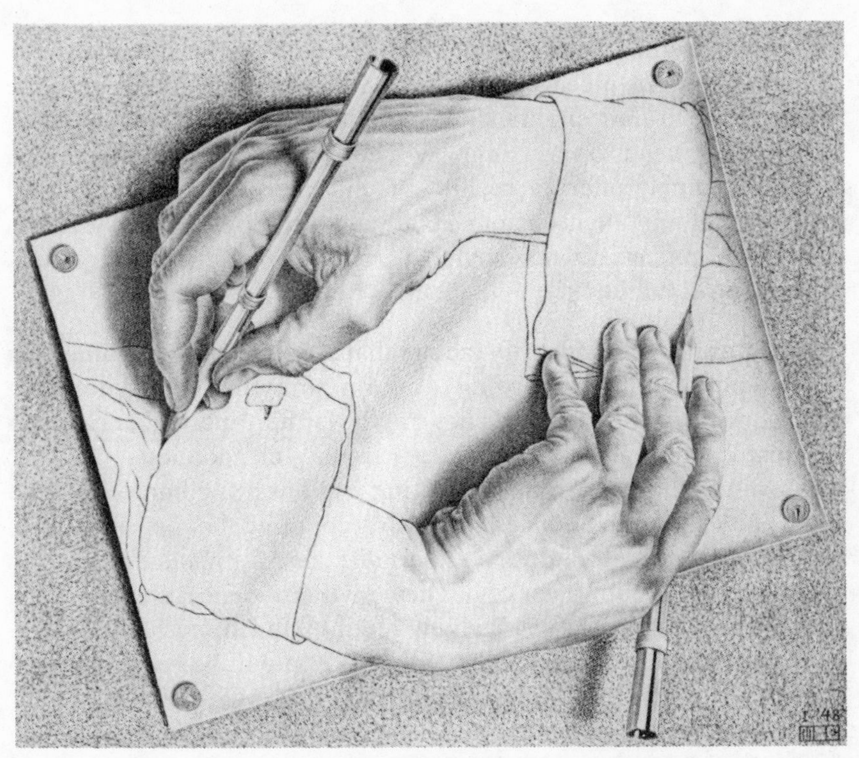

Weaving a Renewed Mythology into Daily Life

my face in the morning and night when I brush my hair and teeth. I expect to enjoy this collage. If a balloon should deflate, I will quietly replace it, with no reproach to myself.

In another ritual, she planned to make a public statement that symbolized her intention to implement her new myth:

> I will be the "balloon lady" at the next Summit Summer Festival. I will write one nice word on each balloon and the children will be surprised to find qualities like *Love, Beauty,* and *Truth* dancing over their heads on a string. I will enjoy the sight very much, and I will lovingly offer each child an understanding of their special quality. If anyone is curious about why I did it, I will answer in a way that reflects my new myth: "Serenity is gained through loving, thoughtful action."

The next task is to identify factors that are supporting or inhibiting your intention to live according to your new myth. One resource that was working to support Meg's new myth was her "incredible richness of close friends who are marvelous models of goodness." Another support was that she lived "in a setting that has less commotion than most people have to endure." She also recognized that her own hope, insight, determination, desire, experience, and faith were all factors that were working in favor of her new myth. Influences she identified that were working against her new myth included old habits, fears, spite, suspicion, jealousy, and neediness. You will be encouraged to review your list with a partner or small group. Meg and her partner identified several specific actions she could take to strengthen the forces that were supporting her chosen mythology, and they found creative ways to deal with some of those that were interfering with it.

At that point she requested another dream, this time asking for guidance on the next steps she might take in implementing her new myth:

> I am in a little room painted jailhouse-green. The walls are metal, the floor is cement with a drain in it, the only seats are metal folding chairs with hard backs. I am seated in the center of a circle. Ugly men and women with harsh voices and hateful expressions are taking turns exposing my sins of commission and omission. One says, "You treated your father shamefully, neglecting him in his last days." Another says, "You have always been self-indulgent and sly." Another accuses me, saying, "You stole from your mother's purse." They go on and on. Some things are petty, others momentous in my life. All are faults, inadequacies, or transgres-

> sions. I feel horrible. Trapped. Without resources. I long for rescue or death. Neither happens and the voices go on and on.
>
> I notice, in my desperation, that there is a door. I measure the distance and decide to try for it. I make it! The door is unlocked—I have only to go through it. I have the sense that there is a sign on the door which reads "PAST." Outside a colt is galloping in a meadow under the benign and amused protection of a mare. I close the old door behind me.

Meg reviewed her dream, her self-statements, and her analysis of the forces that supported the new myth and those that worked against it. Based on this review, she made a contract with her partner in which she specified the actions she would begin to take for bringing her life into closer harmony with her new myth. One of the items in her contract, for instance, was:

> When I hear one of those ugly, repetitious inner voices detailing my badness, I will stop and attend to what is being said. I will then assess if there is any proper action possible to right old wrongs or to learn by what occurred. I will do what is proper if I can see such a course of action. If there is nothing more to learn and no proper action to take, I will redirect my energy to something I have done or am doing well. I will deny energy to destructive ideas by recognizing them and then starving them to death.

In her contract, Meg identified several areas of focus, including monitoring her self-judgments, allowing more vulnerability with others, initiating more intimate and risky conversation with her friends, and listening patiently to other people's points of view. When she and her partner met a week later, Meg recounted her progress in taking these steps and reported a welcome shift in her relationships. Meg and her partner met each week for two months. At each meeting they reviewed her successes, discussed areas of difficulty in carrying out the contract, and revised the contract for the following week. By the end of the second month, Meg felt that inner guidance in support of her new myth—"Serenity is gained through loving, thoughtful action"—had become conscious and accessible to her in many of the same areas of her life in which the isolation and defensiveness of the old myth had caused problems.

BUILDING YOUR NEW MYTHOLOGY INTO YOUR LIFE

The rituals you will perform in this chapter are designed to increase the harmony between your new myth and the way you live your life.

Personal Ritual: Invoking the New Myth in Your "Subtle Body"

There is an extensive tradition in both the East and the West which holds that each person possesses a secondary, nonphysical body, referred to variously as the "subtle body," the "pranic body," or the "etheric body."[3] You can contact this "subtle body" in your imagination. Although you may prefer to think of the subtle body as a metaphor rather than as an actual entity, you can envision it as a bridge between your thoughts and your behavior. By influencing your subtle body with your thoughts, you can subdue patterns of behavior that have been habitual and automatic.

Mental imagery is one way of affecting your subtle body and its manifestations in the physical world. Numerous research studies have confirmed "the fact that vividly experienced imagery, imagery that is both seen and felt, can substantially affect brain waves, blood flow, heart rate, skin temperature, gastric secretions, and immune response—in fact, the total physiology."[4] The following brief exercise provides a concrete demonstration of what we are referring to by the term *subtle body.*[5]

Stand erect and move your head to the right as far as it will go without straining. Measure the degree of rotation by noting precisely where you are staring when the movement stops. Come back to center and raise your right arm, stretching toward the sky. With your right arm overhead, extend the fingers on your right hand and bend back at the wrist. Now stretch all the way down your right side. Next, lower your right arm and stretch your right leg. Extend the toes of your right foot as you bend it at the ankle. Come back to center and again, without straining, measure the degree of rotation by turning your head to the right. You will note that your head rotated farther on the second try, which may be readily explained by the mechanics of the stretching exercise.

Now rotate your head to the left and observe the part of the room you can see when the rotation stops. Come back to center. This time, without moving a muscle, *imagine that you are raising the left arm of your subtle body overhead. Imagine that you are extending the fingers of the left hand and bending it back at the wrist. Now imagine you are stretching all the way down your left side: left arm, left side of chest, stomach, left leg. Still not moving a muscle, imagine that you are stretching your left leg, and extending the toes of your left foot as you bend it back at the ankle. Relax. Again, without straining, measure the degree of rotation by turning your head to the left. Most people will report that their heads also rotated farther after this sequence, even though there was no physical stretching, only mental imagery. To convince yourself that this effect is real, you might repeat the experiment at another time, varying the order and switching the side of your body that you physically stretch and the side you stretch only in your imagination.*

Imagery that is felt in the body has been shown to be effective in assisting people in situations ranging from recovering from an operation to preparing to compete in the Olympics: "The mental rehearsal of a sales presentation or a marathon race evokes muscular change and more: blood pressure goes up, brain waves change, and sweat glands become active."[6] Imagined performance can improve actual performance. The free-throw percentage of basketball players, for instance, has been shown to increase after they imagined themselves practicing perfect shots.

In this ritual, you will use imagery to align your subtle body with your new myth. Study the "Renewed Vision" symbol on your Shield. Find a comfortable position, close your eyes, and begin to relax.

Bring to mind your "Renewed Vision" symbol and the meaning it holds for you. [Pause] Get a sense of what it would feel like to act according to the myth represented by that image. [Pause] Find a plausible situation from your life in which you might behave according to this new myth. You might be expressing an honest opinion in a delicate circumstance, approaching an employer with confidence, or enjoying a quiet moment with a loved one.

Find a scene where it would be useful to act according to your new myth. [Pause] Where are you? Who else is there? What are you doing? [Pause] Focus now on your bodily feelings in this situation. How does it feel to be enacting the new myth? [Pause] Imagine the gestures you might employ and the posture you might assume. [Pause] Feel your words forming in your throat and mouth. [Pause] Continue to "practice" living out your new myth in your subtle body for several minutes. When you are ready, open your eyes and describe the experience in your journal.

Frank reflected on his relationship with his wife:

> I'm much too somber, serious, and negative with Diane, and I decided to create, in my subtle body, more feelings of joy around her. At first, I had difficulty activating these feelings. Then I imagined there was less pressure on me in other parts of my life, and I had all sorts of extra energy. I could feel the aliveness of my new pulsating pink heart flowing throughout my body, and the aliveness infused my subtle body. I liked this preview of how our relationship might change if I were less pressured and more open to that pulsating pink heart.

Mentally practice the new behavior several times each day and imagine that as you carry it out, you are building your new mythology into your subtle body. In the following rituals, you will be shown additional ways of anchoring your new mythology into your subtle body, your thoughts, and your behavior.

Personal Ritual: Cultivating Self-Statements to Support Your New Myth

People, unlike any other creature on earth, are motivated by what they tell themselves—whether critical or compassionate, wise or absurd. Our attitudes, viewpoints, and opinions are expressed in our self-talk, the internal, subvocal statements we say to ourselves. Consequently, a powerful way to facilitate desired changes in your mythology is to identify the self-statements or automatic thoughts associated with the old, dysfunctional myth and to consciously replace them with more constructive self-statements that represent the new myth.

When people change their self-statements, their feelings and behaviors also change.[7] Among the types of irrational self-statements that people frequently use, which are expressions of dysfunctional personal myths, are: "I need everyone to love and admire me," "Whatever I do, I must do perfectly," and "I don't deserve to enjoy myself while others are suffering."

Frank noted that when he thought of a creative project, or even a feasible project, he automatically started to subvocally instruct himself to begin work on the project. His free time was always being crowded out with such projects, which he initiated without considering their costs to his equanimity and personal development. In this ritual, you will be reflecting on habitual self-statements that maintain outmoded patterns of behavior. In your journal, make a heading: "Self-Statements That Support My Old Myth." Find a comfortable position, take several deep breaths, and begin to relax.

Call upon your Inner Shaman. [30-second pause] Exchange words of greeting. Observe. Listen. [Pause] Describe your old myth. Discuss your new understandings of the role it has played in your life.

With your Shaman, identify some of the phrases that tend to maintain that myth. Hold them in your memory or gently rouse yourself so you can record them in your journal as they come to you. List three or four self-statements that seem pivotal in supporting your old myth. When you have completed this task, take respectful leave of your Shaman as you gently return to your waking consciousness.

Identify the self-statements on your list that you believe will be the most difficult to give up. Pitting dysfunctional self-statements or automatic thoughts against the test of rational analysis can help us to distance ourselves from them. For each of the self-statements that you feel may be difficult for you to disengage, write in your journal the answers to these questions:[8]

1. What evidence supports this self-statement?
2. What evidence disputes it?
3. What would happen to me if I no longer heeded it?

Let this reasoning sink in deeply, and refer to it as you work toward altering the automatic thoughts that are keeping you tied to your old myth.

Frank did not think he would easily be able to ignore the inner voice that told him that if he were to remain respectable and successful in his profession, he was required to continually master the tiniest details and exert his full effort at all times. When he challenged this belief, he came to see that success and status were not nearly the issues for him that they once had been. Both were well established; he was proud of his career achievements and people consistently responded to him with respect. He realized he had much more license than he was using to simply "relax and enjoy the ride."

Bring your new myth to mind. You will be identifying the kinds of self-talk that support it. Make a heading in your journal labeled "Self-Statements That Support My New Myth." Find a comfortable position, take several deep breaths, and begin to relax.

Again call upon your Inner Shaman. [30-second pause] Exchange words of greeting. Observe. Listen. [Pause] Use the bodily imagery you developed in the earlier personal ritual to create in your subtle body the feelings you associate with the new myth. Describe your new myth. Discuss your understanding of the role it can play in your life.

With your Shaman, identify some phrases that might support that myth. Hold them in your memory or gently rouse yourself so you can record them in your journal as they come to you. List three or four self-statements that would nourish your new myth. [Pause] When you have completed this task, take leave of your Shaman as you gently return to your waking consciousness.

Among the self-statements that could support Frank's new myth were: "I can always divide my work with breaks that allow me to relax deeply and enjoy tuning into the experience of my senses." He adopted a simple meditation technique to use in situations where he felt tense: "Notice breath. Soften belly. Open heart." Other self-statements included: "I am a worthy human being even if I let this project pass by"; "When I can play, I do play"; and, "I am highly selective about where I expend my perfectionism."

You may feel that some of your new self-statements will be difficult to believe or to follow. If so, adapt the three questions previously listed for examining their validity. It may be necessary to revise some of your self-statements to bring them in line with what you consider reasonable and plausible.

Frank, for instance, could not rationally support one of the statements on his list: "I bolster my enthusiasm for life by seeing only the positive elements when I review a situation." He was able to revise it, however, to: "When I find the positive elements in a situation, I accept them and enjoy them, and I no longer discount them by measuring them against what might have been possible." Continue to formulate and revise your list until you have a set of self-statements that offers you sensible guidance for this new direction in your mythology.

The more you can habitually and concretely build this second list into your automatic thought patterns, the more quickly your behavior will align itself with your new myth. One useful technique is to imagine, for each statement, a situation in which you would feel good acting in accordance with that statement. Construct the situation fully—see pictures, hear words, and feel your physical sensations in the scene. Self-statements that have been linked to images, feelings, and sensations are more potent than thoughts alone. Another aid is to write the list in large and colorful letters and place it where you will regularly see it—on a mirror, on the refrigerator, on your bedroom wall. Repetition strengthens the influence of a self-statement. Use the list as an opportunity for frequently reviewing your new self-statements.

We also suggest that you begin to recognize the self-statements associated with the dysfunctional myth and use a cognitive-behavioral approach called "thought-stopping" when you realize such inner guidance is at play. In thought-stopping, you simply interrupt an objectionable self-statement as soon as you recognize it, and immediately replace it with one that is in line with your intentions. When you recognize a habitual thought or self-statement that supports the old myth, take a deep breath. As you exhale, imagine yourself releasing the thought and your old myth. With the next inhalation, replace that thought with a self-statement that supports your new myth. As you breathe, let the statement imprint itself upon you.

Frank began to pause instances where he normally would have reflexively told his wife he was too busy to do something they would both enjoy. He would then note automatic thoughts that were operating to keep him bound to his work, whether the activity was essential or not. When he identified such thoughts, he replaced them with the self-statement, "When I can play, I do play," and then made his decision.

He also recognized that one of the ways he cut off his passion was by "not being fully present to what is." He realized that he devoted a great deal of his mental energy to ruminating about whether one thing or another was going to go wrong. He made a commitment to himself that whenever he recognized that his mind had drifted into obsessive worry, he would immediately take a deep breath and say to himself: "Notice breath. Soften belly. Open heart." Frank found it useful at the end of each day to log in his journal the old self-statements he had recognized and the new ones with which he replaced them.

Personal Ritual: Ceremonial Enactments of Your New Myth

The steps you have taken to this point have prepared you to affirm and strengthen your new myth through a series of private rituals and a public ceremony in which you will proclaim the new mythology in the presence of people who care about you. Begin with the following private enactment of your new myth:

Standing with your eyes closed, once again invoke your sense of the new myth in your subtle body. [Pause] Find the posture that reflects this mythology—the stance, the feeling of strength, the flexibility, the facial expressions. [30-second pause] Now, recall the situation from the earlier body-imagery exercise in which you acted according to the new myth, or make up a new scene. [Pause] Again, in your subtle body, create a mental pantomime—mentally going through the actions that are an expression of the new myth. [30-second pause] Now open your eyes and "step into" your pantomime. Physically but silently enact the pantomime. [30-second pause] Enact the pantomime again, this time adding words. You may wish to repeat the pantomime a number of times, experimenting with different positions, voice tones, wording, and situations.

Describe this "behavioral rehearsal" ritual in your journal. Frank imagined himself to be intensely involved in a project when his wife comes up to "ask for my car keys because she has misplaced hers again. Where I am usually irritated by such interruptions, I remind myself, 'When I can play, I do play.' I get up, take her by the hand, whirl her around twice, dance her across the room, and we wind up tickling each other and biting one another's necks."

Daily Personal Ritual

The next task is to invent and describe in your journal a ritual you can perform each day that will help to establish the new myth in your life. A daily ritual might involve meditating for a few moments before each meal on a symbol that represents your new myth. It might mean you ceremoniously repeat your pantomime every evening before you retire or in some other way direct your intentions into your subtle body. You might translate your mythic vision into a behavior you can regularly repeat. To implement a myth that allows you to receive help and support from others, for instance, you might each day ask a different person to do a small favor for you. At the end of the day, you could ritualistically mark on a calendar the requests you made that day and the results of having made them.

One woman, whose new myth guided her toward becoming more responsible, took her Power Object, a beautiful stone, and committed herself to carrying it and exploring it every time she went up or down the stairs in her home. The stone was to come with her on every trip. If she forgot it, she would interrupt whatever she was doing to fulfill the rite. In so doing, she was continually renewing her commitment toward greater responsibility, and with each trip up or down the staircase she was communing with her Power Object as well.

A simple and effective daily ritual might be some variation on the following: Each morning, in front of the mirror, direct the feelings you associate with your new myth into your subtle body, assume a posture and facial expression that represents this myth, summarize its guidance in a single statement, and hold a one-minute discussion with the mirror anticipating this day from the perspective of the new myth.

Frank, who found it difficult to get going in the morning, decided to start each day by standing in front of a mirror and finding a posture that symbolized his *old* myth. He would then meditate on the feelings he associated with the new pink heart and would let those feelings pulsate throughout his body until they filled him so completely that he was moved to stretch his body to make room for them. He would imagine he was stretching his whole being into harmony with his new mythology, until he relaxed into a posture that for him was a physical statement of that myth. Finally, he would identify one situation he anticipated that day which was likely to trigger the old myth, and he would envision himself handling it according to his new myth. In your journal, design a single ritual you are willing to perform daily until you decide it has served its purpose.

Public Ritual

You also will plan a transition ritual that marks a public declaration of your new myth. Often, one aspect of such a ritual is to ceremoniously leave the old myth behind. You could, for example, find a photograph of yourself during a period when you were in the grips of the old myth, or create a drawing representing that period. In the ritual, you might burn the photograph or drawing with a friend there to witness, scattering the ashes and drinking a toast to your new myth as it is symbolized on your Shield. Frank brought a dozen pink roses to his wife along with a letter he had just written turning down a new account he normally would have accepted, even though it clearly would have overtaxed him. He showed her the new enlivened pink heart on his Shield, which happened to be the identical shade of the roses. And he promised that he would say yes to her next three invitations to do something together.

At the most basic level, your ritual could simply involve having someone who cares about you witness your daily ritual or the behavioral enactment you did earlier. In a more ambitious observance, you might involve a number of friends, assigning each of them parts in the behavioral enactment so that it becomes more like a skit or play. If, for instance, your new mythology tells you to behave more assertively, the enactment might have others playing your employers, unsympathetic coworkers, judgmental friends, or perhaps an unscrupulous auto mechanic and his boss, in creating a scene in which your interpersonal actions are more effective. Another kind of ceremony might involve simply making a statement of your intentions at a gathering of certain intimates, or sharing a creative expression of your new myth, such as your Shield, a drawing, poem, or new set of clothes. You may wish to embellish the ritual with candles, food, song, and dance.

A poignant ritual was carried out by a woman whose mythology had grown out of a childhood that was afflicted with molestation and parental alcoholism. In her new mythology, she had come to an integration of toughness and compassion. She timed the ritual to coincide with a Thanksgiving gathering in which her husband, brother, sisters, nieces, nephews, and children were all present. After announcing, as they gathered in the living room following dinner, that she was performing a ritual to commemorate a change in the mythology she was living out, she showed them her Shield. She used the symbolism on her Shield in describing her life as an emerging drama whose purpose was to teach her *both* the compassion and the toughness that characterized her new myth. She described how the critical events of her life opened her to the wisdom of this new mythology, and she told her personal Fairy Tale, emphasizing how the theme of the entire adventure was to help the heroine learn the new mythology.

Everyone was deeply moved, and some were stunned, as she metaphorically disclosed family secrets that had been concealed for decades. With everyone's rapt attention, she potently ended the ritual by presenting her eldest daughter—as a legacy for her future offspring—with her Shield, a tape recording she made while telling her story, and a letter to a male descendant and another to a female descendant, four generations off, describing her new myth and how she came to it.

Once you have designed a public ritual that seems appropriate and pleasing to you, make plans in your journal for carrying it out. Be aware of the mood you wish to create, design the event with that mood in mind, and communicate to the participants the importance of the event. Also, ask one or more of the participants to serve as a partner or support group for you in carrying out your new mythology. Select people you perceive to be resourceful, caring, and accepting. Specific suggestions as to how to work with your partner or support group will be included in the final rituals in this chapter.

Personal Ritual: Creating an Ecology that Supports Your New Myth

One of the most venerable principles in modern psychology is that people will seek out and repeat behaviors that are rewarded and avoid behaviors that are punished. You are more likely to change maladaptive behavioral patterns when they are no longer reinforced. In this ritual, you will identify the rewards and punishments in your environment that promote or hinder behavior that is in accordance with your new myth. By making changes that favor your new myth, you will prepare an ecology, a balance of relationships with your environment, in which it is more likely to flourish.

Consider how the behavior of your family, friends, coworkers, or acquaintances sustains your old myth or reinforces the desired behaviors associated with your new myth. Identify actions you can take so the desired behaviors are more frequently reinforced. You might encourage the people whose behavior supports your new myth to keep reinforcing it, or arrange to spend more time with them, or ask others to provide similar support. Conversely, you might ask certain people to stop reinforcing the behaviors that arose out of the old myth. One woman, who wanted to change what she perceived as her "tendency to mother other people," asked her friends to stop praising her for being so helpful to everyone. Frank started to form friendships with people who knew him outside of his professional identity, hoping to reinforce the development of other parts of his personality. Enlisting people who care about you to support behavior that is consistent with your new myth helps build it into your life.

A second way of changing the reinforcers acting on you is to shift your priorities. If your new myth instructs you to make more time for your inner development, but in addition to your work and family responsibilities, you coach a soccer team, are organizing a recall drive against the local mayor, sit on five community boards, and subscribe to a dozen popular magazines, the new myth will have little chance to thrive until your commitments change. In setting priorities, an underlying principle is that the relative strength of a social reinforcer is related to what you value. As your values change, you will see that the activities you find reinforcing also change. You may spend many hours every week happily doing tedious chores for a cause in which you passionately believe, but then find yourself resenting the time and effort as your dedications change. Priorities are tangible statements in the world that reflect the myths you held when you established them. As you evolve, however, unexamined priorities may quietly keep you locked in a mythology you have outgrown.

A third focus is to change the reinforcers you draw to yourself. Suppose you are hoping to become more accepting of other people, but spend most of your spare time in a militant campaign for or against abortion in your local community. Whatever the virtues of your crusade, your choice of activity is decidedly not creating an interpersonal atmosphere that is supportive of living according to your desired myth. Changing a guiding myth often pits us against difficult ethical choices of which we might previously have been oblivious. In directing more of his energies toward his personal life, Frank was tugged by his sense of social responsibility.

Many reinforcers and punishments are symbolic, meeting psychological rather than only practical needs. The culture teaches us to attach our sense of adequacy or our self-esteem to particular kinds of symbols, such as money, position, or beauty. As the qualities to which your sense of self-worth is attached shift from those conditioned by your culture to those chosen by a deeper voice, your life is likely to bring you richer satisfactions. A man whose self-esteem is contingent on the number of women he can attract may find that as he becomes more psychologically mature, he begins to derive an unanticipated sense of fulfillment from the depth rather than the number of his relationships.

Frank identified several internal and external conditions that were reinforcing his new myth:

- The playful presence of my wife
- I've distinguished myself enough so that I no longer have to struggle for professional success
- I am increasingly restless with tasks that don't hold meaning for me
- I know that beneath my shyness and obsessiveness is a very passionate and playful man

Conditions that were acting to negatively reinforce the new myth included:

- I feel I don't have a right to enjoy my life if I'm not achieving prodigiously
- I do receive additional recognition and commissions when I overwork
- When I try to have fun, I usually feel awkward and the experience seems empty
- Most of my friends are also high achievers whom I know mainly through my work, and I haven't developed other kinds of friendships

Use what you have learned through this program about creating personal rituals to invent a ritual that will lead you to construct a "List of Reinforcers." The list will specify the rewards and punishments that cause your life to be more or less aligned with your new myth. Identify the positive and negative reinforcers in your environment, and also the symbolic reinforcers that operate within you, such as Frank's feeling that he had to produce prodigiously to earn pleasure. You might sit down and simply make the list, giving it a ritualistic flair by using pleasing colors and attractive paper as you create it. You might take an imagery journey and consult your Inner Shaman before completing the list. Or you might get together with a friend who can help give you perspective as you analyze the forces in your environment that are influencing your efforts to implement your new myth. Give serious consideration to this important task of identifying the factors that strengthen or obstruct the development of your new myth. In the following personal ritual, you will refer to your List of Reinforcers as you decide where to focus your conscious efforts for effecting changes so that behavior that is in line with your chosen myth is rewarded more and punished less.

Dream Focus: A Next-Step Dream

Review your journal to see if any of your recent dreams has suggested a next step for implementing your new myth. If they have not, you may attempt to incubate such a dream by first reviewing what you have done to this point in the chapter. Then repeat ten to twenty times before you go to sleep this statement: "I will have a dream about how to live my myth, and I will remember my dream." Record and work with any dreams or early morning insights.

Frank reported a dream in which he was romantically pursuing a woman at a drive-in fast-food restaurant, which reminded him of a high school hangout where he recalled having had many "intense and erotically charged adolescent-type feelings." As he established eye contact with the woman, he suddenly realized that she was his wife. Their eyes met with the palpable charge that he had for the chase. He woke up feeling confirmed in his resolve to bring greater passion to his marriage.

Personal Ritual: A Contract for Living Your New Mythology

Patterns that have long been part of your life do not necessarily transform themselves just because you recognize that change would be valuable. One of the most potentially reinforcing sources of support for implementing new modes of thought and behavior is to establish accountability with someone who cares about you. As part of the "public ritual" you performed earlier, you were asked to select one or more people who could provide such support. If you have not yet done this, identify such a person or persons to help you review your progress, serve as a sounding board, and plan new actions on a continuing basis. If there is no one available who could effectively serve you in these ways, you can go through the following instructions by using your Inner Shaman or your journal as a surrogate partner.

At first Frank was going to ask his wife to be his partner, but he decided that because she was already such a key figure in the areas he wished to change, it would be better to be accountable to someone else. It happened that he had a colleague who had recently joined a men's consciousness group and who was talking about many issues that were similar to those emerging while Frank was exploring his personal mythology. When he asked this colleague to serve as his partner, the man readily agreed.

"Behavioral contracts" are used to specify new behaviors that are associated with desired goals. They are statements of intent to perform specific, measurable actions that are steps toward reaching a goal. Behavioral contracts provide reinforcement for learning these behaviors and for beginning to make them habitual. In the behavioral contract, accountability becomes a form of support. The following ritual involves creating a behavioral contract. It gives structure to the way you will have your partner assist you.

You are to make a contract with your partner that specifies the actions you will take to begin to implement your new myth. Later you will review your experiences in attempting to fulfill the contract. You also will consider at that point what you learned from your efforts and how you might best revise the contract. A behavioral contract should propel you into the challenges of the new myth without overwhelming you with unreasonable expectations.

After discussing with your partner the possible actions you might take, label a new page of your journal "My Contract" and put the date at the top of the page. Each point in the contract should be specific, stating, if possible, *where, how, with whom,* and *when* you will carry out the action: "I will have spoken with Sheldon, Constance, and the guy from the Historical Society by Tuesday to identify at least four potential volunteer activities that would stimulate my intellect." Putting specifics in your contract provides you and your partner with criteria for evaluating the results of your efforts. While your behavioral contract may specify any areas you choose, it is particularly recommended that you focus on three topics already covered in this chapter: a daily ritual; making changes so your new myth will be reinforced more frequently; and monitoring your self-statements so that your new myth is better supported and your old myth is less frequently activated.

With your partner, review the experiences you have had to this point with your daily ritual. What has been valuable and what has not been valuable? Devise, with your partner, a personal ritual you are willing to carry out each day that will consistently reinforce your new myth in your subtle body and in your behavior. Frank enjoyed his morning stretching ritual but also found that it became mechanical when he did it every day. He decided that he would do the stretching ritual on his days off. On the way to work, he would contemplate his heart image and bring its energy to the spirit of his work and to the decisions he had to make that day.

Also review your List of Reinforcers with your partner. Assess what you have learned from your initial attempts to shift the positive and negative reinforcers that affect your new myth. With your partner, decide what other actions would strengthen one or more of the promoting forces and minimize or eliminate one or more of the inhibiting forces. Some features will seem easy to change and therefore good targets; others, although less accessible, may still seem important for your attention. Start with one or two areas. Describe a first step in bringing about a change. Because the contract will be updated on a regular basis, you need specify only initial steps that can be accomplished within a short period of time.

One of Frank's goals was to spend more time with his wife, whom he saw as the single person most likely to be able to provide effective support for his new myth. He decided his first step that week would be to go into work late on his wife's day off and to bring her to a restaurant for a leisurely breakfast. Shortly afterwards, he had an opportunity to take a more substantial action. He had been working two years to secure an account that would be very challenging to manage, extremely demanding, but also one that would pay well and offer high prestige. He had been ready to jump at the opportunity for a long time. But when he received the contract, he found that he was reluctant to sign it. He had the feeling that he was about to sign away all of the promises he had recently made to himself.

He decided to wait a few days and live with the implications of taking the project. He talked the issue over with his partner, the colleague who was in the men's group. They came up with what seemed to Frank to be a radical idea: He referred the account to the most prestigious investment firm in the area. The fact that he was in a position to be able to make that referral was a boost for his reputation and his standing in the professional community, so the move was not without some practical benefits. More important, in terms of his new mythology, it was a significant commitment to bringing more peace and intimacy into his life.

In addition to your personal ritual and your analysis of reinforcers, review with your partner the list of self-statements that support your old myth. What feelings, words, and behaviors on your part can serve as cues to signal that your old myth is operating? Write these items under the heading "Traces of My Old Myth." Become so familiar with these cues that whenever they occur, you will be likely to recognize them. Make a contract with your partner about what you will do when you become aware of one of these cues at a given moment. You might, for instance, use the thought-stopping technique described earlier and replace the old self-statement with a self-statement associated with your new myth.

Frank was determined to stop a pattern of piling one project on top of another in a way that crowded out any sense of accomplishment and pleasure. He identified the "endpoints" of various projects, and when he reached them, he would monitor the inner voice that automatically directed him to the next task at hand. He listed several simple rewards, ranging from taking a brief walk to watching a video to taking a day off from work, and whenever he reached an "endpoint," he would instruct himself to stop and treat himself to one of the activities on that list. He also decided that he had better get his partner's help in monitoring the self-statements he would use to evaluate his success with his behavioral contract. He agreed to measure his progress in the first week in terms of *any* new experiences that felt good to him, and he pledged to interrupt any thoughts about how much more he might have accomplished.

By the time you and your partner have completed the ritual of creating a contract, you will have identified several activities you plan to initiate. Your behavioral contract will specify concrete actions you can accomplish in the immediate future. Name names, indicate the number of times you will carry out an action, describe anticipated situations. Be so specific that when you and your partner review these plans, it will be clear which goals you accomplished. In making your contract, you and your partner should be particularly cautious about specifying steps that are too ambitious. Anticipate obstacles to successfully fulfilling the contract, and make plans about how to meet those obstacles when you encounter them. Arrange to meet with your partner again in about a week. Use the instructions in the following personal ritual to structure the way you and your partner review your attempts to support the new myth and to assess what can be learned from any obstacles that emerged.

An Ongoing Ritual: Creating a Feedback Loop as Your Mythology Evolves

In this ritual, you will create an active feedback loop as you begin to implement the new myth you have formulated. You will be drawing upon a technique called "action research."[9] Social scientists sometimes employ action research when helping community groups transform their goals and values into effective measures. You can use some of the basic principles contained in this method as you mobilize your intention to implement your new myth. Action research generally begins with a systematic assessment of a situation that needs to be changed. The central concept in action research is that ongoing feedback is critical for mobilizing effective action. Constructively changing a social system is not seen as a one-shot endeavor. Even the most carefully considered attempts are best viewed as practical research that produces information which can be used in planning subsequent action. After carefully defining precisely what changes are desired, action research proceeds through five basic stages: (1) fact-finding to assess possibilities for change and obstacles to change; (2) planning specific actions for bringing about the desired change; (3) carrying out this plan; (4) evaluating the results of the actions that were taken; and (5) feeding this information back to the individuals concerned in order to begin another round of the cycle.[10]

By the time you meet with your partner to review your progress, the first three stages already will have been completed. The action research model gives a structure for reviewing what has occurred and what to do next. Attempts at changing an established system are not expected to go exactly as planned, and the results of such attempts are used to gather new information. Future attempts can thus be revised and made more effective. In this way, an ongoing feedback loop is established: plans are made, action is taken, results are analyzed, and new plans are formulated. Outcomes are valued according to the learnings they produce as well as the actual changes they accomplish. We advise that you adopt this perspective in each of your review sessions with your partner. One of the most informative ways to understand your own mythic system is to make attempts to change it and observe what takes place.

A hazard of becoming aware of your counter-myth is that the counter-myth sometimes seems so appealing that there is a natural desire just to live according to it. Such leaps often meet with failure and discouragement, and when they do, they may have the paradoxical effect of strengthening the old myth. Going through the steps of this program provides an alternative that allows you to retain some of the promise and inspiration of the counter-myth, while integrating it into a well-considered myth that is more attainable. As you review your contract, you are likely to find areas in which you still have not struck a workable balance. Consider whether parts of your contract that you were unable to carry out were untenable because the new myth is not quite realistic or fitting for you. It is often necessary to make revisions in the myth from one meeting with your partner to the next. This is a natural and expected adjustment, and the action research model can help you to monitor areas where such changes are required.

Plan your first review meeting with your partner so it will include some ceremony and ritual—perhaps through the sharing of food or a special atmosphere. Consider which items from your contract you attempted to carry out and what resulted. What do these results suggest about future plans? How should the contract be revised? Also review the total process. Was the contract too ambitious? Or not challenging enough? Were you able to become motivated to carry it out? Did you and your partner correctly anticipate and plan for obstacles? Finally, remain alert to how the old myth may have influenced even the way you attempt to change it.

Frank's old myth caused him to be overly ambitious in envisioning his goals, and his contract was no exception. As he pushed toward meeting its terms, he found himself starting to approach the activities with a sense of drudgery. His plan to measure his progress according to small gains got lost in the shuffle. He was gaining little creative insight, and he was discouraged by the time of the first review. His partner, however, pointed out the way his old myth was trapping him and helped Frank recognize the pattern, see the irony in it, and ease back into the program. Noting how his self-discipline was stifling his passion even in this attempt to rekindle that passion, Frank revised his contract. He developed an image where he would "use my mind as a machete to carefully clear away the weeds in my life that are crowding out my passion, but I will not get so obsessed with clearing the weeds that there is no time to enjoy the garden." His second contract included fewer assignments, and required that he devote specified periods of time to savor the successful completion of each item.

With your partner, review your experiences in carrying out the first contract and, based on your new insights, create a second contract. Again, be as specific as possible in describing each task you agree to do, and decide when you will hold your next meeting. The action research model keeps your awareness attuned to your mythology as you express it in the world, and it fosters ongoing monitoring and adjustments. We suggest that you continue the process on a weekly basis, with your partner or in your journal, for as long as implementing the new myth seems important in your development.

Some people become discouraged at this point because they find it more difficult to fulfill their contracts than they had anticipated. Ask your partner to help you affirm the steps you have taken in expanding your awareness, and to use the action research perspective for revising your contract so it will be in closer correspondence with what you are actually able to accomplish. Even if you are just beginning to achieve changes in the desired directions, you are already living with a greater awareness of the mythic dimension of your inner life. Do not allow the complexities of implementing mythic changes in your outer life to obscure the importance of the inner changes you have already made. Also keep in mind that it is easier to articulate a new myth than it is to live it. We've not yet found a person who couldn't conceptualize a new mythology which, to some degree, resolved the underlying mythic conflict. That is basically a mental task. Integrating the new myth into your life, however, is a task that challenges your total personality, may push the limits of your environment, and will require sustained effort, experimentation, and awareness.

No human growth process moves in a neat and orderly sequence, such as the steps that can be identified for facilitating that process. The five-stage model you are now completing has assisted a wide range of individuals to encounter their mythic roots, but the system is only a tool to be adapted to your own pace and direction. Some people return to earlier stages of the program to repeat one of the rituals, such as the "Dialogue" or "Power Object." About six months after completing the program, Frank felt that he had reached a plateau and wanted to renew his focus. He reread his journal and decided to make a number of adjustments. He found a new Sequel for his Fairy Tale, and he repeated many of the subsequent rituals as well. The excerpts from his journal presented in these chapters were the most recent entries for each ritual.

In closing this guide to our five-stage model, we wish to emphasize that just as the development of your personal mythology is an unending process, you may use this five-stage approach any number of times. People who have gone through our workshops more than once have had vastly different experiences each time. You will also find ways to streamline and customize the approach as you become more familiar with the methods. It is not, for instance, necessary to create a new Personal Shield or Autobiography each time you explore a mythic conflict. The personal rituals are simply devices for turning inward and establishing a harmony between your efforts and the natural five-stage process by which myths develop. The more you use these methods, the more you will understand the principles behind them and be able to adapt them to a regular discipline of stepping back and focusing on how your mythology is unfolding. The following chapter will further crystallize your understanding of those principles. Your personal myths are an ongoing legacy from your past that extends into your future, and the more effectively you are able to attend to them, the richer that legacy will be for you.

7

Your Evolving Mythology

While in the life of the human race the mythical is an early and primitive stage, in the life of the individual it is a late and mature one. What is gained is an insight into the higher truth depicted in the actual; a smiling knowledge of the eternal, the ever-being and authentic.

—THOMAS MANN[1]

In the program you have just completed, you drew upon a mythological perspective as you reached toward a higher order of understanding. By bringing the clouding effects of limiting personal myths into your awareness, you have been increasing your power of inward choice. You have focused your energies toward resolving emotional conflicts that have kept you bound to outdated mythic images, and you are envisioning new directions for your future.

In this chapter, we present a theoretical framework to supplement the experiential understanding you developed as you worked with your personal mythology. We want to leave you with a scientifically informed perspective and explicit reference points as your mythology continues to evolve. We have synthesized pertinent psychological literature in formulating an overview of the four sources of personal myths, the four modes of myth-making, and the ways myths change over the course of life. The chapter closes with a review of the program from the vantage of the Inner Shaman and a synopsis of seven principles that govern the development of a personal mythology.

THE SOURCES OF YOUR PERSONAL MYTHOLOGY

Your mythology is the product of four interacting sources. Biology, culture, and personal history are the most obvious. A fourth source is rooted in transcendent experiences—those episodes, insights, dreams, and visions that have a numinous quality which seems to expand our comprehension and inspire our behavior. For Philip Wheelwright, "the very essence of myth" is "that haunting awareness of transcendental forces peering through the cracks of the visible universe."[2]

Biological Sources

Personal myths, like all mental representations, are coded in the cerebral cortex. The structure of your brain evolved through the millennia, and one of nature's greatest miracles is in the way the human brain came to support the complex processes that allow us to form mythological explanations of our experiences. Some researchers believe there is an area of the brain that instantly, and with no volition, constructs explanations of why a particular event or behavior occurred. According to neuropsychologist Michael S. Gazzaniga:

> We seem to be endowed with an endless capacity to generate hypotheses as to why we engage in any behavior. In short, our species has a special brain component I will call "the interpreter." Even though a behavior . . . can be expressed at any time during our waking hours, this special interpreter accommodates and instantly constructs a theory to explain why the behavior occurred. . . . This special capacity, which is a brain component found in the left dominant hemisphere of right-handed humans, reveals how important the carrying out of behaviors is for the formation of many theories about the self.[3]

Thus, the moment-by-moment creation of explanations, a rudimentary form of myth-making, appears to be a natural activity of the brain. The brain represents the world with verbal and pictorial symbols and employs narrative as it expands such explanations into personal myths. The capacities for explanation, symbolism, and narrative can carry you into the past or the future, transport you to nearby or faraway locations, and deliver you to realms imaginary or real. They are rooted in your biology and are building blocks for your ability to think mythically.

The patterns by which children learn to speak are so universal that a "deep structure," which determines the rules of grammar and the basic forms of language, is thought to be tied to the organization of the human brain.[4] Just as certain rules of grammar seem to be based

Your Evolving Mythology

on biological predispositions that make up the "deep structure" of language, it is likely that a "deep structure" of myth-making, which governs the patterns by which all people find guidance and meaning, also has a biological basis. The anthropologist Claude Lévi-Strauss contended that the patterns observed in cultural myths reveal a universal logic that is literally embedded in the "structure of the mind."[5]

Cultures spanning all ages and places have indeed developed myths and rituals whose configurations are similar. Carl Jung documented universal themes both in the artistic and literary legacies of various cultures and in the reveries and dreams of his clients.[6] He referred to these innate dispositions for specific kinds of thought and behavior as "archetypes," and he believed that they reflect a genetically coded maturational plan whose nature is revealed to consciousness through dreams, art, and other expressions of the inner self.

Archetypes serve as the "deep structures" of personal myths. Erich Neumann believed that archetypes are not only a "main constituent of mythology," but that they determine the growth and development of the individual's consciousness as well. "Consciousness evolves by passing through a series of 'eternal images,' and the ego, transformed in the passage, is constantly experiencing a new relationship to the archetype."[7] Neumann proposed that an innate sequence of archetypes unfolds to guide the psychological development of the individual from birth to maturity. As the principles of one archetype become outmoded and ineffectual, another archetype stands ready to assume the task of organizing experience and guiding the individual to the next stage of maturation. The Hero archetype, for instance, propels adolescents away from their associations with the Great Mother archetype, manifest in the home and family, and outward toward the world of self-determination. Thus the archetype that originally bonded the child to the mother is superseded by an archetype with the theme of separation and autonomy.

The notion of a genetic basis to the symbols that propel personal behavior and cultural themes has, not surprisingly, been controversial. The appearance of universal symbols in cultures separated by time and space is, nevertheless, difficult to explain, and evidence from such diverse fields as psychiatry, anthropology, ethology, and sociobiology has converged to lead some experts, such as psychiatrist Anthony Stevens, to suggest that archetypes "have been subject to the essentially biological processes of evolution no less than the anatomical and physiological structures [that] first established the truth of Darwin's theory."[8] Other explanations hold that archetypal images reflect a more subtle order of reality, a "collective unconscious" that the human brain can access in a manner analogous to the way a radio, depending on where it is tuned, can bring in Mozart's "Flute and Harp Concerto" or "Truckin' " by the Grateful Dead.

A more firmly established biological influence on your developing mythology is your temperament. Individual differences in such qualities as activity level, inclination toward approach or withdrawal, and intensity of reactions are observable within weeks of birth and retained into adulthood.[9] A person who is by temperament attuned to and more trusting of thoughts will create a very different mythology from another who is more oriented toward feelings. Mr. Spock of "Star Trek" and jolly old St. Nick will develop vastly dissimilar mythologies based on temperament alone. Temperament also influences which societal myths you will find agreeable. If, by temperament, you are quite introverted, you will enjoy greater serenity in a family whose mythology supports solitude than in one that pushes you into a high degree of social activity. The inherited effects of temperament may be highly specific. Identical twins, separated at birth and reunited several decades later, may find that they share the same favorite foods, drive the same style of car, and have married similar spouses.[10]

Physiological imbalances caused by drugs, brain injury, or hormonal irregularities have been implicated in depression, hyperactivity, and psychosis, and they can have an obvious impact on personal myths as well. Another factor in the development of your mythology is stress. Stress upsets the brain's chemical balance and may interfere with perception and thought. Because many of the critical decisions that shape personal myths are made under conditions of duress, it can be of great value to rework those decisions under more optimal conditions, just as you have been doing in this program.

Cultural Sources

Joseph Campbell described four basic human urges.[11] The impulse to eat (with the corresponding requirement that food must be killed because all life feeds on life) and the impulse to procreate are the two primal biological compulsions. A third, the motivation to conquer, "is not of any such primal urgency, but of an impulse launched from the eyes, not to consume, but to possess."[12] When not adequately channeled by the culture's myths and rites, these primal urges "become terrific, horrifying, and destructive."[13] The fourth urge, compassion, is also an impulse launched from the eyes rather than the immediate urgency of the organs. It appeared late in the evolution of species, yet the higher mammals already evidence compassion in their play and in the care of their young. A primary responsibility for the myths of a society is to direct these primal urges for the good of the community. Campbell notes that all mythological systems direct the "expansive faculty of the heart" toward the collective, "while deliberately directing outward every impulse toward violence."[14]

Human behavior, unlike that of most species, is regulated by symbols and internal speech rather than instinct. To a large extent, the words and images people generate for themselves are reflections of their culture's mythology. Imagine how differently a child growing up on the streets of the Bronx will think and feel compared to a child growing up in a Samoan village, the Kalahari Desert, or even upstate New York. Education, politics, business, religion, and family are among the institutions that instill the collective mythology into the individual's personal mythology. The family has first claim on molding the development of the individual's guiding mythology, and it provides a microcosm as the person unfolds into the wider community. A commentary from the *I Ching,* perhaps the oldest existing book on the planet, portrays the family as society in embryo: "It is the native soil on which performance of moral duty is made easy through natural affection, so that within a small circle a basis of moral practice is created, and this is later widened to include human relationships in general."[15]

According to Dennis Anderson and Steven Bagarozzi, who have investigated the clinical implications of family myths, families actively select and adopt as their own "those cultural myths whose various components and symbols have meaning and importance for each family member."[16] Certain themes will grow out of the family's unique history while others will be shared by most families within a culture. In industrialized countries, enormous emphasis has been placed upon acquiring material goods, as satirized by the bumper sticker "He Who Dies with the Most Toys Wins." Progress has been defined according to myths that emphasize the subjugation of nature, the accumulation of power and wealth, and the invention of technological marvels.

What seems natural in one culture may seem unnatural or even perverse to people who live by a different mythology. In the tradition of the Lakota Sioux, for example, our wanton exploitation of the environment is seen as a prophesied step toward the end of life as it has been known ("a thick cloud hangs over the people . . . many plants and animals will die").[17] Before the Chinese revolution, daughters of the noble classes had their feet bound, which ultimately rendered them unable to walk. The practice bestowed status because it accentuated the ownership of servants, who could carry the women where they wanted to go. Of course, it also ensured that the women were unable to roam. In the United States, high heels and tuxedos are required for many occasions where one expects to be served, and an endless series of fads from "hula hoops" to "pet rocks" became, in a brief moment of celebrity, compelling purchases for countless numbers of people. As a graffiti poet put it, "Culture is ubiquitous, that's why people act ridiculous." Customs that seem strange to an outsider are accepted without question within the culture and possess a symbolic significance that is perfectly sensible in the logic of the local mythology.

Anthropologist Edward Hall explains that the human nervous system is structured in such a way that the logic which governs behavior and perception comes into consciousness only when there is a "deviation from plan." This is why the most important "rules governing behavior, the ones that control our lives, function below the level of conscious awareness and are not generally available for analysis."[18]

Psychologist Charles Tart uses the term *consensus trance* to describe the habitual, automated manner of "normal" consciousness.[19] A characteristic of the consensus trance is "a retreat from ordinary sensory/instinctual reality to abstractions about reality."[20] Although we may like to think of ourselves as being free of automated behavior, the consensus trance is an integral part of efficient psychological functioning. It allows us to move through our days without the stress and strain of having to make methodical decisions for every option life presents. But, according to Tart, it also is a state of partially suspended animation that "involves a loss of much of our essential vitality."

The consensus trance reflects the assumptions that are embedded in the culture's mythology. Its contour is, for each individual, shaped by a personalized adaptation of the society's unquestioned assumptions. The consensus trance is induced in part through continual exposure to the mythic images reflected in the culture's institutions, laws, art, and folkways. It embodies the hidden assumptions that are at the basis of our understanding of the world, and it programs much of our behavior. Just as people who are hypnotized still can carry on a conversation, get a drink of water, or sing a popular song, most people ordinarily function quite well within the restricted awareness of the consensus trance. Members of a social group usually do not realize the limitations of the group's world view because it is all they have known, and those around them operate within a similar structure. In these ways, cultural myths serve to define the boundaries of our awareness, often banishing novel perceptions, intuitions, and thoughts to the far corners of the psyche.

Hall emphasizes that it is not that we should "be in synch with, or adapt to" our culture, but that cultures "grow out of synch with" the people they are there to serve. He targets bureaucracies as a major "stumbling block on the road to the future." In Hall's view, "We have enshrined organization at the expense of the individual, and in so doing forced the individual into molds that are not appropriate."[21] He suggests that the times compel us to learn to transcend our culture and embark "on the difficult journey beyond culture."[22] He believes that "the greatest separation feat of all is when one manages to gradually free oneself from the grip of unconscious culture."

To accomplish this, Hall proposes that we obtain greater exposure to other cultures in order to more fully recognize, as well as transcend, our own. In fact, he tells us that to survive, all cultures need one another. It is indeed an extraordinary turn of history that so many cultures can cross-fertilize one another to the extent that is now possible. This, Hall believes, is the key to taking the critical step "beyond culture."

This book has presented another approach for freeing yourself "from the grip of unconscious culture." Rather than traveling to other lands to obtain a perspective on your cultural myths, you have embarked upon an inner voyage with a mythic itinerary. By increasing your familiarity with the deep world of your own mythology, you gain a basis for making comparisons with the mythology expressed by your culture, and thus a vantage point for attaining a new perspective on it. While myths that have been programmed by biology, culture, and personal experience are not easy to change, when you come to understand the role they are playing in your life, you increase your ability to chart your own destiny. Through the personal rituals in this program, you have acquired a vehicle for temporarily peering beneath your personalized version of the consensus trance, examining the assumptions of the mythology that shaped it, and beginning to transform that mythology.

Personal History

From birth onward, you accumulate a legacy of experiences, some of which are formative in your evolving mythology. Certain episodes, such as winning a mathematics contest, being invited to the prom by the class president, or getting fired from a job, can be pivotal to your developing identity. Critical incidents are particularly formative in the lives of children. The child's identity depends on the answers given to such questions as "Who am I?" "What is the meaning of my early memories?" "What is my place in the adult world?" and "What will I do in the future?" An adolescent's "identity crisis" reworks these answers. And the adult "midlife crisis" takes the person yet further into more refined and subtle levels of these questions.[23]

According to object relations theory, a contemporary revision of Freud's psychology, infants initially regard the world and everything in it as a part of themselves.[24] As they become able to make a distinction between themselves and the environment, the realms of "I" and "not-I," self-relations and object relations are created. These internal representations of self and environment establish the core models around which the child's mythology will be elaborated.

Object relations theorists are particularly concerned with the relationship between the incomplete accomplishment of childhood developmental tasks and many of the psychological problems of adults. When you are in a situation that arouses an emotionally charged internal representation of issues from your past, your perceptions and behavior are affected. You tend to unconsciously project certain memories, feelings, and beliefs into such circumstances. If your mother was extremely critical and you meet someone who reminds you of her, the internal representations you project onto that person may cause you to be defensive, submissive, or hostile. Your choice of a mate may *have to* correspond with a certain hair coloring, voice tone, or tendency to dominate, though the model may be outside your awareness. We project both our internal conflicts and our fondest dreams onto the canvas of our outer lives.

Stephen Johnson, a psychologist who integrates object relations theory with approaches that focus on the way emotional conflicts become lodged in the body, emphasizes the human organism's need for self-expression.[25] Character type is related to the way parents and other significant people in our early years support or thwart our self-expressions: assertion of our right to exist, to satisfy our needs, to become independent from others, and to express love. Inevitably, there were some ways the environment suppressed our expressions of self, and there were other ways that we were punished for what we did express. As children, we had to cope with or attempt to evade these constraints. Where we did not succeed, we felt threatened, rejected, or stifled, and reacted with anger, fear, or grief. In response to these feelings, we created compromises by suppressing our need for autonomy, denying our needs for nourishment and support, or holding back our need to give and receive love. To maintain these strategies for coping, we may have adopted illusions about the world and integrated these illusions into our evolving mythology.

Many of the myths developed in childhood determine the way we live in the world. If your accommodation to a harsh parent was to deny your feelings, you may have unwittingly come to experience the world through your intellect. Your internal representations would be relatively void of the feeling dimension. If your accommodation was to be placating or overly compliant, your internal model may portray you as being inadequate to manage your own affairs and guide you to live through other people. If your accommodation was to turn your anger against yourself, you may consistently represent yourself as unworthy and be unjustly self-punishing.

Your initial adjustment to frustrated needs and potentials is at the core of your mythology and also reflects itself in your body. According to some psychotherapists, "all unresolved emotional conflicts become structured in the body in the form of chronic muscular tensions" that affect outlook and behavior.[26] Johnson describes how in people who were deprived of physical or emotional nourishment, the natural rage at deprivation may be "held back, literally in the jaw, throat and arms, while the eyes often betray the very real longing which the person experiences unconsciously."[27] In people who were adequately nourished but whose autonomy was thwarted—where the parent withdraws attention, support, or approval when the child expresses independence—the body is often undeveloped, undercharged, and characterized by restricted movement and breathing. Children whose parents expected too much of them may have been unable to come to terms with their own limitations, resulting in a "puffed-up" quality in the head and upper chest, as if the body were trying to live up to the false self-image in posture and musculature.[28] In people whose will was crushed by a controlling parent, the muscles of the face, throat, neck, thighs, and pelvic floor may be chronically constricted in a manner that blocks direct assertion, while the eyes reveal prolonged suffering.

Your personal mythology reflects the psychological adjustments you made to adapt to the circumstances you faced in your early years, and it is revealed in your body and your style of life. As you mature, your mythology evolves in tandem. Your ability to successfully respond to the ongoing challenges that life presents increases as your mythology becomes more flexible, balanced, and complete.

Transcendent Experiences

Some experiences engender awesome feelings, radiant insights, remarkable healings, or exceptional performances. They take us beyond our ordinary sense of existence. Such moments of transcendence may occur during meditation, prayer, or intensive psychotherapy.[29] They may result from viewing a newborn baby or an awesome work of art, hearing an inspirational sermon or piece of music, or making intimate contact with one's child or one's beloved. A funeral, a personal "near-death" episode (recall Fred's story described in chapter 1), or a graduation ceremony also may elicit such experiences. They may occur in a dream, in a desert, or on a crowded street. A superior performance during a sports event may accompany a sense of transcending one's ordinary limitations. The rapid recovery from a disease may follow a vision that filled life with a renewed sense of purpose.

Carl Jung emphasized that spiritual questions are especially important during the second half of a person's life, but transcendent experiences may have a definitive effect at any point. At least fifty percent of those Americans surveyed have reported experiences in which they felt a shift onto a level of reality that brought them spiritual insights, revelations of a deeper truth, or contact with something sacred.[30] Transcendent experiences vary in their strength and significance. Their most profound form is in the full-blown mystical or religious experience; such experiences may be described as "bliss," "rapture," "ecstasy," "satori," "nirvana," or "enlightenment." William James examined the impact of such experiences and reported that "mystical states of a well-pronounced and emphatic sort *are* usually authoritative over those who have them. . . . Mystical experiences are as direct perceptions of fact for those who have them as any sensations ever were for us."[31] While transcendent experiences, for most people, are not an everyday occurrence, when they do take place, they are deeply felt and often have a significant effect on the individual's developing mythology.

Transcendent experiences may reveal archetypal images, and they can shift a personal myth within moments. An atheist may become a believer; a miser may become a humanitarian; an alcoholic may renounce drinking; a misogynist may become a feminist. The new personal myth may be fragile and persist only a few days or continue throughout a lifetime. Experiences that transcend ordinary consciousness may take a violent turn and produce mass murderers who claim their actions were "dictated by God," or they may evoke an outpouring of great art, music, poetry, or prose. Such experiences are more likely to have long-lasting effects on your mythology when you can find an explanatory framework for them within your culture or reference group, when they are compatible with other myths you hold, and when their guidance leads to concrete results that demonstrate their validity.

When a transcendent episode occurs, the individual is challenged to incorporate into his or her existing mythology the new understandings or inspiration that the episode bestowed. Mother Teresa recounts an occasion as a young nun and schoolteacher, riding on a train in India, when she "heard God" tell her that her life's work was to bring love to the poorest of the poor. The basis of such experiences has been vehemently debated. But they cannot properly be reduced to conventional conceptions of biology, and they appear to transcend culture and personal history. Mother Teresa's experience on that train ride was more than just a product of her upbringing and education. She did not simply *think* that she should help the poor, or *feel* that she should work with the impoverished. Like many saints before her, she had an electrifying sense of spiritual guidance that dramatically set her life on an unpaved course that has inspired millions.

A moral and spiritual realm that transcends sensory knowledge is discernible in every human society and stands at the very heart of each culture's mythology. The transcendent experiences of inspired leaders often provide a culture with its most compelling knowledge about this realm. Buddha, Lao-tzu, and Zoroaster, the first reported sages who claimed to attain a spiritual "oneness" with creation, lived about six hundred years before the Christian era, but the impact of the transcendent experiences that shaped their lives still reverberates in cultures around the world.

Interactions Among the Sources

All four of these sources interact as your mythology evolves. Certain biological inheritances that might be of minor consequence, such as facial features, skin color, or breast size, may take on great significance in your mythology if your culture defines them as either signs of beauty or inferiority. Powerful experiences from your past may have been etched into your physiology. A character trait such as a highly emotional style of expression may be rewarded in some families, leading to a strong sense of personal worth, while it may be severely penalized in other families, resulting in a personal mythology that is self-negating. Particular temperaments are more suited to one economic or political system than another. Some cultures, for instance, expect individuals to take initiative and distinguish themselves, while others expect each person to blend in and never call forth "comment from his neighbors."[32] Mystical experiences, characterized by their ineffable nature, are usually interpreted largely within the symbolism of the person's prior religious and cultural beliefs.

The way that romantic love typically develops illustrates the interplay of the four sources of personal myths. Physiological responses to odor, sight, touch, and sounds are strongly conditioned by the culture's images of beauty and attractiveness. The overbearing role of romantic considerations in an adolescent's perceptions and interests is fueled by a stampede of hormones. All this occurs within the culture's implicit and explicit models of romantic love, which are continually offered, often in conflicting form, through such institutions as school, church, screen, and song. The relationship between your parents also provided a tangible model (or counter-model) of love. Interactions with your opposite-sex parent further shaped your understanding of how males and females relate. Each new involvement that had erotic overtones, and each observation of other people who were intimately involved with one another, may have contributed to or revised your expectations regarding romantic love.

The first experience of "falling in love" is usually rich in sensual and emotional stimulation. It may shatter all previous images, or raise them to a more profound level. But the contrast between the ethereal feelings accompanying a new love relationship and the practical difficulties involved in blending your life with another's usually requires your mythology to undergo further and sometimes drastic revision. In the case of romantic love, as well as life's other adventures and ordeals, the four sources of your myths work together, sometimes provoking conflict and sometimes bringing harmony as your understanding of your self and your world progresses.

MODES OF MYTH-MAKING

The four sources also work together in establishing the dominant modes you will use in the myths you construct. We have identified four basic modes of myth-making, which can be called the visionary, aesthetic, rational, and compassionate modes.[33] The modes used in creating a myth are reflected in the character of the myth. Each of us is unique not only in the *content* of our personal mythology, but also in the *manner* by which we create it. We each utilize a particular combination of the four modes in formulating our myths. Myths differ not only in the information they are conveying, but also according to the mode by which they organize and convey it. We would go so far as to say that it is such differences in mode that make human communication so difficult not only among people of widely disparate cultures but between intimates who speak the same language and have similar backgrounds.

A given personal myth may be created through any of the modes (visionary, aesthetic, rational, and compassionate) or any combination of them. Each mode holds potential strengths and liabilities. For most people, one or two modes dominate in the myths they produce. They trust these modes more, feel compatible with them, and intuitively know how to use them.

The *visionary mode* is oriented toward seeing possibilities and envisioning how to achieve them. It is the most future-oriented mode. Visionary myths are created around a guiding image. The image reflects the person's hopes, ideals, and values. It points the way to a better future according to those values. The myth may express itself in mental pictures, internal dialogue, or an intuitive "knowing." It often involves a complex scenario that determines choices and directs passionate behavior. The kind of mythology created in this mode is exemplified by the visionary political leader. When Martin Luther King, Jr., announced, "I have a dream," he was etching a social vision that guided political change.

Most people express some degree of the visionary dimension in the personal myths that direct their major choices about career and family. It is through this dimension that the myth orients you to where you are going in your life and shows you how to get there. For some, however, this mode may be vague and indistinct, while for others it may provide a detailed blueprint that is adhered to rigidly. When the visionary dimension is too faint, the myth fails to direct you toward actions that actualize your values. When it is too dominant, the myth keeps you trapped within the limits of its vision, obscuring other possibilities and making it difficult for you to adjust it to new information or open yourself to the vision of others. You may have found through your work in the program that guiding images which you once barely perceived have become stronger and more distinct. Or you may have found that images which once firmly governed your choices were challenged and perhaps discredited. Your guiding images were probably strengthened by the program if you are less developed in the visionary mode, and softened if it is a more dominant mode for you.

Myths created primarily in the *aesthetic mode* have an artistic quality. They place a high value on experiences that gratify the person's sensibilities. With a strong aesthetic dimension, the myth itself becomes a work of art that is pleasing to the myth-maker, and life, too, is experienced as a work of art. An extreme example of this mode would be the consummate artist Salvador Dali, who has lived each day as if he were creating an artistic masterpiece and performed each action as if he were in a theatrical drama. Most people who have gone through our program have found that the very act of examining and working with their personal myths enhances their aesthetic appreciation of the mythology they are living out.

A mythology sparse in the aesthetic dimension doesn't nourish your higher sensibilities, nor does it draw upon them in providing you with guidance. The whole enterprise of living is more drab when it is untouched by the aesthetic realm. If this mode is too dominant, however, you may find yourself responding so strongly to what you encounter that the disagreeable elements are amplified many times and you become obsessed with them. You may find it difficult to listen to a neighbor whose voice is too shrill. You may find yourself unable to let go of judgments against yourself or others for minor trespasses, and you may hear devastating criticism where constructive suggestions are being offered. Whatever is discordant is experienced as acutely adversive. As you examined your mythology, you may have found that you were able to identify ways that you characteristically lose your direction by becoming caught in your reactions to what you encounter. If so, a desired outcome of the program would be to bring your aesthetic responses into a better balance with the other modes.

The *rational mode* brings logic to your mythology: the logic of abstraction and generalization, classification and analysis, and cause-effect relationships. It allows you to order your experiences and draw conclusions. It clears a path into uncharted territory that is based upon the knowledge that can be garnered from the terrain you and others have already explored. The power inherent in the rational mode has brought us to the moon and led us to the edge of nuclear cataclysm. A mythology dominated by this mode will reach for the most effective way to pursue whatever we desire, regardless of consequences to which we may be blind. The rational mode is exemplified by brilliant scientists, such as Linus Pauling, who applied judicious logic to pursuits ranging from analyzing the structure of amino acids (which led to his receiving the Nobel Prize for Chemistry) to challenging the testing of nuclear weapons (for which he won the Nobel Peace Prize).

If your mythology is weak in the rational dimension, the conclusions you derive from your experiences will be misleading. Your desires, choices, and behaviors will be based on inaccurate generalizations, selective abstractions, and arbitrary inferences. If the rational mode is overly dominant in your mythology, you may be so fully absorbed in your logical construction of reality that you will miss many other dimensions of life. A narrow rationality may eclipse the realms of feeling and values, as can be seen at the community level where businesses and bureaucrats have overlooked ecological issues, traditional folkways, and the quality of life. You may also be so certain about the correctness of positions rooted in your system of logic that you are unable to comprehend the legitimate strengths of other positions. In examining your own mythology, you may have realized that your logic is frequently overwhelmed by your feelings; you may have come to understand your past in a way that contradicted some of the premises of your guiding mythology; or you may have found that you frequently become paralyzed in conflict between your head and your heart. In any of these cases, you were attending to the rational mode of your mythology.

In the *compassionate mode,* the mythology prompts empathy and elevates it to a guide for action and planning. Empathy that is strongly developed by such a mythology allows a seemingly effortless ability to touch others in ways that matter to them. The mythology supports wholesome relationships and makes them more probable. In their empathy and concern for others, people whose myths are strong in compassion instinctively seed understanding and goodwill in the community. Saintly persons such as Florence Nightingale and Albert Schweitzer exemplify this mode.

People whose mythologies are weak in the empathic dimension tend to be self-absorbed and disengaged from the concerns of others. Their plans and actions are less effective because they cannot accurately assess the feelings of other people. They relate to others as objects and are unable to enjoy the intimacy of equality in a relationship. But for those whose mythology is inundated with compassion unbalanced by the other modes, the urge to respond to other people's needs and pains may be overwhelming. They may be compelled to orient their lives around the needs of others, sometimes losing themselves in the process. In reviewing your personal history, you may have identified times when your mythology led you to be too empathic or not empathic enough. Ask yourself whether your new myth attempts to better attune you to others' needs and feelings, or reminds you to consider your own needs before responding reflexively to those of others.

Achieving a balance among these modes is a core developmental task of adult life. As the modes become more balanced, your mythology becomes more versatile and reliable. The complexity of interactions among the modes is complicated, however, because some modes operate outside of awareness. Competing personal myths may also have been constructed within different modes, perhaps at different times of life. A prevailing myth may have been formed primarily in the visionary mode, while a newly spawned counter-myth, still barely recognized, is primarily a product of the compassionate mode. As you work through the maze of inevitable conflicts between myths with which you identified earlier in your life and emerging myths that pioneer less developed aspects of your personality, your effectiveness and sense of integration will increase as well.

PERSONAL MYTHS ACROSS THE LIFE SPAN

The nature of your personal mythology depends upon your characteristic modes of myth-making, the influence the larger culture exerts upon you, and your point of development in the life cycle. The central issues of your personal myth-making activities are vastly different when you are young than when you are older.[34] Churchill is said to have commented wryly on this subject: "The man who is not a liberal when he is twenty has no heart, and the man who is not a conservative when he is forty has no brain." Just as biological development passes through a continuous series of changes from womb to tomb, the myths we create evolve through a succession of changes from infancy to old age.

Freud outlined a sequence of psychosexual developments in early life, and Erik Erikson described a subsequent progression of psychosocial stages that extend into maturity and old age. Erikson thought of development as a succession of predictable psychosocial crises that he identified in children (trust vs. mistrust, autonomy vs. shame, initiative vs. guilt, industry vs. inferiority), followed through maturity (identity vs. identity confusion, intimacy vs. isolation, generativity vs. stagnation), and ultimately into old age (integrity vs. despair).[35] The hard-earned mythic lessons accumulated during one stage of development are often painfully inadequate and therefore misleading in the next stage. Individuals are forced to grapple in new ways with the requirements and the potentials of their biology, culture, and unique life circumstances.

Robert Kegan uses the symbol of a spiral in his model of "the evolving self," portraying the way people move beyond and then return to certain core issues as they develop.[36] As you go up the spiral, you come to the same issues again and again, but from different vantage points. If, as a child, you made an uneasy peace with people in authority, you may well find, at different points in your life, that you are challenged by issues related to authority, although perhaps at increasingly subtle and refined levels. Familiar difficulties recur, but at a higher level on the spiral. Your evolving mythology, circling from prevailing myth to counter-myth to new myth, corresponds with this pattern. Learning does not cease. As you look backward and detect the spiral pattern, you will see your progress.

In Kegan's scheme, you will for a time be psychologically embedded in the issues of a particular developmental stage. When you progress beyond it, you come to a higher level on the developmental spiral and are presented with new tasks and challenges.[37] The adolescent's evolving identity is immersed in the opinions and judgments of peers, which shape attitudes such as those toward sex, drug use, and school. Eventually, however, teenagers must formulate personal myths that step beyond those of their age mates and are more suited to their unique experiences. Later, as young adults, tasks involving family and career become the preoccupation in further developing one's identity. With a seasoned psychological maturity, the focus of the personal mythology is broadened from primarily individual concerns to include the wider community, responsibility to generations yet unborn, and more comprehensive ethical considerations.

Personal myths may reach points of crisis around any of life's developmental junctures. While other themes are still being worked through, the issues concerning certain developmental questions become "front-page news" during a particular phase of life.[38] The following cases illustrate how one woman's personal mythology shifted concerning her relationship to childbearing, and another's concerning her own mortality.

The first involves an unusually dramatic episode in an extended therapy group. Nancy, a nineteen-year-old lesbian, believed that the transition in her identity during adolescence from heterosexual to homosexual was essentially completed, although she wished to work on underlying feelings of confusion and anger in relationship to her family's rejection of her life-style. Her overriding concerns at the time of the group, however, focused on severe pain in the area of her right ovary and fear of surgery because a medical examination a few days earlier had revealed a growth at that site.

She asked for help with the intense fear she felt around the physical disruption. Initially, the group leader had no intention of exploring any emotional basis of her tumor, hoping, rather, to assist her in relieving some of the tension that seemed to be aggravating the pain. Her presenting problem involved somatic complaints, and a body-based therapeutic approach was used. The events of the subsequent two and a half hours spontaneously revealed the possible involvement of a mythic conflict in the development of her tumor and apparently marked its reversal.

She was asked to lie down on a mat, breathe deeply, and visualize each inhalation traveling to the site of the pain while, with each exhalation, the therapist's hand exerted pressure on her diaphragm. This is a fairly common procedure in body-oriented psychotherapy, which establishes the support of physical contact and sometimes induces a spontaneous release of chronic tension and a flooding of feelings. She was encouraged to make a sound with each exhalation, which was the beginning of an intensive emotional release, resembling at various points an exorcism, death wails, and childbirth.

She reached a crescendo of deep convulsive screaming that was accompanied by a long series of spasmodic movements originating in her abdomen. As these began to subside after a substantial expenditure of energy, her face spontaneously distorted, and she raised her head, neck, and upper back. With her hands six inches from either ear and her fingers so tightly contorted that they almost looked webbed, she elicited a deep hissing sound, all of which was distinctly reminiscent of the possessed adolescent portrayed in the movie *The Exorcist.* A fearsome voice that seemed incongruous with this young woman was loudly hissing the words, "You will have your baby!"

This sort of "possession" by a repressed aspect of the personality is not particularly unusual in such work. As the raging voice continued expressing itself, its theme never varied. The forceful expression seemed to build to the maximum her body could tolerate, finally culminating with her vomiting into a bucket. This was followed by deep sobbing that gradually led to a buildup of sensation in her legs and pelvis. As her feet pushed down into the mat, her body took the posture of a woman giving birth. She struggled with this for some time until there was a cathartic release and she triumphantly lifted an imaginary baby over her head. She was asked to talk with the image and give the image a voice so a dialogue could be established. As she began, she appeared to be increasingly identified with the baby, finally letting her hands down and "becoming" the baby, assuming a fetal position, gurgling, and urinating.

After some time, an aura of peacefulness surrounded her as she gradually returned to her ordinary state of consciousness. She was asked to speak to her tumor and then give the tumor a voice and carry on a conversation. This became a lengthy and moving process in which she came to view her tumor as an expression of an inner desire toward becoming a mother, a wish she had been suppressing in the service of her homosexual identity. She attributed such statements as "I have to be born!" and "You are my mother!" to the tumor. She reached a point where the rage she had been feeling toward the tumor transformed into an acceptance and even an appreciation of the information it was providing about her deeper desires. She then felt equipped to deal with the conflict at a conscious level.

It is interesting to compare this account with Nancy's personal reflections on the experience in a journal entry made some time after the group meeting:

> I felt that being a heterosexual meant having babies. Having babies meant being heterosexual. Being an adolescent and being torn about my sexuality created what felt like a tear in my body. A wound. The wound was in my ovary. My struggle manifested itself in a tumor.
>
> Part of me wanted even then to be fertile. My experience at the workshop was a combination exorcism/birth. There was hate and anger from years of repressing that came out in the form of a face. A red, ugly, hideous face that appeared to me during the most painful moments. I felt like this was my fear conjured up and personified in an image. The image was a monster with teeth who cut me and penetrated me. I was raped by this demon and my rage/tumor was the outcome.
>
> The other image I had during that time was of giving birth to myself. I felt like this was the beginning of my being able to nurture and love myself as a helpless child. The birth was a cleansing, a purity.

The pain had subsided markedly by the end of the session and did not return. Interestingly, a sonogram administered a few days after the session revealed a three- to four-centimeter growth on the site of the ovary, which her physician insisted was an ectopic pregnancy until she convinced him that this was not possible. Within a few weeks the growth had completely disappeared and a five-year follow-up showed no recurrence.[39] While it is unusual for longings that are being repressed by a personal mythology to break through and be integrated in so brief a period, this scenario illustrates the potent forces that can be unleashed when a core area of one's mythology, such as a woman's relationship to childbearing, has been inadequately resolved.

Dealing with the inevitability of death is another issue that begs for creative attention as your mythology evolves. Particularly in a culture that venerates youthful qualities while desperately attempting to escape aging and death, the panic about approaching old age can be overwhelming. Staying focused on the values and aspirations appropriate to youth does not lead to the graceful wisdom of old age seen in cultures whose mythology supports a dignified role for the elderly.

We are all required to live a mythology that is fitting for our stage in life. As Jung put it, "We cannot live the afternoon of life according to the programme of life's morning." Meg had an experience, shortly after completing our program, that became a dominant feature as she worked out her own mythology concerning aging and death.

> Traveling in Northern California, alone, on my birthday, filled with reverence and awe after hiking through a redwood grove, I had a vision of my own death. Laying face down on the cool, fragrant humus of needles and ferns, a shaft of light penetrates the indescribably sacred grove and falls on me. There is a dark square of redwood forest with four guardian trees at the cardinal points. I envision a grave hollowed out among the roots without disturbing them. The roots form an angular cradle. Three men and a woman carry me toward the cavity. One man is my husband, tender, thin, and old. Another is a beloved friend. The third's face is an unrecognizable shadow. The woman is a lovely young stranger.
>
> I know that I am ninety-four. My hair is downy white and my face is brown and wrinkled, like a friendly walnut. My eyes are alert and unafraid. I am dressed in a loose nondescript gown and I have a lemon-yellow scarf around my neck. All my fleshiness used up, my body is light and nearly transparent. There is little of substance left of who I was. They lay me in the cradle of roots and we smile, one at a time at one another. It is clear there is no anguish here. I rest on my earthly cradle and look up at the splendid trunks of the trees. I smell the pungent dampness. My breath leaves my body for the last time. A squirrel runs out on a limb, excitedly, and drops a cone into my bed.

She later wrote about the place that this vision came to have in her life:

> It is not clear to me how much of this mythic revelation is made from fragments of dreams, wish-fulfillment, denial, or sacred vision and time warp. I no longer care. Having been granted such a gratifying hallucination, delusion, holy intuition, or reverie, I find it wisest to believe. I choose, as an educated woman, to keep that myth out in front of me. Because I believe that I will die as envisioned in the forest, I greatly enhance my opportunity to have a good death. Even if I am wrong, I am making my present infinitely more tolerable. If I start thinking of myself as a charred body in Armageddon, I am certainly destroying my present, and I may be contributing to making it happen—nothing productive comes from

> it, there is no good in it. If people didn't get any more rarified than that, than to give themselves a vision of a good death, that could affect all kinds of things: what you eat, the kinds of stress you put yourself under, all the things you have to do to give yourself a good death.

New mythic issues of richer fiber and greater subtlety are poised to arise at each succeeding stage of adult life. You are required to have attained some level of completion with the questions of previous stages to be able to attune yourself to the subtleties of the next. Our program attempts to help you look in both directions, ushering fresh effort into what is not yet completed and sensitively uncovering what is emerging. Here we review the program and the concepts that have been presented. First, a summary of the program is presented from the perspective of the Inner Shaman.

RESPONSIBILITIES OF THE INNER SHAMAN REVIEWED

Just as tribal shamans preserved, transmitted, and transformed their cultures' myths, you have examined the historical roots of your own mythology, learning to recognize how your myths affect your life. From this probing, you have challenged and started to change some of them. In chapter 1, your Inner Shaman was depicted as the personification of inner qualities that could be developed to assist in the evolution of your personal mythology. Three basic responsibilities of the tribal shaman, and corresponding abilities of your Inner Shaman, were discussed. Many of the rituals in the program invoked your Inner Shaman or addressed one of these three areas.

The tribal shaman's first responsibility was to ensure that a connection was maintained between Ordinary Reality and the sacred realities of the Upper and Lower Worlds. Thus uncommon knowledge and powers could be tapped for socially useful purposes. In a manner resembling the procedures used by these shamans to obtain information from the Other Worlds, you have learned to tap into the powers of your unconscious mind and solicit images from the deeper recesses of your psyche. The Paradise and Resolution fantasies, the seeking of confirmation from the "Powers That Be," the dreamwork, and the healing journeys resemble shamanic practices in the way they provide a passage between your waking consciousness and the Other Worlds of your deeper self. The rituals in which you followed a feeling to different time periods are reminiscent of shamanic flights to other realms. Shamans were well aware that every vision they encountered in an altered state of consciousness could not be trusted. Shamanic lore emphasizes the possibility of being deceived or misled by harmful or immature spirits. It counsels that critical judgment is an ally when entering the Other Worlds. As a modern seeker who does not answer to the external authority of a tribal shaman, you are challenged to marshal both your intuition and the power of your rational mind to weigh your intuitive revelations.

The second responsibility of the native shaman was to lead members of the tribe in applying the guiding mythology to new circumstances. You started the program by identifying guiding myths that you could no longer productively apply to your circumstances. You went through a series of personal rituals to systematically revise one of those myths, and in the final stage of the program, you began to apply that new myth to the circumstances in your life. Just as traditional shamans attempted to use their allies in the Upper and Lower Worlds to help and heal individuals, your Inner Shaman helped you to look within for strength in supporting your new direction. The ceremonial enactments of your new myth, the cultivation of self-statements to support it, and the behavioral contract to maintain it are allies that can help empower your new myth.

The third responsibility of the shaman was to assist the tribe in altering a guiding mythology that was failing. When the sea or river no longer yielded fish, when dissension broke out among the people, or when neighboring tribes posed a threat, the shaman was called upon to journey to the Other Worlds, seeking a vision that could revitalize the mythology where it seemed to have lost its power. The shaman lived at the meeting point between tradition and social inventions, guarding tradition but offering new mythic images to society when necessary. The rituals that examined conflicts in your mythology and traced them back to their sources were designed to adjust your developing mythology to the realities of who you have become and the circumstances you face. When you identified your counter-myth, you performed the shamanic function of discerning a new vision and a new direction. The dramatized dialogues allowed you to submit your counter-myth to the lessons of the past before committing yourself to its vision. Your personal Fairy Tale also mediated between the past and the possible, concluding with the portrayal of a new myth that cast off self-defeating elements of the old myth and unrealistic aspects of the counter-myth while incorporating the most positive elements of each.

Tribal shamans, in fulfilling their responsibilities, would make extensive use of body consciousness. In some of their visions, shamans reported that the body became a battleground for the conflict between spirits that would tear them apart and spirits that would piece them together again. They believed that they could transform their bodies into animal and bird forms, and that they could rely on bodily sensations to diagnose illness. While you have not undertaken any task so dramatic in this program, you have identified analogues of your mythic conflict in your body, and you have worked with your "subtle body" in fostering your new myth.

Traditional shamans cultivated a highly disciplined attention. Their abilities to alter their consciousness, travel to other realms of reality, and channel spirit voices were exquisitely developed. You were asked to develop a disciplined attention as well. This discipline will assist you as you work with your dreams, focus upon the significance of bodily sensations, and quiet your mind to attain a fresh perspective that goes beyond the limitations of unexamined myths. Your Inner Shaman can continue to serve as a wise inner witness who, after intimate examination of the way your myths operate, opens you to new possibilities.

PRINCIPLES OF YOUR EVOLVING MYTHOLOGY

Throughout this book, we have offered explanations of the way your personal mythology develops. These principles are summarized here to reinforce your learning in the program and to leave you with a synopsis that you can draw on as you continue to work with your evolving mythology.

Emergence from the mythic premises in which you have been psychologically embedded, and movement to another set of guiding images, is a natural and periodic phase of personal development. Personal myths exist within a psychological ecology of mutation and selection in which even the "fittest" mythic structures must continually evolve if they are to serve us. Not only do circumstances continually change but new developmental tasks also appear throughout adult life. Personal myths that were appropriate and effective during one period of life or at one level of development become inappropriate or dysfunctional at another. As myths grow outmoded, they fail to support your psychological, social, and spiritual needs, and they begin to restrict your emotional development. Psychological growth often requires a shift to a more advanced mythology. The surrounding culture's attitudes regarding such changes, and the rites of passage it provides or fails to provide for supporting them, may promote or inhibit your ability to successfully move through such periods of transition.

Personal conflicts—both in your inner life and external circumstances—are seen as natural markers of these times of transition. When a prevailing mythic structure no longer serves your needs, alternative structures are generated naturally and begin to be revealed in dreams and other windows into unconscious processes. Psychological defenses, however, may prevent you from recognizing features of your experience that are incompatible with the dominant myth, even as it becomes less capable of providing valid guidance. In maintaining a myth that is failing, you will tend to experience increasing conflict that permeates your feelings, thoughts, actions, dreams, fantasies, and the circumstances you draw to yourself. If you treat such difficulties as markers of transition, rather than simply resisting them, you can better mobilize your energies for understanding and resolving the underlying mythic conflict.

On one side of the underlying mythic conflict will be a self-limiting myth rooted in past experience that is best understood in terms of the positive purposes it once served in your life. In the early phases of the program, we attempt to connect current difficulties with past experiences. The old myth is examined for the constructive role it played at an earlier time. By understanding how the old myth developed, it becomes more possible to turn from its guidance while affirming your strengths and embracing the valid lessons the myth once provided.

On the other side of the conflict will be an emerging counter-myth that serves as a force toward expanding your personality and prerogatives in the very areas the old myth was limiting you. Just as your psyche may produce inspiring dreams that point toward new directions for your development, it also creates new mythic images whose guidance may be in direct conflict with more limiting, prevailing myths. Latent qualities of your personality not supported by prevailing myths will naturally push toward expression and a corresponding counter-myth will emerge. Counter-myths are woven from the accumulation of life experiences, from a developmental readiness to accept the society's more advanced myths, and from an unconscious reservoir of primal impulses and archetypal images. Counter-myths are best understood as creative leaps in the psyche's problem-solving activities, but, like dreams, they often serve a wish-fulfillment function that lacks real-world utility. Still, they serve as an impetus to integrate unrecognized impulses and images into your personality and to recapture qualities you have repressed under the constraints of the old myth.

This conflict between the old myth and the counter-myth will naturally progress toward the creation of a new myth that integrates the most trustworthy premises of each. The conflict may be viewed as a subterranean struggle between alternative myths vying to organize your perceptions, thoughts, feelings, and behaviors. Although much of this process will occur outside of awareness, you will tend *consciously* to identify more fully with one of the myths, or some of its elements, than with the other. Meanwhile, also often outside of awareness, it is the natural action of your psyche to work toward resolving the conflict. Techniques that attune you to this process increase your opportunity to participate actively and effectively in formulating a new myth that provides sounder guidance than either of the conflicting myths is able to offer.

Unresolved mythic conflicts reemerge, interfering with the resolution of subsequent developmental tasks. If you were unable at an earlier age to successfully meet the requirements of a particular developmental task, such as resolving the need for affirmation that was not available in your environment, that issue will play a thematic role in your subsequent life. Certain aspects of your mythology become fixated at the level of this unresolved issue and interfere with later developmental steps. It is valuable to use imagery and imagination to enter an earlier period of life where your development was arrested. There you can provide this younger, internalized part of yourself with a rite of passage onto the next developmental tier and into an expanded personal mythology.

Reconciling a carefully conceived new myth with existing attitudes, goals, and life-style becomes a vital task in your ongoing development. Historically, rites of passage provided a relatively unambiguous direction for regulating people's lives. For a variety of reasons, including the increase of individualism in modern Western cultures, this is no longer possible. The need for such direction, however, is no less pressing than in earlier eras as the available myths in our culture are themselves in unprecedented flux. The five-stage model presented in this book can be used at any point in your development. We believe it can lead you to a renewed guiding mythology that is based upon a culturally attuned synthesis of your history, your emerging potentials, and archetypal images that are pushing for expression. The task of weaving this renewed mythology into the fabric of your life can add fresh meaning and purpose to your journey and serve vital functions that cultural rites and rituals no longer adequately address.

In addition, by coming to understand your own mythic processes, you become more adept at understanding the mythology of your society and more able to skillfully participate in its evolution. The Epilogue elaborates on this assertion and its far-reaching implications.

Epilogue

Tending to the Mythic Vision of Your Community

The discord and the malaise of the 20th century are reflected in our images of who we are. The century that has shown us the ultimate brutality and anonymity of Auschwitz and Hiroshima has produced images of identity that are frightening and confusing, fail to affirm life, fail to give us direction, and fail to instill within us the hope that what we feel and believe really matters and what we do really makes a difference.

—DAN P. McADAMS[1]

We close by examining the way mythology, consciousness, and culture evolve in concert. As has been emphasized, a distinguishing feature of the modern era is that people have achieved greater autonomy than ever before in formulating the myths that guide their lives. Here we will outline the historical basis of that assertion and explore social forces that are pushing the collective mythology to further unfold in unprecedented ways. Finally, we will propose that it is possible to become better equipped to actively and creatively participate in the evolving mythology of your culture. Understanding your own personal mythology, as you have been learning to do through these chapters, is an important part of developing that capacity. Furthermore, the paradox that in order to fully develop yourself you must engage with forces that are beyond yourself urges a reflective involvement with the community in which you live.

MYTHOLOGY AND THE EVOLUTION OF CONSCIOUSNESS

Biologist Lewis Thomas noted that "our most powerful story, equivalent in its way to a universal myth, is evolution."[2] One of the most provocative facts about human evolution is that while the structure of the brain has remained essentially unchanged for at least forty thousand years,[3] consciousness has evolved dramatically. For the human species, language and myth-making replaced genetic mutation as the primary mechanisms by which consciousness and societal innovations are carried forward.

Four Epochs

Times of transformation in the nature of the myths people hold are milestones in the evolution of human consciousness and form the heart of human history. Ken Wilber has described four fundamental phases in that evolution. In the current era, Wilber's fourth phase, consciousness is dominated by the rational, self-reflecting, individual ego.[4] In the earliest period, the sense of self was wholly identified with physical being and the primordial forces of nature. If we can think of mythology at all in this period, we would have to think of it in terms of a trancelike identity with the functioning of the body.

Consciousness, according to Wilber, later became separated from the physiological life of the body, but it had not advanced beyond a childlike sense of magically mingling in the world. In this second era, the myths structuring reality were still bound to the body, but an external world was recognized and responsibility for events were magically assigned to it.

With the advent of more complex forms of language, some twelve thousand years ago, the verbal mind climbed out of the body and into a world of extended time. The physical world could now be represented, manipulated, and narrated through mental symbols. With an increased capacity for accumulating and transmitting knowledge about plants and what they required, agriculture became possible. The hunter-gatherer learned to farm and had to sublimate body-bound desires in order to labor for the benefit of the crop. People were using complex, shared symbols to understand and control their impulses and their world. The requirements for sophisticated myths had all been met, and the great cultural mythologies bloomed. The hard-earned insights of elders could be carried in detail to new generations by mythic story and ritual. However, the mental abilities necessary for self-reflection were not yet well developed, so the individual's emerging sense of self was primarily in the image of the society's mythology. Cultural myths reigned supreme.

As the capacities for self-reflection evolved and the individual's assumptions could be tested through deductive reasoning, perhaps only as recently as three thousand years ago, a self-observing aspect of the psyche came into being.[5] This marked the beginning of Wilber's fourth era, which is characterized by the differentiation of the separate, personal ego—the awesome result of the capacity to mentally step back and observe oneself. Self-aware individuals began to live according to increasingly personalized mythologies whose content, once dictated by the culture's mythology, might now be based on the test of unique experience. Individuality became the order of the day.[6] Joseph Campbell has made the distinction that in primitive times "all meaning was in the group," while today "all is in the individual."[7]

The Hero's Journey

Wilber suggests that close examination of the collective mythologies at the beginning of this emergence of the individual ego unequivocally reveals that an entirely different form of myth began to appear—the "Hero Myth." The true hero myths could come into being only after the personal ego had differentiated itself from the collective. Campbell observed that the principle "represented by the freely willing, historically effective hero not only gained but held the field, and has retained it to the present. Moreover, this victory of the principle of free will, together with its moral corollary of individual responsibility, establishes the first distinguishing characteristic" of specifically Western myth.[8] But it is also the exaggerated accent on the personal ego, and the accompanying alienation from nature and community, that is responsible for much of the malaise in contemporary society. Effective solutions must take the mythic proportions of the problem into account.

We turn to Homer's *The Odyssey* to compare the modern heroic journey with a classic prototype. After fighting valiantly in the Trojan War, Odysseus' return is fraught both with clear hazards—the Lotus-Eaters, the Cyclops, the Laestrygonians—and with dangerous delights: the Sirens, Circe, Calypso. Through strength and cunning, Odysseus finds his way back to his kingdom Ithaca, his wife Penelope, and their son Telemachus. He has been away for two decades. Odysseus, representing the eternal quest of the male hero, has longed to return to Penelope and his homeland throughout his journey. Homer tells us that for Odysseus, Penelope is like "the sun-warmed earth" that is "longed for by a swimmer spent in rough waters where his ship went down."

However, classic mythic images of the hero's return do not fit the plight of modern heroes. The individualism of the modern era has made the heroic journey a common rather than elite path in modern Western cultures.[9] The hero's journey has become everyone's venture. Unlike Odysseus, contemporary heroes have lost their connection

Tending to the Mythic Vision of Your Community

with the natural order, and because their homeland is now populated by other disconnected heroes, they are separated from community as well. Odysseus was a singular hero, returning alone to a family who awaited his return. In the contemporary era, many people are engaged in the challenges of the personal heroic quest. The modern Penelope, rather than waiting at home for twenty years, is likely to be on her own heroine's journey. The home for which the alienated hero yearns no longer hosts a community poised to welcome the gift of his or her leadership. So the unfulfilled hero moves on, disconnected from the purpose of the journey, and perceiving no mission other than to soothe a trembling ego, now so small and alone, by toiling for fame, fortune, and other promises of redemption.

The Modern Hero's Dilemma

As more attention was devoted to the emerging ego, the sense of self became less identified with the life of the body or of the community. The inability of the newly emergent ego to integrate its activities with the prior realms of instinct, emotion, and "body-self" is, in Wilber's eyes, the culture's essential dilemma. He points out that "even [Erich] Neumann, arch-champion of the Hero Myth, clearly recognized that the heroic thrust went way too far, and with this, the great revaluation of the feminine begins, its conversion into the negative, thereafter carried to extremes in the patriarchal religions of the West."[10]

Preoccupation with the self as an entity separate from both body and reference group, necessary for the development of rational thought and individuality, became exaggerated. These separations, which were painstakingly achieved, are not easily transcended. The conquering hero of the contemporary era has ripped himself away from Mother Nature, spearheaded by a belligerent personal ego and supported by increasingly sophisticated technology. Wilber explains the dilemma in terms of the relationship of humanity to its biological nature, the mythical "Great Mother":

> The ego, in the necessary course of its emergence, had to break free of the Great Mother or biological nature embeddedness. That is all well and good—the ego, in fact, did manage to break free of its attachment and subservience . . . and establish itself as an independent, willful, and constellated center of consciousness, a feat represented in the Hero Myths. But in its zeal to assert its independence, it not only *transcended* the Great Mother, which was desirable; it *repressed* the Great Mother, which was disastrous. And there the ego—the Western ego—

> demonstrated not just an awakened assertiveness, but a blind arrogance . . . no longer harmony with the Heavens . . . but a technological assault on Nature. . . . It is one thing to gain a freedom from the fluctuations of nature, emotions, instincts, and environment—it is quite another to alienate them.[11]

The ego, according to psychologist Anthony Greenwald, is characterized by biases that are strikingly analogous to totalitarian information-control strategies.[12] Like totalitarian regimes, the ego organizes knowledge in a way that exalts itself, distorts new information, and revises past experiences to justify its own premises. The totalitarian empire resembles the individual ego forged at the community level. Its model for social organization is the "top-down hierarchy," in which an autocratic leader directs the activities of obedient followers, and the strategy for success is "to win by *defeating others.*"[13]

Individual expression was first encouraged for the masses around the fifteenth century, when "the new mood of the Renaissance pushed individualism out into broad new areas and democratized it."[14] The evolution of democratic empires out of autocratic rule has been a vital response to the hero's journey having become a quest of ordinary people rather than only of the phenomenal individual. From a mythological perspective, democracy may be defined as a social arrangement in which the group consciously and collaboratively chooses the mythic visions that are to be collectively embraced. Democracy as a cultural form allows a collectivity of heroes and heroines to form communities that are attuned to the pluralistic needs of freely willing egos. Erich Neumann emphasized that while in the past, individuals endowed with greatness "possessed a consciousness and stood for the collective in the role of leader," the further course of evolution must involve "a progressive democratization, in which a vast number of individual consciousnesses work productively at the common human task."[15]

We are speaking of democracy here, not in a narrow political sense, but in terms of a broad recognition of the right and ability of individuals to participate in the decisions that affect their destinies. No perfect democracy has ever existed. In Athens, women lacked citizenship, and the leisure for freemen to devote themselves to public concerns was purchased through an economy based on slavery. The so-called "people's democracies" in Marxist nations provide for full employment of their citizens and guarantee basic material needs, but they deny significant personal freedoms and political choices. Western "democracies," marred by their competitiveness and inequities, promote an interlocking conformity and alienation.[16] However, trends toward increased participation, decentralization, and connectedness have also been identified in both parts of the world.[17]

Social developments such as the women's movement, and the resulting turbulence in gender roles and family relationships, may be seen as self-corrections in contemporary democracies. As recently as the 1960s, patriarchal rule was still largely unquestioned in the family and the workplace even in Western nations that espoused the ideals of democracy in their political system. The women's movement has been persistently challenging those assumptions. The mythologies that define identity are vastly different for men and women. Whereas male myths have typically focused upon the tasks of *separation* and *mastery* of self over environment, female myths have typically been more concerned with *caring* and *connectedness,* [18] and they may thus point the way for the as-yet uncharted return of the contemporary hero.

Whether in times of stability or upheaval, the family has served as a robust institution for comforting the patriarch who was trapped in his alienation from the greater society. Even in his separation from nature and the larger community, the family provided him with a consoling sense of home and connectedness. Letty Cottin Pogrebin has argued, however, that "the traditional patriarchal family is democracy's 'original sin'; it is the elemental flaw in an otherwise perfectible political system. . . . Very simply, it is impossible to achieve the exalted goals of the democratic dream and the free and full development of every person so long as the basic unit of our society, the family, is undemocratic and unfree."[19] Upheavals in family structure and gender identity are reverberations of increasingly democratic notions in the culture's mythology pushing their way to the family and individual levels, where they lead to radical and unsettling changes.

Available evidence from studies of contemporary families does indeed suggest that the happiest marriages are egalitarian, while marriages typified by one partner's domination are correlated with marital dissatisfaction.[20] In the predemocratic marriage that was the reigning model in the 1950s and earlier, each partner's commitment was toward fulfilling a prescribed set of gender-linked role expectations. In the marriages that seem to be on the edge of social evolution today, the commitment is increasingly toward the integrity of a relationship between equals. Before the dawning of the individualized ego, autocratic rule was a logical arrangement for social relationships. Although the vestiges of such arrangements are still tightly gripped by many families and in many areas of government, they are becoming outmoded. Pogrebin has emphasized that "just as the authoritarian family is the authoritarian state in microcosm, the democratic family is the best training ground for life in a democracy."[21] The democratization of marriage and the equalization of gender and race relationships are, from this perspective, required steps in democracy's continued evolution.

The costs of having placed the individualism of the heroic journey above the values of caring and connectedness continue to mount.[22] A new vision of democracy is urgently needed that can support the individual and at the same time promote a greater sense of community and more harmonious international relationships.[23] Because it is our myths, more than our genes, that have plunged us into our current dilemmas, it is our potential for formulating more effective mythologies that offers us the greatest hope of not following in the wake of the dinosaur, to be heaped upon nature's stockpile of "discarded models."[24]

AN EPOCH IN THE MAKING

According to Jean Houston:

> A new genre of myth is emerging in our time: myths of evocation and potentiation, myths of new ways of being. We must recall the importance and power of the myth for psyche and civilization, for the myth is . . . the coded DNA of the human psyche calling us to reflesh the dream that has been pushed so far away. . . . The myth is always the stimulus, the alarm clock, the lure of becoming. It quickens the heart to its potential and prepares the ground for society's transformation.[25]

Joseph Campbell has suggested that "one cannot predict the next mythology any more than one can predict tonight's dream."[26] Shortcomings and conflicts in the mythology of the times do, however, reveal the problems the next mythology is challenged to correct. The disruption of gender roles, as we have seen, portends the need for greater democratization in the modern hero's mythology. The turmoil around such issues tills the soil for new mythic visions. While no one can reliably predict what new myths will come to dominate in the coming decades, a remarkably diverse group of candidates, from the "New Fundamentalism" to the "New Age," can be seen vying for the cultural spotlight.

Science has been the standard-bearer, the shared pathway to progress among Western cultures. Erich Jantsch noted that Prometheus, "who stole the fire from heaven and set out to establish mankind as a creed of counter-gods, is still the hero of the official Western ideology of progress and dominance through technology."[27] But neither science nor technology has provided lasting security or peace of mind. In the failure of Promethean attempts to establish science as the monolithic religion for a world culture, Jantsch saw another round of frustrated labor for the Western world, taking its place alongside such other visionary solutions as Marxism and America's "missionary zeal" to bring free enterprise to the world. He suggested that Sisyphus, "who struggles to roll his fate on to a platform of eternal rest, but has to recommence over and over again, turns out to be the involuntary sad hero of all those frustrated attempts to create a lasting structure somewhere, anywhere in the human world."[28]

Jantsch emphasized, however, that Prometheus and Sisyphus are not the only myths from which we can choose. They are bound to Western culture, and he pointed to Leibnitz's "perennial philosophy," the cross-cultural tradition of beliefs held by humanity's most universally respected members, as "another myth which has illuminated human life throughout the millennia and across many cultures . . . holding that human life is sharing integrally in a greater order of process, that it is an aspect as well as an *agent* of universal evolution."[29]

Wilber believes that we can identify people who are already living according to the mythology of the coming era. He emphasizes that he described the four epochs in the evolution of consciousness in terms of the average person's experiences and level of awareness. But he also notes that there are individuals whose lives reflect "the growing tip of human consciousness," the most advanced level of their time. Their lives herald stages of consciousness yet to come. The individuality that has become widespread in our culture was first restricted to sanctioned leaders. Wilber speaks of the first ones to live out the next major structure of consciousness as the shamans, sages, and saints who serve as prototypes of the advancing higher levels of consciousness. If Wilber is correct, then the self-actualizing subjects studied by Abraham Maslow may be examples of what is to come. They tended to evidence greater creativity, autonomy, and ability to resolve polarities than their fellows, had more democratic (as contrasted with authoritarian) character structures, and were more able to transcend the ego boundaries of a narrow sense of self. In addition, certain universal values, such as truth, beauty, and justice were stronger in their personal, motivational schemes.[30]

Such qualities may prove to be vital features in the expanded mythic visions we are collectively challenged to pursue. Rollo May believes that three new myths are necessary for our survival: the *"green myth,"* which would depict our proper relation with nature; *women's liberation,* which would ensure the rights and draw upon the talents of all people; and *planetism,* which would represent the world as a place that transcends political boundaries.[31] All three of these themes can be seen as correctives pushing to change the direction of the contemporary hero's journey.

The women's movement and the wanton destruction of natural resources that has accompanied the hero's faltering Promethean phase have already been discussed. In terms of *planetism,* Robert Gilman believes we are already in the midst of a transition from an "Empire era" to a "Planetary era." He observes that late-twentieth-century Western society is a strange blend of institutions and values that clearly belong to the Empire era, and of "other features like global electronic communications and high levels of literacy, that are completely novel."[32] But, especially since World War II, "the contradictions and tensions have grown deeper between (1) our new technological capabilities combined with the continuing spread of individual human rights and capabilities, and (2) the old values and institutions we have inherited from the Empire period."[33]

The fiercely independent Empire, the individual ego writ large, is losing its feasibility as a social form. It is clear that the planet is shrinking, and if we are to survive, we must be concerned with one another's interests. But new models have not proved viable. Odysseus' journey was of the Empire period. Unlike the modern hero, his return was bound to tradition and predictable forms of social organization. But there are also lessons to be learned from *The Odyssey*'s finale. Odysseus returned to find that suitors had not only laid claim to Penelope, they had plundered his house, decimated his provisions, disposed of his resources, and made plans to murder his son and steal his son's inheritance. Odysseus dramatically challenged the suitors and reclaimed his wife, kingdom, and land. Humanity in modern times has indiscriminately misused the earth's resources and placed the inheritance of future generations in jeopardy. The overriding demand facing today's returning hero requires, in the tradition of Odysseus, cleansing a home fouled by unrestrained avarice, putting the household in order, and reinstating the children's birthright to the world's assets. The new hero's challenge is unique in the way it requires both individual ingenuity and collaborative effort.

New possibilities are supported by remarkable technology that has evolved in this century, particularly electronic communications. Marshall McLuhan claimed that the advent of electronic media has begun to break down old allegiances as people everywhere become aware of what is happening in other parts of the world. He predicted that electronic media would abolish space and time insofar as communication was concerned and would enable people to live mythically in a "global village."[34] While it will take more than electronic media to stop the territorial, religious, and racial wars that currently pockmark the earth, the implications of electronic and satellite communication systems for influencing people's mythologies are dazzling.

The first U.S.-USSR "space bridge" in 1982 used a communications satellite enabling people in Moscow and California to talk with one another instantly on a wide variety of topics such as music, education, and peace. This event was a stunning demonstration of how much the world is shrinking and how citizens of the world's two superpowers might be congenially exposed to one another's mythologies and obtain a feeling of neighborliness through electronic technology. McLuhan correctly foresaw that any viable "global village" must be based on a more far-reaching mythology than could have been conceived before the age of electronic media.

Television, radio, telephone, and personal computers allow people to experience and interact with others in spite of their physical separation. Rather than being psychologically isolated in a local town or city, increasing numbers of people are living in an information system that has no physical location.[35] Allegiances that transcend regional and cultural boundaries are created on a global scale; opinions are instantly catalyzed and shared; beliefs and motivations are transformed by new information. Important topics are examined from many angles through increasingly sophisticated talk shows, news specials, and dramatized portrayals of contemporary issues. Never has more information been available about the events that surround us. A media image of ourselves is constantly being reflected back to us, a development in myth-making worth appreciating.

In summary, the trends toward a reconciliation with natural forces, equality in interpersonal relationships, and a global consciousness all move beyond the structure of the heroic mentality. Although robust counter-reactions to each of these trends are conspicuous, analogous to the way your prevailing myth may have more strongly entrenched itself when challenged by a counter-myth, a new archetype is coming into view. It is characterized by a transcendence of the polarities that marked the heroic era, including instinct vs. reason, individualism vs. community, and nature vs. technology. While the emergence of this archetype is obscured by unprecedented anxieties and complexities, we also have grown more capable than ever before of mindfully participating in the evolution of the new mythologies that will shape our collective destiny.

THE MYTHOLOGICALLY INSTRUCTED COMMUNITY

Albert Einstein once observed that "perfection of means and confusion of goals seem to characterize our age. If we desire sincerely and passionately the safety, the welfare, and the free development of the talents of all men, we shall not be in want of the means to approach such a state."[36] According to Eleanor Wilner, "Myth is the necessary first step in the realignment of social order,"[37] and Joseph Campbell spoke of the "mythologically instructed community."[38] He suggested that it is possible to arrive scientifically at an understanding of the life-supporting nature of myths so that, "in criticizing their archaic features, we do not misrepresent and disqualify their necessity."[39]

For Campbell, a problem with the myths of the past has been that their authority rested almost exclusively in emotional experience, while the needs of these times demand myths that are intellectually sustained as well. He proposed that we may turn to depth psychology for help in creating a more intellectually grounded mythology that is attuned to deeper psychological processes.[40] This is in counterpoint to Erich Jantsch's proposal that "we need, above all, ways to emancipate our processes of model/myth formation from the rational level of inquiry, to elevate them to the mythological level where quality and total experience comes into focus."[41] While agreeing with Jantsch that contemporary rationalism needs to become more mythical, Campbell is making the complementary suggestion that for a mythology to serve us today, it must be supported by sophisticated logic.

Science and the Mythologically Instructed Community

Depth psychologists have for a century been inventing and sharpening procedures for probing the unconscious mind. Other social scientists have developed sophisticated methods for studying the sources of the collective myths we hold and anticipating where they are leading us. The scientific method converges with electronic information systems to make it more plausible for the myths that shape community life to be rationally examined than ever before.

Pollster Daniel Yankelovich, for instance, was able to articulate the culture's "new rules" based upon a scientific analysis of social trends and public attitudes.[42] Psychologist David McClelland has, over the past several decades, conducted an important series of studies of the underlying mythic forces that shape a culture's behavior. He has identified relationships among the imagery in popular literature (i.e., the operative cultural myths), motivation, and subsequent societal events (economic output, political violence, participation in warfare).[43] As social scientists become more able to reliably identify specific attitudes and images that historically have preceded war or economic collapse, they are making a potentially momentous contribution to the knowledge base of a democratic society.

McClelland is discouraged, however, over the obstacles to bringing empirical knowledge about human behavior to benefit public policy. As Albert Einstein noted, "All of us who are concerned for peace and the triumph of reason and justice must be keenly aware how small an influence reason and honest good will exert upon events in the political field."[44] Melvin Konner goes even further, cautioning that "the political experience of this century convincingly proves that almost any scientific theory about behavior can be bent to the purposes of evil, and used by someone to support his wicked, selfish, occasionally psychotic acts, up to and including wholesale slaughter."[45] History insists that knowledge and goodwill are not enough. Humanity is required to squarely face and more effectively deal with its dark side.

The Dark Side from a Mythological Perspective

Erich Neumann spoke of the necessity of "a creative relationship between the dark instinctual side of man's nature and the light side represented by the conscious mind." He emphasized that the shadow side of personality is an essential component of creative vitality.[46] Classically, rituals were agents for inner work that carried the psyche through the passages of life and transformed its dark forces into productive energies. Psychiatrist Stanislav Grof notes that senseless tragedy can be wrought when certain archetypal themes govern a people unchecked. He believes that the expertise is available for constructively teaching people to encounter the roots of their own intrapsychic turmoil and violence. He has proposed that "the task is to create safe and socially sanctioned situations in which certain toxic and potentially dangerous elements of the human personality structure can be confronted and worked through without any harm or damage to others or society as a whole."[47]

The creative potential of the individual's "dark side" sometimes foreshadows an evolutionary breakthrough in the culture's mythology. Neumann observed that "not infrequently a sensitive person falls ill because of his incapacity to deal with a problem which is not recognized as such by the world in which he lives, but which is, in fact, a future problem of humanity which has confronted him and forced him to wrestle with it."[48] A study of humanity's changing self-image came to a similar conclusion: "Often those individuals who bring the new reconceptualizations to society have had personal problems that were similar in form or were significantly related to those of the larger society. In resolving their own problems, they presented viable resolutions to the problems of their culture."[49]

By establishing more opportunities for sensitive people to work out their troubles in tandem with a society that is attuned to the mythological basis of deviant or disruptive behavior, psychological conflict could take on constructive meaning for the society. This kind of awareness also would sensitize people to leaders and social movements that are working out archetypal themes unchecked. Grof cautions against the appeal to the individual's unresolved intrapsychic problems by politicians who convert their own emotional turmoil into a program of revolutionary violence. Political leaders ideally should be those who have undergone substantial exploration of their own unconscious motivations and have reached an advanced level of emotional maturity. For Grof, the real problem is to raise the consciousness of the general public so that it is capable of recognizing public figures whose policies mask their own inner conflicts. From his perspective, adequate time and space must routinely be appropriated by the culture so that its members could be encouraged to engage in such a process. Destructive aspects of the psyche could thus be played out in a protected arena, and the culture could assume a mythic rather than a mechanistic posture in confronting the developmental crisis of its members.

The Five-Stage Model and Social Change

The program you just completed provided a model and a set of personal rituals for working through your own developmental crises with a mythological perspective. The five-stage model can be adapted for systematically participating in social change as well. Organizational consultant Anne Dosher has described the "reflexive relationship" between the myths of individuals and the myths of organizations and community groups.[50] Dosher uses a mythological framework to demonstrate in a practical manner the recognized principle that philosophy and symbol undergird organizational effectiveness.[51]

For instance, Dosher helps management become attuned to the organization's operative mythology and able to assess its consequences. She uncovers organizational ties with the personal myths of the early founders. She helps the organization's members to acknowledge and celebrate these mythic roots, and sometimes to ritualistically bid them farewell. The informal rewards and negative sanctions that reflect the organization's mythology are delineated, and the fit between the organization's mythology and the personal mythologies of its staff is examined. Dosher also identifies competing myths—both within the organization, and between the organization's mythology and that of the broader culture. Such conflicts are often at the basis of organizational crises. If the organization can grasp the mythological dimension of the crisis and respond creatively, it is more likely to emerge revitalized and capable of constructively adjusting its course.

Dosher's interventions frequently include ritual, such as when "the shadow sides of living myths are codified, recorded and ceremoniously burned as a way of 'exorcising' dysfunction."[52] Her approach parallels our five-stage model for working with the individual's mythology, in that she (1) identifies the myths operating in areas of organizational difficulty, (2) traces the historical roots of prevailing myths and recognizes emerging myths, (3) mediates between competing mythologies, (4) delineates, and (5) implements new mythic images that can constructively move the organization forward.

To the extent that working with the individual's mythology holds implications for making interventions at the social level, our five-stage model can be used as a preliminary framework. An implication of the first phase of the model ("Recognizing When a Guiding Myth Is No Longer an Ally") is that where there is social conflict and unrest, underlying discord in the culture's mythology is frequently influencing external conditions. The different sides of the conflict are often forcefully expressed by specific religious, ethnic, or political groups. Tracing the historical roots of mythic conflict can reveal a great deal about a social problem and the failing myths that are maintaining it. The natural resistance to giving up a long-standing myth must also be heeded. Abraham Lincoln described the essential dilemma of this first phase when he warned, "The dogmas of the quiet past are inadequate to the stormy present," and he beckoned the country toward a new mythology: "The occasion is piled high with difficulty, and we must rise with the occasion. As our case is new, so we must think anew and act anew."[53]

Often, however, we cannot find new guiding images that promise to remedy the chaos left in the wake of failed myths. Rollo May has used the term *mythoclasm* to describe what occurs when a guiding truth becomes bankrupt.[54] At such times, people are forced to reckon with shortcomings of principles they once venerated. They are shaken to ease their grip on myths that no longer serve their best interests. And they are challenged to remain alert. According to the historian of religion Mircea Eliade, the sacred often bursts forth into the profane at the darkest hour, purifying and reordering the world.[55] By learning to sense the mythological conflicts at the basis of social unrest, you are able to keep yourself more attuned to the deeper and sometimes surprising forces at play.

The implication of the second phase of our program ("Bringing the Roots of Mythic Conflict into Focus") for working with social processes is that the mythological basis of each side of the conflict, once identified, can be productively examined. Both an historical understanding and an ability to find a prototype of the conflict within yourself are useful. As discussed earlier, social scientists have developed sophisticated procedures for analyzing the relationship between mythic imagery and cultural trends. The willingness to find the other side of the conflict within oneself sometimes requires coaxing. Psychologist Carl Rogers has suggested that leaders in international negotiations should not criticize an adversary's position before having stated the opponent's view to the satisfaction of the other. Rogers demonstrated such prospects, with impressive results, in conflict -resolution efforts with opposing groups in some of the world's most difficult trouble spots, such as Northern Ireland, South Africa, and Latin America.[56]

Examining the forces acting upon your own mythology can deepen your understanding of the mythological basis of conflict in your community. For instance, where one of your long-standing personal myths is in conflict with a counter-myth, you may find within yourself both the inclination to stay with the old and familiar and the impetus to alter your mythology. Such inner conflict is mirrored at the social level in the perennial tension between conservatives and progressives. Conservatives function to defend and *conserve* what is of value from the mythologies of the past, even as the forces of change carry a society into the future. Liberals focus on change, reform, and *progressive* ideals with an eye toward a better future, but sometimes lose touch with important customs and traditions from the past. Both leanings can be found within each of us; if we can establish a balance between them within ourselves, we will be better able to support our culture in its need both to conserve worthwhile practices and to innovate new social forms.

Exploring your inner depths attunes you to the mythological underpinnings of diverse social patterns and conditions. There is evidence, for instance, that the classical hero's journey may exist in primitive recesses of the psyche as well as in the guiding models provided by cultures. Joseph Campbell, who described the hero's journey based on his comparative studies of mythologies throughout history, notes his "amazement" upon reading of psychiatrist John Weir Perry's studies of psychosis[57] and discovering that sometimes "the imagery of schizophrenic fantasy perfectly matches that of the mythological hero journey" as he had outlined it more than a decade before.[58]

Because of these powerful internal mythic forces, Grof recommends in-depth self-exploration on the part of leaders who would complement what they are doing in the external world with systematic inner searching.[59] Policymakers could be educated to find both sides of an ideological conflict within themselves. Even if the process did not change their ideology, it would increase the likelihood of empathy and respect for their opponent's position, thus enhancing their capacity for creative collaboration.

The processes corresponding with the first two stages of our model would include uncovering the mythological basis of a difficulty in your community, identifying its manifestation in the myths of dissonant groups, tracing its history, recognizing its analogue within yourself, and investigating the constructive impulses and destructive potentials contained within each side of the conflict. The principle corresponding with the third stage of our program ("Conceiving a Unifying Mythic Vision") is that where there is conflict in the community's mythology, the individuals and groups involved are served by working toward an understanding of the deeper layers of their differences and using this understanding to expand their own positions. Raising the level of discourse to the mythological level makes it more likely for each side to appreciate the actions the other side has taken. And from the perspective of this larger picture, it becomes evident that it is in the interests of each side to be concerned with the needs of the other. This can help conflicting groups to envision a "superordinate goal"—a mutually beneficial outcome that transcends the separate interests of either group.[60]

Cooperation between opposing groups is maximized when both recognize a superordinate goal, desirable for both groups but attainable only through cooperation. One of Einstein's cherished hopes was for the creation of a federation of nations designed specifically for preventing war. Such an organization would shape world politics because this would be the only organization entitled to have an army, and it would have jurisdiction in international disputes. Einstein did not believe that individual countries would disarm voluntarily without the sanction and protection of such a larger arbitrating authority.[61] Superordinate goals lead to conditions in which actions that benefit the individual or subgroup simultaneously benefit the collective.

Superordinate goals are also at play in anthropologist Ruth Benedict's important concept of *synergy.*[62] In cultures with a high degree of synergy, the society is organized so that an individual, in one act, serves his or her own advantage as well as that of the community. In groups that are low in synergy, social arrangements create a pronounced opposition between the needs of the person and the needs of the group. Benedict found that "high synergy" societies were secure, benevolent, and high in morale; "low synergy" societies were insecure, surly, and low in morale.

Social action that produces a far-reaching beneficial impact is often high in synergy. Clara Barton once noted that the greatest benefits of the Red Cross, which she founded, lie not in its past service, but "in the possibilities it has created for the future; in the lessons it has taught; in the avenues to humane effort it has opened, and in the union of beneficent action between people and Government." In promoting societal or international cooperation, the amount of synergy embodied in a particular action—the degree to which it is capable of promoting superordinate goals among groups with diverse mythologies and opposing interests—is a sensible measure of its social advantage. Such a measurement could be used as a criterion for assessing new visions as they are being translated into action. Another imaginative criterion is the Iroquois Indian practice of asking how a policy decision would affect the seventh generation to come. Such perspectives increase the chances of a mythic conflict reaching resolution.

The final two stages of our program ("From Vision to Commitment" and "Weaving a Renewed Mythology into Daily Life") involve choice and dedication to action. As you attempt to implement the new guiding mythology that you have painstakingly crafted through this program, you will undoubtedly run into obstacles you had not anticipated. Success comes in starts and stops. Progress seems slow because we are all constructed so that we can envision possibilities long before we can attain them. At our best, we monitor our expectations so we won't be disenchanted in the very process of facilitating our self-development. And this is but a microcosm of the complex challenges faced by individuals who seek to catalyze their community into refining and expanding its mythic vision. Planned social change may seem excruciatingly slow, but an understanding of its mythic dimension can provide a consoling perspective and practical knowledge of the underlying forces at work.

Overpopulation, for example, is often identified as "perhaps the gravest threat to future world peace."[63] Yet even where policies and programs designed to limit population growth have enjoyed widespread support, progress often falters. Successful programs can, however, be identified and studied. In 1965, Singapore's population growth was 22 percent more rapid than Ethiopia's; through free family planning and various economic sanctions and incentives, the country had slowed the rate to half of Ethiopia's within a decade.[64] Singapore reached zero population growth in 1986, and by 1987 the country's leaders were calling for *more* children per family. To use a mythological perspective in designing a program to limit population growth in another country, the Singapore program could be scrutinized for the way it managed to interface with the culture's mythology to gain such cooperation. A local adaptation of that model, attuned particularly to the social forces already working to counter overpopulation, might be introduced into a new community as a well-articulated alternative myth. The succeeding stages of conflict and resolution could be observed and articulated, as in the action research model described in chapter 6. Thus, as the community moves forward with an understanding of the mythological dimension of the task it has undertaken, it can also adjust its course with reliable information.

The overriding mythic theme of our era is that the hero's solitary journey has led us onto a path that can only be transversed by heroes who cooperate in their respect for the planet and for one another. Recognizing our interdependence with people around the globe has become urgent both for our personal and our collective security. This development begs for superordinate goals that inspire us to take decisive action toward international understanding and cooperation. In pondering the paradox that there is "so much evil in the world, but so few evil men," Abraham Maslow observed that "the voice of the divine within is counterposed *not* by the voice of the devil within but by the voice of the timid."[65] We would add that effective work with your own myths and the myths of your society is a skillful reply to both the voice of the devil and the voice of the timid.

Each of us is challenged to direct our strength and wisdom toward creating mythological harmonies within ourselves; within our families; within our organizations; within our nation; within the world. And as we reconcile our logic with our intuition, our egos with our shadows, our old myths with our new ones, and our personal needs with those of our community, we also pave the way for a world steeped in contradictions to move forward in greater peace and creative harmony.

Appendix A
Enhancing the Program

To participate creatively in the evolution of your personal mythology requires time, focused concentration, and a willingness to explore material that may be discomforting. Based on our substantial experience with the obstacles people face when they attempt to work with their personal myths, a number of strategies are offered here to enrich your experience in the program.

Building habit patterns that support self-exploration. Working with your personal mythology requires new habits that are similar to those involved in establishing a regular practice of exercise, meditation, yoga, or any similar discipline. Habits of thinking, such as keen observation and patience, and habits of doing, such as reflecting in a journal and working with dreams, can be cultivated. You may not be able to use your willpower to achieve profound insights on command, but you can marshal it toward creating the time and the conditions that will support effective inner work. Stepping out of the routines and stresses that normally occupy your mind and into protected space permits you to connect more deeply with your inner self. Setting aside a regular time for contemplation and self-exploration builds habitual responses that can aid you in your intention to do this work.

Creating a special place for inner work. The place you choose for these efforts should provide a comfortable and inspiring atmosphere while protecting you from distractions such as television and telephone. Be aware of lighting and sounds as you create your environment. You can work in an easy chair, at a desk, or from pillows on the floor. Some people have built altars in the corner of a crowded living room. Native American tribes consecrate important places as sacred, using particular sites for blessing a hunt or ceremony. We suggest you treat your own work space with similar reverence.

Inspirational prompts. You can use candles, incense, objects from nature, and inspirational works of art, literature, or music to enhance the atmosphere of your work space. Besides setting a mood, these may be particularly valuable to focus upon when you are feeling resistant to continuing the work or when you need a break. Reflecting upon inspiring materials can give you refuge if the program becomes uncomfortably intense, yet you will still be building the habit of regular inner work. If you find yourself resisting a personal ritual, it may be wise to take a recess and turn to one of these inspirational objects. One client would browse through an 1893 edition of Walt Whitman's poetry when she felt bogged down, and this frequently led to fresh inspiration and motivation. A man who was inclined to become lost in a welter of words that took him off on tangents found it grounding to meditate on a beautiful polished rock his daughter had given him. If you do not force yourself, and at the same time keep your inner life stimulated, you are likely to be drawn effortlessly back to the program.

Retreats. Many of the world's great religious leaders received their inspiration while in solitude, often in the desert or mountains. Inspiration can come when you remove yourself, psychologically as well as physically, from ongoing workaday concerns and create a conducive environment. A weekend retreat can provide a fertile setting for engaging yourself in the program offered here.

Speaking your inner experiences. If you have trouble following or keeping your concentration on the guided imagery journeys, you will increase your success markedly by telling your experience as it is occurring to a partner or speaking it into a second tape recorder. This will not only keep you alert and on track during the experience but will also make it easier to recall or retrieve the details of your inner journey.

Staying physically vibrant. If you are feeling weary or run-down, the energy available to you will not take you to your creative edge. Rest, good nutrition, and exercise are the first order of business. Physical exercise in particular can bypass ordinary thought patterns, increase nonlinear thinking, alter perceptions, and open you to fresh experience and insight (the "runner's high"). Swimming, jogging, bouncing on a jumper, or other properly paced aerobic exercise after a sedentary day at work can sharpen you for the mental effort required by this program.

Working with others. Other people can lend a different perspective and greater objectivity. They may perceive blind spots that are invisible to you, yet central to your development. The program may be used alone, with a partner, as the focal point of a personal mythology study group, under the supervision of a therapist, or as the basis for clinicians or other qualified leaders to design their own personal mythology classes and workshops. Working with others can help you tap into the healing qualities of relationship and community. If you make yourself accountable to another person, you are also more likely to confront your resistances directly than to unknowingly allow them to sabotage your efforts.

"Leaderless" women's groups, men's groups, adult children of alcoholics groups, and other self-help groups can use this book to lead their members into a productive exploration of their personal myths. When we work with a group, we divide it into subgroups of three or four people. Guided imagery instructions are given to the entire group as participants go through the experience simultaneously but individually. They then discuss in their small support group what occurred and what it means. Exploring your personal mythology with others can intensify the potency of the techniques and provide support and perspective.

If you work with another person, we strongly urge that you start by reaching an agreement on ground rules, such as respecting each other's personal defenses and honoring each other's privacy by maintaining confidentiality. This is not a time to "play therapist" in the sense of probing for hidden feelings or dark secrets the other may be avoiding, offering uninvited interpretations of the meaning of the other's experiences, or giving advice. When you challenge your established patterns of thought and behavior, you need acceptance and emotional support. If you are planning to conduct the program with a partner or a group, the most sensible posture is to agree to listen receptively to one another's experiences, offer nonjudgmental support, and provide an active sounding board. Maintaining the balance of engaging in mutual problem solving and not becoming intrusive can be enhanced by discussing (prior to the program) what kind of support you will want from your partner, and building in a feedback system so that you can let your partner know if you are getting what you need.

Intensifying personal rituals through progressive relaxation. Each imagery ritual begins with a brief induction for relaxing and tuning yourself inwardly. You can deepen your experience with the rituals by taking the time to tape and use the following longer induction,[1] which brings you deeper into the part of yourself usually accessed only in dreams. Begin by sitting or reclining in a safe, secluded space where you are unlikely to be interrupted.

Settle in comfortably—feeling warm, secure, and well supported. [Pause] Thank your body for its hard work and good service. [Pause] Find the parts of your body that need special attention, healing, or rest. Picture a warm, wise hand filled with a fragrant ointment gently touching and acknowledging those parts. Focus your attention and sense the melting, calming relaxation that comes into those sore and tired places. [60-second pause]

All is well with you as you set off on this journey of self-discovery. You are always able to move and adjust yourself, yawning and stretching, rearranging until your body is peaceful and satisfied. Use any sounds in the environment as a reminder to bring your attention back to the instructions.

Your facial muscles—forehead, eyes, cheeks, mouth, and jaw—yield to gravity by softening and melting. Blood flows freely through your skin, tingling your scalp and enlivening your face. At your own pace, breathe deeply seven times, exhaling completely. Be aware of your entire head—face, scalp, eyes, ears, mouth, jaw. You are vitally alive and relaxed. [60-second pause]

Your neck, the bridge between head and body, has worked very hard and welcomes this peaceful time. The heavy load is at rest and nothing is demanded of your neck or throat. You are grateful for all the air and nourishment they have carried for you. The healing hand sensitively massages around your neck and its muscles. You sigh, content. Take seven deep breaths, at your own tempo, becoming increasingly aware of softening your throat and neck. [60-second pause]

Your chest, ribs, back, spine, shoulders, lungs, and heart are working together to bring breath into you as they have all of your life. Focus on each—ribs all the way around, back, spine, shoulders, lungs, heart—as you find the tired places. Take seven good breaths, at your own pace, exhaling completely and resting between inhalations. With each breath you are increasingly aware of the healing hand, which again finds the wounded, weary parts, nourishing them with tender touch. Be generous with yourself, allowing time for the healing to happen. [90-second pause]

Your pelvis, hips, buttocks, genitals, belly, muscles, and deep organs deserve the attention you are giving them. Sense their needs and strengths. Give thanks for their good service. With seven breaths, as before, experience in sensation and visualization the wonderful, lov-

ing hand healing your hurts and soothing your restlessness. [90-second pause]

Your arms, hands, legs, and feet are ready to rest and be appreciated. Move your awareness to the muscles and joints of your arms, hands, legs, and feet, opening and freeing each in turn. One by one, discover and thank the muscles and joints in your arms [20-second pause]; your hands [20-second pause]; your legs [20-second pause]; and your feet [20-second pause]. The healing hand will touch away your pains as you take seven deep breaths, exhaling your tiredness, hurt, and disillusion. [60-second pause]

With each of the next ten suggestions, you will become more able to relax and to move into the experience you have chosen. You are always free to return to ordinary consciousness simply by opening your eyes and exhaling deeply, and you are just as free to explore the landscape of your unconscious. You will recall all you need of this experience, and you will emerge from it with insight and power. This is your mythology, entirely your own creation.

ONE, you are able fully to focus on the instructions. You are conscious, alert, and curious.

TWO, your body remembers the healing it has received and sinks pleasurably into full relaxation.

THREE, your breathing deepens as your lungs become quieter and more efficient. Your chest rises and falls in gentle rhythm. The air moves softly through your nose and throat.

FOUR, your heart pumps at a peaceful, efficient rate, sending oxygen and nutrients to every part of your body. Trace this flow with a vivid sensation of refreshment reaching every cell.

FIVE, your deep organs—heart, stomach, liver, kidneys, and the others—have silently served you, and you are grateful as you visualize and sense their appreciation of your attention.

SIX, your buttocks, genitals, and belly are butter-soft. Deliciously comfortable. How good you feel!

SEVEN, your thighs, calves, ankles, and leg joints are heavy and happy, relieved of effort and demand.

EIGHT, your head, face, neck, and shoulders are contented and easy, feeling good.

NINE, deeply relaxed, you feel the comfortable sensations of warmth and heaviness within you and a pleasant tingling on your skin.

TEN, fully relaxed. Your body is vital and comfortable. Your best energy is available for the journey of self-discovery you have begun.

Progressive relaxation slows your metabolism, quiets your mind, increases your receptivity, and deepens the guided imagery experience that will follow it. At the close of any ritual that you begin by using this induction, count yourself out from TEN to ONE instead of from FIVE to ONE as the text indicates. By practicing this technique regularly, you can develop within yourself the ability to reach a deeply relaxed and peaceful state at will.

Appendix B
A Primer for Working with Your Dreams

With the publication of *The Interpretation of Dreams* in 1899, Freud brought the mystery of dreaming into the reach of scientific investigation. While he recognized that the meaning of a dream is often well concealed, he considered dreams "the royal road to the unconscious." Carl Jung insisted that the dream symbol typically *reveals* insights rather than concealing information from the dreamer. As a result, Jung went beyond Freud in having his clients write down their dreams and in asking them to play a central role in dream interpretation.

Working with dreams can be a useful way of making contact with underlying feelings, conflicts, and motivations because the dream, as Freud said, is probably the most direct route to unconscious experience. A number of excellent books are available that provide detailed guidance for examining your own dream life.[1] The next few pages provide brief guidelines for working with dreams in a way that is oriented toward understanding your personal mythology.

Myth-making Activity Through Your Dreams

Many depth psychologists believe that dreams are best understood as an unfolding of the psyche and should not be distorted by intellectual interpretations. In a similar manner, you can learn to sense, without being overly intellectual, the relationship between the patterns you find in your dreams and your developing personal myths. Dreams serve to mediate between your daily experiences and your underlying myths. Working with your dreams can reveal changes in your mythology that are occurring outside your awareness.

A woman had a recurrent dream about crossing a bridge that was in a forest. That was the only scene in the dream, but it was accom-

panied by a feeling of enormous frustration. She was asked to imagine that she was having the dream again. This time, however, she was told to "redream" the dream from the point of view of the bridge. She closed her eyes, relaxed, imagined she was *the bridge, and was soon sobbing softly.*

She explained that her initial reaction was one of great satisfaction because she was helping people get from one part of the woods to another. But then as people kept walking over her, she felt old and creaky, as if she were going to collapse and break apart. Then she realized that she really was *the bridge. The bridge represented the fact that she was always serving her husband, waiting on her children, caring for her aged parents, and doing little for herself. She was living according to the dictates of a personal myth that had her reflexively serving others, underfoot, unaware, and unappreciated. She realized that if she kept doing this,* she *was going to creak and fall apart.*

The dream helped her to realize that a part of her was suffering because of her unquestioned compliance to an image of the role of wife and mother that she had held since childhood. Her dream was telling her the importance of revising that guiding image, and it spoke to her by dramatizing her myth in a way that led her to realize the harm it was causing.

When the consequences of your mythology are harmful, or when your daytime experiences are inconsistent with your mythology, your dreams may work to adjust the mythology. Or they may reinterpret your circumstances or experiences to better fit existing myths. Dreams may support or challenge an existing myth, foster or inhibit a counter-myth, or focus upon conflict between the two.[2] You can understand your dreams better in terms of your personal mythology, and you can understand your personal mythology more fully through the instruction of your dreams.

Suggestions for Remembering Your Dreams

Some people spontaneously remember a dream or two almost every morning. Most do not. A few simple techniques can assist recall. Just before falling asleep, breathe deeply, relax, and repeat ten to twenty times: "I will remember a dream when I wake up." We suggest you place a tape recorder or a pen and your journal beside the bed. Record your dreams immediately upon waking. Dreams are often fragile and transitory, and you may lose the dream if you wait even for a few minutes.

If you wake up without recalling a dream, you might shift your body into a different position, especially a position in which you might have had a dream. Or you might remain alert during the morning because a trivial incident or association can take you back to a dream. Even if you can remember only a single fragment, or a fleeting feeling with which you awaken, record it. Sometimes the process of simply starting to write or speak the dream expands your initial glimpse into a much more complete recollection. There is a saying that a dream is like a tiger—if you catch even a trace of it, you have it by the tail and can pull it into view, stripe by stripe.

It may take several days of giving yourself the recommended instructions before you start recalling your dreams. Do not become discouraged. The program is designed so that your dreams are a supplementary rather than a central focus of the work. Also, as you repeat this process for several nights, you will be developing habit patterns that support dream recall.

We will mention two additional methods that can help with dream recall, although they are more intrusive. While alcohol and most drugs tend to reduce dreaming, some people claim to have found that their dream recall is enhanced by the ingestion of certain herbal teas and other natural substances. Vitamin B-6, for instance, is believed to increase dream recall. If there are no contraindications to your using B-6, occasionally taking between 50 mg and 250 mg with dinner (do not take more without medical supervision) may facilitate dream recall. Another technique is to set an alarm clock to go off early so you will be more likely to awake mid-dream and also have additional time to work with your dream. Although these are not recommended as a regular practice, they may on occasion be useful.

Even if you do not recall a dream on a particular morning, your attempt promotes new insights. Often people will ask for a dream that clarifies a certain issue, and they will wake up not with a dream but with a new understanding of the problem. Rather than becoming disappointed or self-critical if you do not remember your dreams, simply set aside a few protected minutes upon awakening and remain alert for whatever comes. Nor should you be concerned if the meaning of a particular dream is not initially clear to you. Several techniques for dream exploration follow, and others can be found in the recommended books.

Ways of Working with Your Dreams

Carl Jung suggested: "If we meditate on a dream sufficiently long and thoroughly, if we carry it around with us and turn it over and over, something almost always comes of it."[3] Keeping your attention focused on a dream is likely to induce a greater understanding of its meaning. The techniques offered here are, in a sense, ways of creatively turning the dream "over and over." The oldest and most frequently used method of working with dreams is simply to repeat the dream to yourself or to tell it to another person. Recording dreams in a journal serves a similar function. Five additional techniques for working with your dreams follow.

Review via dream elements. Some researchers have identified several categories of dream content.[4] One way of attending to a dream is to review it in terms of these categories. This process often helps the dreamer see new relationships among parts of the dream and may also bring additional aspects of the dream into memory. Ten possible dream categories include: *characters* (friends, famous people, strangers, mythical creatures); *nature* (trees, birds, stars, water); *objects* (clothing, weapons, computers, buildings); *emotions* (anger, love, fear, loneliness); *sensations* (warmth, pain, sound, smells, taste); *settings* (your home, nineteenth-century France, midnight, outer space); *solitary activities* (running, eating, watching TV, sewing); *interactions* (having a conversation, playing Ping-Pong, making love, fighting a duel); *modifiers* (small, pretty, purple, old, tall); and *outcomes* (failure, victory, confusion, incompleteness). While no single dream is likely to have all ten categories represented in it, the list may remind you of important aspects of the dream. Also, if you record your dreams on a regular basis, you may find that certain elements regularly repeat themselves, revealing patterns that you can explore just as you would explore an individual dream symbol.

Identifying with one of the elements. Many clinicians who work with dreams believe that each image represents an aspect of the dreamer. The woman who "became" the bridge was using an approach to working with dreams that is based on this assumption.

In this technique, you select a tangible element from the dream—usually one that is particularly puzzling, troubling, or ominous—and identify with that person, place, thing, quality, or activity. One way of identifying with the dream element is to "redream" the dream. If a bear rug in the dream puzzles you, close your eyes and imagine that you are having the dream again. But this time, imagine that you are the bear rug. What is the rug thinking and feeling as the dream proceeds? Perhaps your rug will feel stepped on and ignored. Or perhaps your rug is a resource that can transform itself into the living animal when you have a need for strength.

A second method of identifying with the dream element is to role-play it, using the technique called "creative projection" introduced in chapter 2. If you were exploring the bear rug, you would assume the role of the rug and literally act out the dream, giving the rug a voice and gestures and, in your imagination, interacting with other elements as the dream proceeds. As you enact the plot of the dream, remain alert to any impulses you may have to examine other dream elements.

After finishing the dream as you dreamed it, you can extend the role play. The element with which you are identifying can have an imaginary dialogue with another dream element. The bear rug, for instance, might begin such a dialogue by asking the room in which it is placed, "Why are you so cold?" You would then "become" the room, answer, and proceed with a dialogue between them.

Free association to a dream element. You also can freely associate to a particular dream image, writing down everything that comes to mind. Perhaps you dreamed about a robot. As quickly as you can, list all of your associations with "robot"—for example, "mechanical, efficient, futuristic, cold, programmed." You may come to understand some of these associations in the context of the entire dream, the context of recent events in your life, or the context of the work you are doing with your personal mythology. If you are working with a partner, you might have your partner ask you a series of questions as a naive interviewer. For example, imagine that your partner has just arrived from another culture and needs to have everything explained. Your partner could ask such questions as "What is a robot?" If the answer is, "A mechanical person," your partner might ask, "What do you mean by mechanical?" Have your partner continue the process, moving so rapidly that you will need to express yourself spontaneously, without the opportunity to preplan your responses.

Another variation of this approach is to imagine that you are interviewing the dream element. You can ask the bear rug or the robot what it is doing in your dream and what it is trying to tell you, and then let the image answer.

Extending the dream. Sometimes you will wake up with a dream that feels unfinished or in some other way seems unresolved. With this technique, you simply redream the dream in your imagination just as you remember it, and then carry the plot beyond the dream's actual stopping point. You extend the dream toward a new ending. For instance, you might have the bear rug become animated, leave the cold room, and discover what is beyond it.

Critical focus. With this technique, you again redream the dream in your imagination, as if you were watching a motion picture. This time, however, you "freeze" the action where the scene changes, a new character appears, or there is a shift in the emotional tone. Examine that scene in detail and then continue. This gives you a chance not only to observe the action carefully at critical points but also to enter the dream, examine its elements, and even question the elements about their role in the drama, as if they were actors.

Your dreams can provide fresh insight into the mysterious workings of your unconscious mind in an intriguing blend of literal and symbolic language. While they may not reveal a perfectly clear picture of your personal mythology, they can provide enticing clues into its dynamics.

Appendix C
When the Program Becomes Unsettling

A sensitive issue in presenting some of the exercises in this program is that any tool that is useful for psychological exploration can stir up strong emotions or uncover dormant psychological problems. We have made every effort to present the program in such a way that you can pace it according to your particular needs and sensitivities. The personal rituals presented here have been tested with more than two thousand people in our consultations, workshops, and seminars, as well as with the individuals who worked with earlier drafts of the book. In no instance have serious adverse effects been reported. Rather, we have received requests for techniques that would intensify some of the exercises, and a few such methods were outlined in Appendix A.

However, interpersonal support is built into face-to-face settings. If you should feel discouraged or unsettled as you proceed through the chapters, and if those feelings persist after you have utilized the suggestions given below, we strongly recommend that you find appropriate support or professional assistance.

Some people have repressed important life issues for years. If these issues are on the verge of breaking through one's defenses, nearly any intense experience can trigger a reaction. For some, it might be seeing a powerful film; for others, it might be an argument with a loved one or a volley of criticism from a friend. What should be done if you become too upset?

For some people, psychotherapy is long overdue. However, a number of practical "psychological first aid" procedures are available, and in most cases one or more will suffice:

Shift your focus. Simply put the book away and shift activities. Listen to music, work in your garden, telephone a friend, take a walk, turn on the television.

Honor your body. Involve yourself in invigorating physical activities such as swimming, running, dancing, jumping on a trampoline, cleaning your house, or waxing your car. Regularly discharging pent-up or stagnant energies is an excellent form of emotional self-care.

Quiet your mind. Meditate or use a relaxation technique such as the one described in Appendix A.

Protect yourself mythically. Visualize your Inner Shaman nurturing you or use your Personal Shield for emotional protection, as described at the end of chapter 2.

Find support from another person. Share intimately with someone who appreciates the task you have accepted and whom you can use as a sounding board. Being valued in the darkest part of your struggle makes that struggle more endurable.

Be kind and patient with yourself. Shift your perspective, keep your humor, and call upon your creativity. Find the ironies and the lessons even in memories and insights that may at first seem dismal and upsetting. The awareness that is upsetting you is still new. The creative responses you will engage to meet it are still being mobilized. Remember, as Abraham Maslow used to say, "Anything worth doing is worth doing awkwardly at first!"

Newly conceived personal myths can provoke discomfort even as they begin to improve your life. For change to occur, the old mythic system must destabilize. Because the program is oriented toward identifying and changing areas of your personal mythology that are not serving you well, you have been asked to explore memories and feelings that may be difficult and unpleasant. It is typical, in fact, to encounter frailties and weaknesses that were not previously recognized. Although realistic adjustments to your self-concept will be valuable, it is equally important to attend to your self-esteem. Along with the methods presented above, acknowledge to yourself that you have willingly entered a realm that holds difficult as well as inspiring material, and appreciate your own courage.

A Stress Release Technique

We also have found the following stress release technique to be helpful in diminishing the effects of a past emotional trauma. This technique, which is based on Chinese medicine, is being used increasingly in settings ranging from emergency rooms to the Olympics.[1] Its effect is to clear the meridians (the energy pathways on which acupuncture points are supposedly situated) of stress-related energy blockages. Experiment with this simple self-help procedure when working with your personal mythology becomes overly stressful.

Keeping the troubling emotion or memory in your awareness, place the palm of one hand across your forehead. Place your other hand over the protrusion at the back of your head, just above the line of your ears. Gently hold your head between your hands as you continue to experience the emotion or memory. Continue for at least a minute. You will feel yourself beginning to relax and surrender. Notice how the feelings of stress gradually diminish, even as you keep the memory in your mind. You may also feel sensations of energy streaming through your body and down your legs. Know that your hands are activating points that naturally defuse the stress reflex conditioned to the memory.

This technique stimulates a physiological response that is believed to neutralize some of the effects of emotional stress that can build during a traumatic event, or in this case, a traumatic memory or disturbing insight. The memory or insight remains, but the noxious electrochemical consequences of post-traumatic stress that had been associated with it may be alleviated.

While we are focusing here on the limitations and possible hazards of self-guided exploration, we want to reemphasize the potential benefits of actively working with your personal mythology. Out of the creative chaos of examining your life story will come fresh perspectives for living a more harmonious and vital existence. We believe that such exploration is one of the most powerful, yet gentle, ways of facilitating the development of your personality.

Notes

Prologue

1. Naomi Goldenberg, *Changing of the Gods: Feminism and the End of Traditional Religions* (Boston: Beacon, 1979), p. 47. **2.** Frances G. Wickes, *The Inner World of Choice* (Englewood Cliffs, NJ: Prentice-Hall, 1963), p. ix. **3.** Ibid., p. 1. **4.** Hans Kohut's "self psychology" (*The Restoration of the Self,* New York: International Universities Press, 1977), while derived in a very different context, shares many of the premises of our model. **5.** Henry A. Murray, ed., *Myth and Mythmaking* (New York: George Braziller, 1960), pp. 335–339. **6.** Sam Keen, *The Passionate Life: Stages of Loving* (New York: Harper & Row, 1983), p. 23. **7.** Wanda Urbanska, *The Singular Generation: Young Americans in the 1980s* (Garden City, NY: Doubleday, 1986). **8.** Rollo May, *Love and Will* (New York: W. W. Norton, 1969), pp. 13–14. **9.** Ernst Kris, "The Personal Myth: A Problem in Psychoanalytic Technique," *Journal of the American Psychoanalytic Association,* 1956, *4,* 653–681. **10.** Carl G. Jung, *Memories, Dreams, Reflections* (New York: Random House, 1961). **11.** James Hillman, *Re-Visioning Psychology* (New York: Harper & Row, 1975), p. 20. **12.** Ibid., p. 154. **13.** This study was conducted by David Feinstein at The Johns Hopkins University School of Medicine, Department of Psychiatry and Behavioral Science, between 1970 and 1972. Different aspects of the project were supervised by Joel Elkes, M.D., Donald C. Klein, Ph.D., and Carl E. Young, Ph.D. **14.** A. David Feinstein, "Personal Mythology as a Paradigm for a Holistic Public Psychology," *American Journal of Orthopsychiatry,* 1979, *49,* 198–217. **15.** Stanley Krippner, chair, "Personal Myths and Psychotherapy," symposium conducted at the 87th Annual Convention of the American Psychological Association, New York, 1979. **16.** Feinstein, "Myth-Making Activity Through the Window of the Dream," *Psychotherapy in Private Practice,* 1986, *4,* 119–135; Feinstein, "The Shaman Within: Cultivating a Sacred Personal Mythology," in Shirley Nicholson, ed., *Shamanism: An Expanded View of Reality* (Wheaton, IL: Quest, 1987), pp. 267–279; Feinstein and Krippner, "Personal Myths—In the Family Way," in Steven A. Anderson and Dennis A. Bagarozzi, eds., *Family Myths: Psychotherapy Implications* (New York: Haworth Press, in press); Feinstein, Krippner, and Granger, "Myth-Making and Human Development," *Journal of Humanistic Psychology 1988 28* (3); Krippner, "Dreams and the Development of a Personal Mythology," *The Journal of Mind and Behavior,* 1986, *7,* 449–462; Krippner, "Shamanism, Personal Mythology, and Behavior Change," *International Journal of Psychosomatics,* 1987, *34*(4), 22–27; Krippner and Bruce Carpenter, "The Interface Between Cultural and Personal Mythology in Three Balinese Dreams," in Ruth-Inge Heinze, ed., *Proceedings of the Second International Conference on the Study of Shamanism* (Berkeley: Independent Scholars of Asia, 1985), pp. 104–113. **17.** George A. Kelly, *The Psychology of Personal Constructs,* Vols. 1 and 2 (New York: W. W. Norton, 1955). **18.** Jerome Bruner, *Actual Minds, Possible Worlds* (Cambridge, MA: Harvard University Press, 1986). **19.** Carl R. Rogers, *On Becoming a Person* (Boston: Houghton Mifflin, 1961). **20.** Abraham H. Maslow, *The Farther Reaches of Human Nature* (New York: Viking, 1971). **21.** Frieda Fordham, *An Introduction to Jung's Psychology* (Baltimore: Penguin, 1953). **22.** Gerald M. Rosen, "Guidelines for the Review of Do-It-Yourself Treatment Books," *Contemporary Psychology,* 1981, *26,* 189–191. **23.** At press time, we know of three doctoral dissertations in process that attempt to evaluate various aspects of our model.

24. Onno Van der Hart, *Rituals in Psychotherapy: Transition and Community* (New York: Irvington, 1983). 25. See, for example, descriptions of Anna Halprin's work with ritual and dance, such as her *Circle the Earth Manual: A Guide for Dancing Peace with the Planet* (Kentfield, CA: Tamalpa Institute, 1987), and descriptions of "empowerment groups" in Joanna Rogers Macy's *Despair and Personal Power in the Nuclear Age* (Baltimore: New Society Publishers, 1983). 26. Robert Johnson, *Inner Work: Using Dreams and Active Imagination for Personal Growth* (New York: Harper & Row, 1986), p. 25, italics deleted. 27. Ira Progoff, *At a Journal Workshop* (New York: Dialogue House Library, 1975).

1

1. Joseph Campbell, *The Hero with a Thousand Faces.* 2nd ed. (Princeton: Princeton University Press, 1968), p. 3. 2. Ibid., p. 11. 3. David Feinstein and Stanley Krippner, "Personal Myths in the Family Way," in Anderson and Bagarozzi, eds., *Family Myths: Psychotherapy Implications.* 4. This personal ritual is patterned after an exercise developed by Jean Houston, whose seminars and writings we respectfully acknowledge for their service in awakening people to the mythological realm. 5. Paraphrasing a Joni Mitchell lyric. 6. Mark Shorer, *William Blake: The Politics of Vision* (New York: Holt, 1946), p. 29. 7. Joseph Campbell, *Historical Atlas of World Mythology.* Vol. 1 (New York: Harper & Row, 1983). 8. Harry Levin, "Some Meanings of Myth," in Henry A. Murray, ed., *Myth and Mythmaking* (New York: George Braziller, 1960), pp. 103–114, p. 106. 9. Joan Marler, "The Mythic Journey" (an interview with Joseph Campbell), *Yoga Journal,* November–December 1987, pp. 57–61. 10. Carl G. Jung, *Two Essays on Analytical Psychology,* trans. H. G. and C. F. Baynes (New York: Dodd, Mead, 1928). 11. James Hillman, *Revisioning Psychology* (New York: Harper & Row, 1975), p. 146. 12. Erich Neumann, *The Origins and History of Consciousness,* trans. R. F. C. Hull (Princeton: Princeton University Press, 1970), p. 210. 13. Albert Upton, *Design for Thinking* (Stanford: Stanford University Press, 1961), p. 11. 14. Henry A. Murray, "American Icarus," in Arthur Burton and Robert E. Harris, eds., *Clinical Studies of Personality* (New York: Harper & Row, 1955), pp. 615–641. 15. Abraham H. Maslow, *The Farther Reaches of Human Nature* (New York: Viking, 1971). 16. Colin Martindale, *Cognition and Consciousness* (Homewood, IL: Dorsey Press, 1981). 17. Jean Houston, *The Search for The Beloved: Journeys in Sacred Psychology* (Los Angeles: Jeremy P. Tarcher, 1987), p. 104. 18. Jerome Bruner, "Myth and Identity," in Murray, ed., *Myth and Mythmaking,* pp. 276–287, p. 286. 19. Houston, *The Search for The Beloved,* pp. 105–106. 20. Roberto Assagioli, *Psychosynthesis* (New York: Random House, 1965). 21. David Feinstein, "The Shaman Within: Cultivating a Sacred Personal Mythology," in Shirley Nicholson, ed., *Shamanism: An Expanded View of Reality* (Wheaton, IL: Quest, 1987), pp. 267–279. 22. Michael Harner, *The Way of the Shaman: A Guide to Power and Healing* (New York: Bantam, 1980). 23. Joseph Campbell, *The Masks of God.* Vol. 1: *Primitive Mythology* (New York: Viking, 1969).

2

1. Carl G. Jung, "The Theory of Psychoanalysis," in R. F. C. Hull, ed. and trans., *The Collected Works of C. G. Jung.* Vol. 4: *Freud and Psychoanalysis* (Princeton: Princeton University Press, 1961, first published 1913), para. 451. 2. See Dan P. McAdams, *Power, Intimacy, and the Life Story: Personological Inquiries into Identity* (Homewood, IL: Dorsey Press, 1985). 3. Motifs from classical mythology have been used as frameworks for self-exploration in, for instance, Jean Shinoda Bolen's *Goddesses in Everywoman* (New York: Harper & Row, 1983), Robert Johnson's *Ecstasy* and his trilogy *He, She,* and *We* (Harper & Row), and Jean Houston's *The Search for The Beloved* (Los Angeles: Jeremy P. Tarcher, 1987). 4. We are grateful to Melanie Morgan, a colleague who uses this framework in her own personal mythology workshops. 5. See Jean Houston, *Lifeforce: The Psycho-Historical Recovery of the Self*

(New York: Delacorte, 1980). **6.** Rollo May, *Love and Will* (New York: W. W. Norton, 1969), p. 281. **7.** Ken Wilber, *Up from Eden: A Transpersonal View of Human Evolution* (Garden City, NY: Anchor/Doubleday, 1981). **8.** Aldous Huxley, *The Perennial Philosophy* (New York: Harper & Row, 1970, first published 1945). **9.** The case presentations are drawn from our clinical practice, seminars, and the journals of those who tested earlier drafts of the book. We have altered names and other identifying details and in some instances asked people to edit their journal accounts for clarity. **10.** This method is patterned after a Gestalt therapy technique developed by Fritz Perls. It is reminiscent of the Jungian technique of active imagination combined with psychodrama, the therapeutic approach developed by Jacob Moreno. One of Perls's students, Peg Elliott, has dubbed the technique *creative projection,* the term which we use. **11.** Ernest Jones, *Papers on Psycho-Analysis,* 4th ed. (Baltimore: Wood, 1938). **12.** Steven E. Locke and Douglas Colligan, *The Healer Within: The New Medicine of Mind and Body* (New York: Dutton, 1986). **13.** This method is adapted from a hypnosis technique called the "affect bridge" developed by John Watkins ("The Affect Bridge: A Hypno-Analytic Technique," *International Journal of Clinical and Experimental Hypnosis,* 1971, *19,* 21–27).

3

1. Anthea Francine, *Envisioning Theology: An Autobiographical Account of Personal Symbolic Journeying as a Source of Revelation* (Unpublished Master's Thesis. Berkeley: Pacific School of Religion, June 1983), p. 45. **2.** Sam Keen and Anne Valley Fox, *Telling Your Story: A Guide to Who You Are and Who You Can Be* (New York: Signet, 1973), p. 158. **3.** Francine, *Envisioning Theology,* p. 77. **4.** Richard Gardner, *Therapeutic Communication with Children: The Mutual-Storytelling Technique* (New York: Science House, 1971). **5.** See Eugene Gendlin, *Focusing* (New York: Bantam, 1978).

4

1. John Bowlby, *Loss* (New York: Basic Books, 1980). **2.** Ken Wilber, *Up from Eden: A Transpersonal View of Human Evolution* (Garden City, NY: Anchor/Doubleday, 1981), p. 206. **3.** Ibid., p. 21. **4.** Richard Cavendish, *An Illustrated Encyclopedia of Mythology* (New York: Crescent, 1980), p. 11. **5.** Cited in Charles Hampden-Turner, *Maps of the Mind* (London: Mitchell Beazley, 1981), p. 98. **6.** Roberto Assagioli, *Psychosynthesis* (New York: Viking, 1965). **7.** Ralph Metzner, "Alchemy and Personal Transformation," *The Laughing Man,* 1981, *2*(4), 53–57, p. 55. **8.** Erich Neumann, *Depth Psychology and a New Ethic,* trans. Eugene Rolfe (New York: Harper & Row, 1969), p. 138. **9.** Ibid., p. 147. **10.** Liliane Frey-Rohn, *From Freud to Jung: A Comparative Study of the Psychology of the Unconscious,* trans. Fred E. & Evelyn K. Engreen (New York: Delta, 1974), p. 267.

5

1. William Irwin Thompson, *Passages About Earth: An Exploration of the New Planetary Culture* (New York: Harper & Row, 1974), p. 174.

6

1. See Michael J. Mahoney and Diane B. Arnkoff, "Cognitive and Self-Control Therapies," in Sol I. Garfield and Allen E. Bergin, eds., *Handbook of Psychotherapy and Behavior Change,* 2nd ed. (New York: Wiley, 1978), pp. 689–722. **2.** See Albert Bandura, *Principles of Behavior Modification* (New York: Holt, Rinehart & Winston,

1969). **3.** See Jean Houston, *The Possible Human* (Los Angeles: Jeremy P. Tarcher, 1982), p. 11. **4.** Ibid. **5.** This exercise, which comes out of the work of Moshe Feldenkrais, was taught to us by Ilana Rubenfeld. **6.** Jeanne Achterberg, *Imagery in Healing: Shamanism and Modern Medicine* (Boston: New Science Library, 1985), p. 3. **7.** Mahoney and Arnkoff, "Cognitive and Self-Control Therapies." **8.** Adapted from Albert A. Ellis and Robert A. Harper, *A New Guide to Rational Living* (Los Angeles: Wilshire, 1976). **9.** Kurt Lewin, *Resolving Social Conflict* (New York: Harper, 1948). **10.** Ibid.

7

1. From "Freud and the Future," a speech delivered by Thomas Mann in celebration of Freud's eightieth birthday on May 9, 1936, in Vienna, where Mann described what he called the "lived myth." Excerpted in Henry A. Murray, ed., *Myth and Mythmaking* (Boston: Beacon, 1968), pp. 371–375. **2.** Philip Wheelwright, "Poetry, Myth, and Reality," in A. Tate, ed., *The Language of Poetry* (Princeton: Princeton University Press, 1942). **3.** Michael S. Gazzaniga, *The Social Brain: Discovering the Networks of the Mind* (New York: Basic Books, 1985), p. 5. **4.** Noam Chomsky, *Reflections on Language* (New York: Pantheon, 1979). **5.** Claude Lévi-Strauss, *Structural Anthropology* (New York: Penguin, 1979). **6.** Carl G. Jung, ed., *Man and His Symbols* (Garden City, NY: Doubleday, 1964). **7.** Erich Neumann, *The Origins and History of Consciousness* (Princeton: Princeton University Press, 1973, first published 1954), p. 16. **8.** Anthony Stevens, *Archetypes: A Natural History of the Self* (New York: William Morrow, 1983), p. 47. **9.** Alexander Thomas and Stella Chess, *Dynamics of Psychological Development* (New York: Brunner/Mazel, 1980). **10.** Constance Holden, "The Genetics of Personality," *Science*, 1987, *237*, 598–601. **11.** Joseph Campbell, *The Inner Reaches of Outer Space: Metaphor as Myth and as Religion* (New York: Alfred van der Marck, 1986), p. 12. **12.** Ibid., p. 14. **13.** Ibid., p. 13. **14.** Ibid., p. 16. **15.** Richard Wilhelm and Carey F. Baynes, trans., *The I Ching or Book of Changes* (Princeton: Princeton University Press, 1967), p. 144. **16.** Dennis A. Anderson and Steven Bagarozzi, "The Evolution of Family Mythological Systems: Considerations for Meaning, Clinical Assessment, and Treatment," *Journal of Psychoanalytic Anthropology*, 1982, *5*(1), 72. **17.** From the oral teachings of Wallace Black Elk as reported by anthropologist William Lyon. **18.** Edward T. Hall, *Beyond Culture* (Garden City, NY: Anchor/Doubleday, 1976), p. 43. **19.** Charles T. Tart, *Waking Up: Overcoming the Obstacles to Human Potential* (Boston: Shambhala, 1986). **20.** Ibid., p. 85. **21.** Hall, *Beyond Culture*, pp. 207–208. **22.** Ibid., p. 240. **23.** Dan P. McAdams, *Power, Intimacy, and the Life Story* (Homewood, IL: Dorsey Press, 1985). **24.** Margaret S. Mahler, Fred Pine, and Anni Bergman, *The Psychological Birth of the Human Infant: Symbiosis and Individuation* (New York: Basic Books, 1975). **25.** Stephen Johnson provides a theoretical integration of "the object relations and ego psychology schools and of characterological theory which derives primarily from Reich, Lowen, and other bioenergetic theorists" in his *Characterological Transformation: The Hard Work Miracle* (New York: W. W. Norton, 1985). **26.** Alexander Lowen, *Bioenergetics* (New York: Penguin, 1976), p. 183. **27.** Johnson, *Characterological Transformation*, p. 32. **28.** Ibid., p. 37. **29.** Stanislav Grof, *Beyond the Brain: Birth, Death and Transcendence in Psychotherapy* (Albany: State University of New York Press, 1985). **30.** Andrew Neher, *The Psychology of Transcendence* (Englewood Cliffs, NJ: Prentice-Hall, 1980). **31.** William James, *Varieties of Religious Experience* (New York: Crowell-Collier, 1961, first published 1902), p. 332. **32.** Ruth Benedict, *Patterns of Culture* (New York: New American Library, 1934). **33.** There are parallels between these visionary, aesthetic, rational, and compassionate models of myth-making and Jung's four psychological functions (intuiting, sensing, thinking, and feeling, respectively) and the four representational systems described in neurolinguistic programming (visual, auditory-tonal, digital, and kinesthetic, respectively). **34.** A longitudinal study by Daniel J. Levinson, *The Seasons of a Man's Life* (New York: Ballantine, 1978), popularized in Gail Sheehy's *Passages: Predictable Crises of Adult Life* (New York: Bantam, 1977), investigates the character of these changes. **35.** Erik H. Erikson, *Identity and the Life Cycle*, 2nd ed. (New York: W. W. Norton, 1980). **36.** Robert

Kegan, *The Evolving Self: Problem and Process in Human Development* (Cambridge, MA: Harvard University Press, 1982). **37.** Ibid., p. 31. **38.** McAdams, *Power, Intimacy, and the Life Story,* p. 12. **39.** David Feinstein, "Conflict Over Childbearing and Tumors of the Female Reproductive System: Symbolism in Disease," *Somatics,* 1982, *4*(1), 35–41.

Epilogue

1. Dan P. McAdams, *Power, Intimacy, and the Life Story: Personological Inquiries into Identity* (Homewood, IL: Dorsey Press, 1985), p. 1. **2.** Lewis Thomas, *The Lives of a Cell* (New York: Bantam, 1974), p. 142. **3.** Joseph Campbell, *The Inner Reaches of Outer Space: Metaphor as Myth and as Religion* (New York: Alfred van der Marck, 1986), p. 12. **4.** In this discussion, we follow Ken Wilber's synopsis of Jean Gebser's major "epochs" in the growth of consciousness and his astute synthesis of that model with the thinking of Joseph Campbell, Ernst Cassirer, Sigmund Freud, Julian Jaynes, Carl Jung, Erich Neumann, Jean Piaget, and L. L. Whyte, presented in Wilber's *Up from Eden: A Transpersonal View of Human Evolution* (Garden City, NY: Anchor/Doubleday, 1981). **5.** Julian Jaynes, *The Origins of Consciousness in the Breakdown of the Bicameral Mind* (Boston: Houghton Mifflin, 1976). **6.** John Weir Perry, *The Heart of History: Individuality in Evolution* (Albany: State University of New York Press, 1985). **7.** Joseph Campbell, *The Hero with a Thousand Faces,* 2nd ed. (Princeton: Princeton University Press, 1968), p. 388. **8.** Joseph Campbell, *The Masks of God.* Vol. 3: *Occidental Mythology* (New York: Viking, 1964), p. 24. **9.** Campbell, *Hero with a Thousand Faces,* **10.** Wilber, *Up from Eden,* p. 189. **11.** Ibid., pp. 187–188. **12.** Anthony G. Greenwald, "The Totalitarian Ego: Fabrication and Revision of Personal History," *American Psychologist,* 1980, *35,* 603–618. **13.** Robert Gilman, "The Human Story," *In Context,* 1985, *12,* 18–25, p. 23. **14.** Ibid., p. 24. **15.** Erich Neumann, *The Origins and History of Consciousness* (Princeton: Princeton University Press, 1973), p. 434. **16.** Robert N. Bellah, Richard Madsen, William M. Sullivan, Ann Swidler, and Steven M. Tipton, *Habits of the Heart: Individualism and Commitment in American Life* (Berkeley: University of California Press, 1985). **17.** Among the many provocative discussions of the changes that can be identified in contemporary consciousness are Morris Berman's *The Reenchantment of the World* (New York: Bantam, 1984), Riane Eisler's *The Chalice and the Blade: Our History, Our Future* (New York: Harper & Row, 1987), and John Naisbitt, *Megatrends* (New York: Warner, 1982). **18.** Carol Gilligan, *In a Different Voice* (Cambridge, MA: Harvard University Press, 1982). **19.** Letty Cottin Pogrebin, *Family Politics: Love and Power on an Intimate Frontier* (New York: McGraw-Hill, 1983), pp. 18–19. **20.** B. Gray-Little and N. Burks, "Power and Satisfaction in Marriage: A Review and Critique," *Psychological Bulletin,* 1983, *93,* 513–538. **21.** Pogrebin, *Family Politics,* p. 18. **22.** Edward E. Sampson has made the distinction between a one-sided *self-contained individualism* and an *ensembled individualism* that completes the circle by promoting community values in "The Debate on Individualism," *American Psychologist,* 1988, *43*(1), 15–22. **23.** Jane J. Mansbridge, *Beyond Adversary Democracy* (New York: Basic Books, 1980). **24.** Arthur Koestler, *Janus: A Summing Up* (New York: Random House, 1978), p. 5. **25.** Jean Houston, "The Psycho-Historical Recovery of the Self," in Stanley Krippner, ed., *Into the Mythic Underworld* (Special Issue of the *Association for Humanistic Psychology Newsletter,* April 1982), p. 8. **26.** Campbell, *The Inner Reaches of Space,* p. 17. **27.** Erich Jantsch, "Introduction and Summary," in Erich Jantsch and Conrad H. Waddington, eds., *Evolution and Consciousness: Human Systems in Transition* (Reading, MA: Addison-Wesley, 1976), pp. 1–8, p. 1. **28.** Ibid., p. 1. **29.** Ibid., pp. 1–2. **30.** Abraham H. Maslow, *Motivation and Personality,* 2nd ed. (New York: Harper & Row, 1970) and *Toward a Psychology of Being,* 2nd ed. (Princeton, NJ: Van Nostrand, 1968). **31.** Rollo May, *The Cry for Myth* (New York: W. W. Norton, 1989). **32.** Gilman, "The Human Story," p. 23. **33.** Ibid., p. 25. **34.** Marshall McLuhan, *Understanding Media: The Extension of Man* (New York: McGraw-Hill, 1964). **35.** Joshua Meyrowitz, *No Sense of Place: The Impact of Electronic Media on Social Behavior* (New York: Oxford University Press, 1985), p. 140. **36.** Albert Einstein, *Einstein: A Portrait* (Corte Madera, CA: Pomegranate Artbooks, 1984), p. 64. **37.** Eleanor

Wilner, *Gathering the Winds: Visionary Imagination and Radical Transformation of Self and Society* (Baltimore: The Johns Hopkins University Press, 1975), p. 32. **38.** Campbell, *Hero with a Thousand Faces,* p. 384. **39.** Joseph Campbell, *Myths to Live By* (New York: Viking, 1972), p. 10. **40.** Joseph Campbell and Chungliang Al Huang, "The Sword and the Flute: Mythologies of War and Peace." Seminar sponsored by the Esalen Institute, March 18–23, 1984. **41.** Erich Jantsch, *Design for Evolution: Self-Organization and Planning in the Life of Human Systems* (New York: Braziller, 1975), p. 205. **42.** Daniel Yankelovich, *New Rules: Searching for Self-Fulfillment in a World Turned Upside Down* (New York: Bantam, 1981). **43.** David C. McClelland, *Human Motivation* (Glenview, IL: Scott, Foresman, 1985). **44.** Einstein, *Einstein: A Portrait,* p. 76. **45.** Melvin Konner, *The Tangled Wing: Biological Constraints on the Human Spirit* (New York: Harper & Row, 1982), p. 419. **46.** Erich Neumann, *Depth Psychology and a New Ethic,* trans. Eugene Rolfe (New York: Harper & Row, 1969), pp. 146–147. **47.** Stanislav Grof, *Beyond the Brain: Birth, Death, and Transcendence in Psychotherapy* (Albany, NY: State University of New York Press, 1985), p. 413. **48.** Neumann, *Depth Psychology,* p. 30. **49.** O. H. Markley, "Human Consciousness in Transformation," in Erich Jantsch and Conrad H. Waddington, eds., *Evolution and Consciousness: Human Systems in Transition* (Reading, MA: Addison-Wesley, 1976), p. 218. **50.** Anne W. Dosher, "Personal and Organizational Mythology: A Reflexive Reality," in Krippner, ed., *Into the Mythic Underworld,* pp. 11–12. **51.** Terrence E. Deal and Allan A. Kennedy, *Corporate Cultures* (Reading, MA: Addison-Wesley, 1984). **52.** Dosher, "Personal and Organizational Mythology," p. 12. **53.** Cited in David P. Barash and Judith Eve Lipton, *The Caveman and the Bomb: Human Nature, Evolution, and Nuclear War* (New York: McGraw-Hill, 1985), p. 259. **54.** Rollo May, *Freedom and Destiny* (New York: W. W. Norton, 1981). **55.** Mircea Eliade, *The Sacred and the Profane: The Nature of Religion,* trans. Willard R. Trask (New York: Harcourt, Brace & World), 1959. **56.** A number of activities of the Peace Project, which Rogers helped establish at the Center for the Study of the Person, are described in a special "Citizen Diplomacy" issue of the *Journal of Humanistic Psychology,* 1987, *27*(3). **57.** John Weir Perry, *Roots of Renewal in Myth and Madness: The Meaning of Psychotic Episodes* (San Francisco: Jossey-Bass, 1976). **58.** Campbell, *Myths to Live By,* p. 208. **59.** Grof, *Beyond the Brain.* **60.** Muzafer and Carolyn W. Sherif, *Groups in Harmony and Tension* (New York: Octagon, 1966). **61.** Einstein, *Einstein: A Portrait.* **62.** Ruth Benedict, "Synergy: Patterns of the Good Culture," *American Psychologist,* 1970, *72,* 320–333. **63.** Konner, *The Tangled Wing,* p. xiv. **64.** Laura Ackerman, "The Successful Animal: Fertility Rights," *Science* 1986 *86,* 7(1), 55–56. **65.** Abraham H. Maslow, *The Journals of Abraham Maslow,* ed. Richard J. Lowry (Lexington, MA: Lewis, 1982), pp. 299–300.

Appendix A

1. This induction is patterned after Edmund Jacobsen's classic method of *Progressive Relaxation* (Chicago: University of Chicago Press, 1938).

Appendix B

1. See, for instance, *Dreamworking: How to Use Your Dreams for Creative Problem-Solving* by Stanley Krippner and Joseph Dillard (Buffalo, NY: Bearly, 1988); *Inner Work: Using Dreams and Active Imagination for Personal Growth* by Robert A. Johnson (New York: Harper & Row, 1986); *Working with Dreams* by Montague Ullman and Nan Zimmerman (Los Angeles: Jeremy P. Tarcher, 1985); and *The Dream Workbook* by Jill Morris (Boston: Little, Brown, 1985). **2.** David Feinstein, "Myth-Making Activity Through the Window of the Dream," *Psychotherapy in Private Practice,* 1986, *4,* 119–135. **3.** C. G. Jung, "The Practice of Psychotherapy," in R. F. C. Hull, ed. and trans., *The Collected Works of C. G. Jung.* Vol. 16: The Practice of Psychotherapy (Princeton: Princeton University Press, 1966), p. 42. **4.** See Calvin S. Hall and Robert L. Van der Castle, *The Content Analysis of Dreams* (New York: Appleton-Century-Crofts, 1966).

Appendix C

1. This technique was taught to us by Donna Eden, a Touch for Health Instructor and practitioner of natural healing.

Suggested Readings

Baumeister, Roy F. *Identity: Cultural Change and the Struggle for Self.* New York: Oxford University Press, 1986.

Bellah, Robert N.; Madsen, Richard; Sullivan, William M.; Swidler, Ann; and Tipton, Steven M. *Habits of the Heart: Individualism and Commitment in American Life.* Berkeley: University of California Press, 1985.

Berman, Morris. *The Reenchantment of the World.* New York: Bantam, 1984.

Bettelheim, Bruno. *The Uses of Enchantment: The Meaning and Importance of Fairy Tales.* New York: Random House, 1977.

Blumenberg, Hans. *Work on Myths* (trans. Robert M. Wallace). Cambridge, MA: MIT Press, 1985.

Bolen, Jean Shinoda. *Goddesses in Everywoman: A New Psychology of Women.* New York: Harper & Row, 1984.

Bruner, Jerome. *Actual Minds, Possible Worlds.* Cambridge, MA: Harvard University Press, 1986.

Campbell, Joseph. *The Hero With a Thousand Faces.* 2nd ed. Princeton: Princeton University Press, 1968.

Capra, Fritjof. *The Turning Point: Science, Society and the Rising Culture.* New York: Bantam, 1982.

Carlsen, Mary Baird. *Meaning-Making: Therapeutic Processes in Adult Development.* New York: W.W. Norton, 1988.

Charme, Stuart L. *Meaning and Myth in the Study of Lives.* Philadelphia: University of Pennsylvania Press, 1984.

Eisler, Riane. *The Chalice and the Blade: Our History, Our Future.* New York: Harper & Row, 1987.

Erikson, Erik H. *Identity and the Life Cycle.* 2nd ed. New York: W. W. Norton, 1980.

Feinstein, David, and Mayo, Peg Eliott. Rituals for Living and Dying: From Life's Wounds to Spiritual Awakening. San Francisco: Harper & Row, in press.

Gebser, Jean. *The Ever-Present Origin* (trans. Noel Barstad). Athens, OH: Ohio University Press, 1986.

Grof, Stanislav. *The Adventure of Self-Discovery.* Albany, NY: State University of New York Press, 1988.

Harman, Willis. *Global Mind Change: The Promise of the Last Years of the Twentieth Century.* Indianapolis: Knowledge Systems, 1988.

Heuscher, Julius E. *A Psychiatric Study of Myths and Fairy Tales: Their Origin, Meaning and Usefulness.* 2nd ed. Springfield, IL: Charles C Thomas, 1974.

Hillman, James. *The Dream and the Underworld.* New York: Harper & Row, 1979.

Houston, Jean. *The Search for The Beloved: Journeys in Sacred Psychology.* Los Angeles: Jeremy P. Tarcher, 1987.

Johnson, Robert A. *Inner Work: Using Dreams and Active Imagination for Personal Growth.* New York: Harper & Row, 1986.

Johnson, Stephen M. *Characterological Transformation: The Hard Work Miracle.* New York: W. W. Norton, 1985.

Jung, Carl G., ed. *Man and His Symbols.* Garden City, NY: Doubleday, 1964.

Kegan, Robert. *The Evolving Self: Problem and Process in Human Development.* Cambridge, MA: Harvard University Press, 1982.

Konner, Melvin. *The Tangled Wing: Biological Constraints on the Human Spirit.* New York: Harper & Row, 1982.

Krippner, Stanley, and Dillard, Joseph. *Dreamworking: How to Use Your Dreams for Creative Problem-Solving.* Buffalo, NY: Bearly, 1988.

London, Herbert I., and Weeks, Albert L. *Myths That Rule America.* Washington, D.C.: University Press of America, 1981.

McAdams, Dan P. *Power, Intimacy, and the Life Story.* Homewood, IL: Dorsey Press, 1985.

May, Rollo. *The Cry for Myth.* New York: W. W. Norton, 1989.

Metzner, Ralph. *Opening to Inner Light: The Transformation of Human Nature and Consciousness.* Los Angeles: Jeremy P. Tarcher, 1986.

Mindell, Arnold. *Working with the Dreaming Body.* New York: Routledge & Kegan Paul, 1985.

Murray, Henry A., ed. *Myth and Mythmaking.* Boston: Beacon, 1960.

Neumann, Erich. *Depth Psychology and a New Ethic* (trans. Eugene Rolfe). New York: Harper & Row, 1969.

Pearson, Carol S. *The Hero Within: Six Archetypes We Live By.* New York: Harper & Row, 1986.

Perry, John Weir. *Roots of Renewal in Myth and Madness: The Meaning of Psychotic Episodes.* San Francisco: Jossey-Bass, 1976.

Robertson, James Oliver. *American Myth; American Reality.* New York: Farrar, Straus & Giroux, 1980.

Sarbin, Theodore R., ed. *Narrative Psychology: The Storied Nature of Human Conduct.* New York: Praeger, 1986.

Singer, June. *Boundaries of the Soul: The Practice of Jung's Psychology.* Garden City, NY: Anchor/Doubleday, 1973.

Slochower, Harry. *Mythopoesis: Mythic Patterns in the Literary Classics.* Detroit: Wayne State University Press, 1970.

Smith, Huston. *Beyond the Post-Modern Mind.* Wheaton, IL: Quest, 1984.

Stevens, Anthony. *Archetypes: A Natural History of the Self.* New York: Quill, 1983.

Tart, Charles T. *Waking Up: Overcoming the Obstacles to Human Potential.* Boston: Shambhala, 1986.

Thompson, William Irwin. *The Time Falling Bodies Take to Light: Mythology, Sexuality, and the Origins of Culture.* New York: St. Martin's Press, 1981.

Valle, Ronald S., and von Eckartsberg, Rolf, eds. *The Metaphors of Consciousness.* New York: Plenum, 1981.

Vaughan, Frances E. *Awakening Intuition.* Garden City, NY: Doubleday, 1979.

Villoldo, Alberto, and Krippner, Stanley. *Healing States.* New York: Fireside/Simon and Schuster, 1987.

Walsh, Roger N., and Vaughan, Frances, eds. *Beyond Ego: Transpersonal Dimensions in Psychology.* Los Angeles: Jeremy P. Tarcher, 1980.

Watzlawick, Paul, ed. *The Invented Reality: How Do We Know What We Believe We Know?* New York: W.W. Norton, 1984.

Whitmont, Edward C. *The Symbolic Quest: Basic Concepts of Analytical Psychology.* Princeton: Princeton University Press, 1969.

Wilber, Ken. *Up from Eden: A Transpersonal View of Human Evolution.* Garden City, NY: Doubleday, 1981.

Index

The institutional support of Innersource in the development of this book is gratefully acknowledged.

ABOUT THE AUTHORS

David Feinstein, Ph.D., specializing in clinical and community psychology, is director of Innersource, an innovative health care and education center in Ashland, Oregon. He has taught at The Johns Hopkins University School of Medicine, the California School of Professional Psychology, and Antioch College. He is coauthor of *Rituals for Living and Dying: A Guide to Spiritual Awakening*, and has lectured and consulted widely on the application of a mythological perspective to personal, organizational, and social change.

Stanley Krippner, Ph.D., is professor of psychology at Saybrook Institute in San Francisco and director of the Center of Consciousness Studies. In a dozen volumes and more than 700 articles, he has investigated developments in consciousness research, education, and healing. He has served as president of the Association for Humanistic Psychology, the Parapsychological Association, and the American Psychological Association's Division of Humanistic Psychology.